The Washington Lobby

The Washington Lobby

Fifth Edition

Congressional Quarterly Inc.

Congressional Quarterly Inc., an editorial research service and publishing company, serves clients in the fields of news, education, business, and government. It combines specific coverage of Congress, government, and politics by Congressional Quarterly with the more general subject range of an affiliated service, Editorial Research Reports.

Congressional Quarterly publishes the *Congressional Quarterly Weekly Report* and a variety of books, including college political science textbooks under the CQ Press imprint and public affairs paperbacks on developing issues and events. CQ also publishes information directories and reference books on the federal government, national elections, and politics, including the *Guide to Congress*, the *Guide to the U.S. Supreme Court*, the *Guide to U.S. Elections*, and *Politics in America*. The *CQ Almanac*, a compendium of legislation for one session of Congress, is published each year. *Congress and the Nation*, a record of government for a presidential term, is published every four years.

CQ publishes *The Congressional Monitor*, a daily report on current and future activities of congressional committees, and several newsletters including *Congressional Insight*, a weekly analysis of congressional action, and *Campaign Practices Reports*, a semimonthly update on campaign laws.

The online delivery of CQ's Washington Alert Service provides clients with immediate access to Congressional Quarterly's institutional information and expertise.

Printed in the United States of America

Library of Congress Cataloging in Publication Data

The Washington lobby.

Bibliography: p.
Includes index.
1. Lobbying--Law and legislation--United States.
2. Lobbying. I. Congressional Quarterly, inc.
KF4948.Z9W37 1987 328.73'078 86-29030
ISBN 0-87187-408-3

Editor: Colleen McGuiness.
Contributors: Robert Benenson, Jacqueline Calmes, Nadine Cohodas, Joseph A. Davis, Harrison Donnelly, John Felton, Pamela Fessler, Stephen Gettinger, Steve Pressman, David Rapp, Eileen Shanahan, Paul Starobin, Tom Watson.
Cover: Richard A. Pottern.
Graphics: cover - Uniphoto/Julie Houck; pp. 5, 8, 61, 97 - Ray Driver; pp. 17, 140 (Kasten) - Jim Wells; pp. 18, 53, 73, 115, 119 - George Rebh; pp. 21, 187 - Library of Congress; p. 45 - AP/Wide World Photos; pp. 95, 105, 107, 169 - Sue Klemens; p. 110 - Murray H. Sill; p. 129 - Bureau of Reclamation/E. E. Hertzog; p. 132 - Pacific Power & Light Co.; pp. 140 (Danforth, Gorton), 149 - Ken Heinen; p. 144 - Marvin T. Jones; p. 153 - Black Star/David Turnley; p. 193 - Gamma-Liaison.
Bibliography: Genevieve Clemens.
Index: Bernice Eisen.

Table of Contents

The Washington Lobby

1

Lobbying

From abortion to Zaire security aid, every conceivable issue has attracted the attention of competing interest groups, and across the country they and their lobbyists have become a potent force in the political process. Their ranks include the traditional rich and powerful Capitol Hill lobbies, as well as the many grass-roots coalitions that derive power from their numbers and determination.

"America is no longer a nation. It is a committee of lobbies," wrote Charles Peters, editor in chief of the *Washington Monthly.* The goals these groups espouse are diverse and, from their point of view, their causes just.

Although their objectives may differ, the various groups pressuring Congress in the 1980s increasingly were using similar, often highly developed, strategies to get what they wanted. At one time lobbying may have meant a persuasive soloist pleading his case to a senator or representative; but as often as not the contemporary lobbyist depended far less than his predecessors on individualistic methods and more on coordinated, indirect techniques made possible by modern means of communication.

As it grew in size and sophistication, the lobbying profession lost much of the stigma attached to it from past scandals and the activities of unscrupulous influence peddlers. But concern lingered that some individuals and groups, despite their polish and adherence to laws and proprieties, might be having too much sway in Congress, to the detriment of the public interest.

Peters continued in his article to say that "Politicians no longer ask what is in the public interest, because they know no one else is asking. Instead they're giving each group what it wants. . . ." In his farewell address to the nation delivered January 14, 1981, President Jimmy Carter also expressed concern about the proliferation of single-interest groups, which he said was "a disturbing factor" that "tends to distort our purposes, because the national interest is not always the sum of all our single or special interests."

But comments like these have produced little in the way of restrictions on lobbies or the way they operate. The dilemma for would-be reformers was that lobbying derives from basic American rights, and any efforts to control it must avoid any entanglement with those rights.

Constitutional Protection

Lobbying has been recognized as a legitimate, protected activity from the earliest years of the United States. The First

Amendment to the Constitution provided that "Congress shall make no law . . . abridging the freedom of speech or of the press; or the right of the people peaceably to assemble and to petition the Government for redress of grievances."

But there is a potential for corruption and conflict of interest inherent in protecting the rights of groups to petition, and James Madison was credited with foreseeing it. In *The Federalist* (No. 10) he defended the need for a strong federal government to act as an effective counterbalance: "Among the numerous advantages promised by a well-constructed union," he wrote, "none deserves to be more accurately developed than its tendency to break and control the violence of faction. . . . By a faction, I understand a number of citizens, whether amounting to a majority or minority of the whole, who are united and actuated by some common impulse of passion, or of interest, adverse to the rights of other citizens, or to the permanent and aggregate interests of the community."

By the early nineteenth century, corruption and conflicts of interest were commonplace and, although they discomforted many, were taken as a matter of course. Abundant evidence accumulated that venal and selfish methods often were used to get legislative results. Chief among the indiscretions was bribery, where legislators traded influence for money.

The term *lobbyist* came into usage about this time, and the unsavory reputations of the early practitioners gave the word a pejorative sense that lobbyists have been trying to shake ever since. By 1829 the phrase *lobby-agents* was being applied to special favor-seekers hovering in the New York Capitol lobby at Albany. By 1832 the term had been shortened to lobbyist and was in wide use at the U.S. Capitol. Newspaper reporters and political cartoonists compounded the lobbyists' stereotypical image by portraying them as sinister, portly, cigar-smoking individuals who held legislatures completely in their control.

An often-cited example of a conflict-of-interest problem arose in the 1830s when Congress became embroiled in President Andrew Jackson's battle with the Bank of the United States. It was disclosed that Daniel Webster, then a senator from Massachusetts, enjoyed a retainer from the bank. On December 21, 1833, Webster complained to bank president Nicholas Biddle: "My retainer has not been renewed or refreshed as usual. If it is wished that my relation to the Bank should be continued, it may be well to send me the usual retainers."

Over the years, often in response to lobby scandals, Congress tried to control influence buying, passing lobby registration and disclosure laws. But the effectiveness of those laws continued to be disputed into the 1980s.

Nevertheless, lobbyists gradually gained a more positive image. The public began to recognize that pressure groups and their agents perform some important and indispensable jobs. Such services today include helping to inform both Congress and the public about problems and issues, stimulating public debate, opening a path to Congress for the wronged and needy, and making known to members the practical aspects of proposed legislation — whom it would help, whom it would hurt, who is for it, and who is against it. The result of this process has been considerable technical information produced by research on legislative proposals.

Growth of Lobbying

Despite the deep and pervading sense of ambivalence that surrounded their profession, lobbyists continued to be attracted to Washington in the twentieth century. Their legions grew steadily after the New Deal of the 1930s, paralleling the growth in federal spending and the expansion of authority into new areas. Over the next four decades the federal government became a tremendous force in the nation's life, thus expanding the areas where changes in federal policy could spell success or failure for special interest groups.

Then in the 1970s a series of congressional reforms opened up meetings, diminished the seniority system, forced more publicly recorded votes, and increased the power of subcommittees. Power once concentrated in the leadership and held by committee chairmen was diluted among many members, as well as in the ranks of professional staffers that had swelled throughout the 1960s. Lobbyists found they had to influence more people, members and staffers, to get something accomplished.

Because of the unspecific — and some would say unenforceable — lobby registration laws, it was impossible to come up with an exact number of lobbyists in Washington. But whether they referred to themselves as political consultants, lawyers, foreign representatives, legislative specialists, consumer advocates, trade association representatives, or government affairs specialists, there were an estimated 10,000 to 20,000 people lobbying in Washington by the mid-1980s — either periodically or throughout the year. Even the lower end of this estimate showed a dramatic increase from the figure of 4,000 estimated for 1977.

According to Robert H. Salisbury in the second edition of *Interest Group Politics,* "The result of the most extensive effort to identify all the individuals who represent group interests of every kind is a list published annually that by 1984 included some 10,000 names. By no means were all these people officially registered as lobbyists, but even with the various loopholes that enable individuals to avoid registration, the number registered reached 7,200 by 1985, up from 3,400 just ten years earlier. Some 850 people registered in 1985 as agents of foreign governments and firms, more than 20 percent greater than in 1982."

Variety of Techniques Open to Lobbyists

A Washington lobby group wants results. It pursues them wherever they are likely to be found in the governmental process.

Many organizations, directed by professionals in the art of government, focus major efforts at key points where decisions are made and policy interpreted into action. They use the methods they deem appropriate for the circumstances within the limits of their resources, group policies, and ethical outlook.

If a group loses a round in Congress, it can continue the fight in the agency charged with execution or in the courts. A year or two later, it can resume the struggle in Congress. The process sometimes continues indefinitely. On a long-range basis, groups strive to build up what they consider a sympathetic or at least neutral attitude in places of power where their particular interests are affected.

Coalition Organizing

The concerted exercise of influence is as old as government itself, but most lobbyists agree that during the 1970s and into the 1980s coalition lobbying became a commonplace ritual in Washington. The ad hoc coalition, the working group, the alliance, the committee — these became the routine format of all but the most obscure lobbying campaigns.

While the movement toward coalitions had accelerated after World War II, it was far from new even then. As early as 1950 the House Select Committee on Lobbying Activities said in a report: "The lone-wolf pressure group, wanting nothing more from other groups than to be left unmolested, is largely a thing of the past."

Cooperative Efforts

The explosion of the lobbying business, aimed at comprehending and staunching the flow of government activism, meant many voices competing for the ear of Congress. One advantage for lobbyists and members alike was that collective lobbying allowed a sorting out of competing aims before going to Congress, almost like lawyers settling a case out of court.

And so although at one time a lobbyist may have individually pleaded his case, by the 1980s a person with a cause found his first task was to persuade members of his own organization or group to support him, then to line up help from natural allies in other interest groups. These ad hoc lobby coalitions often are composed of a mix of corporate, association, and business federation lobbyists, as well as unions and any other interests that can be enticed into a marriage of convenience. Allies on one issue sometimes become opponents on the next one.

These temporary alliances do their initial work off Capitol Hill, in a community possessing its own committees, leadership, staff, communications network, service organizations, and culture. Participants contribute time, legal help, printing and mailing costs according to their resources and their stake in the battle.

Ideally, before the lobbyist approaches a member, compromises within the coalition have been made, congressional sponsors for the bill have been identified, legislation has been drafted to satisfy a wide range of allies, priorities have been assigned, and a strategy has been mapped out. When the lobbyist finally does go to Congress, he is likely to be in a team of two or three — perhaps with one individual representing the member's district — selected to dramatize the breadth of support for, or opposition to, the legislation.

Although labor, consumer groups, environmentalists, arts and education advocates, charities, and many other groups merge into short-term alliances, business groups clearly demonstrate superior mastery of the technique, helped along by money and a naturally cohesive political outlook. A historic example of the broad coalition was the protectionist bloc, which was effective in raising protective U.S. tariffs to their highest point ever in 1930. More recently, coalitions labored to protect favored programs from Reagan budget cuts.

Enacting Legislation

Traditionally, the best-known coalitions have been directed primarily at stopping new government initiatives — a federal consumer protection agency, a common situs picketing bill, or labor law reform legislation. Successfully ushering legislation through Congress always has been a much more ambitious task than preventing passage, which can be accomplished by a single subcommittee blockade or a crippling amendment.

This developed by design. The bicameral structure of the legislative branch and the constitutional separation of powers gave a considerable natural advantage to defensive lobbying efforts. Political scientist David B. Truman wrote that these structures "operate as they were designed, to delay or obstruct action rather than to facilitate it." He added: "Requirement of extensive majorities for particular kinds of measures and the absence of limits on the duration of debate have a like effect as do numerous technical details of the parliamentary rules. Finally, the diffuseness of leadership, and the power and independence of committees and their chairmen, not only provide a multiplicity of points of access . . . but also furnish abundant activities for obstruction and delay, opportunities that buttress the position of defensive groups."

By combining their knowledge and resources, members of coalitions improve

their chances of overcoming the natural obstacles to new legislation, and they have a better chance of killing bills they oppose. In the early 1980s lobby coalitions increasingly were on the offensive to move legislation and to roll back existing laws.

"Up until now, you didn't have a chance to get things passed. All you were trying to do was put out the fires your opponents started," said R. Hilton Davis, who had served as vice president of legislative and political affairs for the U.S. Chamber of Commerce. Davis said he believed the arrival of a Republican administration and Senate majority as a result of the 1980 election, along with several years of practice at team-building, were responsible for that chance.

A notably successful collective effort was one mounted by the Alaska Coalition, which in 1980 won passage of the lands bill that preserved much of the state from development.

Direct Lobbying

The changes in Congress that occurred in the 1970s worked to enlarge the job of Washington lobbyists. They not only had to become more active — to communicate their messages to a much broader range of members and staff — but they also had to adopt more effective techniques. As access to members became more available, more groups formed to protect or enlarge their turf and competition between lobbyists increased.

Lobbyists using the direct approach continued to meet with members of Congress and their staffs, provided in-depth information, and gave testimony at congressional hearings. But their methods became more sophisticated, relying more on information than on personal connections.

One legislative aide observed: "I think there's a new breed of lobbyist around. There's less of the slap-on-the-back, 'I've been dealing with you for 15 years, let's go duck hunting' kind of approach. Now it's 'Here's a 20-page paper full of technical slides, charts showing the budget impact, a table on how it meets the threat situation and some language in case you'd like to introduce an amendment.' "

Access Prerequisite

A lobbyist's strategy focuses on the interaction between his group and those on Capitol Hill and in the executive branch. To communicate with the power brokers, the advocate first needs access. So whether he is a partner in a Washington law firm or an in-house employee of a union, trade association, or business, more often than not the lobbyist already has close ties with Congress. Many lobbyists have spent time as staff aides on Capitol Hill, and some were members of Congress.

Although debate continues on whether contacts are what ultimately count, many people believe that insider credentials are a good investment. Charles Black, a one-time campaigner for presidential candidate Ronald Reagan and a member of a political consulting firm, put it this way: "No. 1 is the access — to get them in the door and get a hearing for the case. The second thing is the development of the case and how to present it. Knowing the individuals personally, knowing their staffs and how they operate and the kind of information they want . . . that kind of personal knowledge can help you maximize the client's hearing."

It also is possible to gain access by taking part in the Washington social circuit. Some lobbyists become well known, even notorious, for giving lavish dinner and cocktail parties.

Until his downfall in the 1977-78 "Koreagate" scandal on Capitol Hill, South Korean lobbyist Tongsun Park was a noted Washington host. "His flamboyant social style earned him enormous good will and access in the Washington political community," noted a Washington commentator. "That could often be cashed in for reciprocal good will and generosity toward the country he represented."

Another help in opening doors is the sheer size of the interest group represented, such as the senior citizens' lobby. As Norman Ornstein and Shirley Elder wrote in *Interest Groups, Lobbying and Policymaking*: "Beyond the direct political translation of size into votes, a large group representing many citizens has a built-in legitimacy; it 'speaks' for a sizable part of America, not just for a handful of individuals." When a large group speaks out loudly and vehemently, as the National Rifle Association does, its cause must be taken seriously by lawmakers.

Prestige alone also provides a strong incentive for members of Congress and their staff to listen. The Business Roundtable, a group composed of the chief executive officers of major corporations such as General Motors, IBM, and AT&T, can feel confident that its leaders will be heard when they present their opinions and requests on Capitol Hill.

Information and Expertise

Access is crucial, but knowledge and technique are just as critical because lobbyists traditionally have provided information as well as expertise to hard-pressed members and committees. According to Ornstein and Elder, political expertise and reputation are essential to the successful lobbyist: "Knowledge of the ins and outs of the legislative process — including the important stages of the process, the relevant committees and subcommittees, the key actors, the best moments to act or withdraw, the personal characteristics, strengths, and weaknesses of members and staff — is vital to a group's legislative success. . . ."

Direct lobbying most often begins at the committee or subcommittee level, as approval of a measure by a congressional panel usually ensures final passage. Except on highly controversial issues, committee decisions are almost always upheld by the full chamber. A thorough lobbyist provides to the committee and its professional staffers extensive background and technical information on the issue of interest, precise legislative language for a proposed bill or amendment, lists of witnesses for the hearings, and the name of a possible sponsor for the bill.

The decentralization of power in Congress, resulting in the expansion in the number and importance of subcommittees, directly affected the lobbyist's job. As the number of people having power increased, so did the number of pressure points. It became advantageous for an interest group to have a supporter in power. Thus in the Congresses of the 1980s it was not unusual for a lobbyist to back a particular member for a slot on a favored committee, or for a leadership position on a panel.

Also, as "sunshine" laws and rules opened markup sessions, hearings, and conferences to the public, the lobbyist no longer was left hovering outside the closed door excluded from the action; rather he could be right there watching every move — in many cases suggesting legislative language and compromise positions. This kind of help is especially useful during consideration of highly technical legislation. Also, recorded votes on amendments, and open knowledge of who introduced them, makes it easier for the lobbyist to monitor the action and apply pressure where most needed.

Political scientist Lester W. Milbrath in his book *The Washington Lobbyists* noted that "failure to locate such key persons (members and staff) may result in the sending of many superfluous messages, and if the key persons cannot be persuaded, there is a high likelihood that the decision will go adversely."

It also behooves the successful lobbyist to be accurate and complete, alerting the member to any negative aspects of the legislation he seeks to advance. Former White House aide Douglass Cater said in *Power in Washington*: "The smart lobbyist . . . knows he can be most effective by being helpful, by being timely, and, not least, by being accurate. According to the testimony of lobbyists themselves, the cardinal sin is to supply faulty information which puts a trusting policy-maker in an exposed position."

Ornstein and Elder expressed a similar opinion: "A group's or lobbyist's political reputation — as an honest political broker and honest information source, as well as the general reputation for political influence — is a crucial element in political success."

Most contemporary lobbyists carefully avoid approaches that the member could interpret as threatening or as constituting excessive pressure. An adverse reaction by a member could lead to unfavorable publicity or even a damaging congressional investigation.

Political scientist Donald R. Matthews described the lobbyist as a "sitting duck — their public reputation is so low that public attack is bound to be damaging. . . . To invite public attack, or even worse a congressional investigation, is, from the lobbyist's point of view, clearly undesirable." Matthews added: "It is the threat of and use of these countermeasures which help explain why so little lobbying is aimed at conversion. A lobbyist minimizes the risks of his job, the cause which he serves, and his ego by staying away from those senators clearly against him and his program. For, of all types of lobbying, attempts at conversion are most likely to boomerang."

Grass-Roots Techniques

In conjunction with direct lobbying, many organizations seek to mobilize constituents into pressuring senators and representatives. High election turnovers gradually have created a Congress less wedded to old loyalties and more skittish about constituent pressures. This trend contributed to the current prominence of indirect, "grass-roots" lobbying — inducing constituents back home to bring pressure on Congress.

Constituent Power

Confirming what has come to be conventional wisdom in the lobbying trade, the public relations firm of Burson-Marsteller interviewed 123 congressional staffers and found that constituent letters, telegrams, and calls counted more than anything else in influencing their bosses.

Nearly every trade association or public interest group of any stature has developed its own grass-roots network to ensure that what its Washington lobbyists say is reinforced by an outpouring from back home. For those interests that do not have such a network, a thriving intermediate industry has grown up that promises clients it can take a whisper of public interest and amplify it into a roar of public pressure.

Traditional grass-roots pressure meth-

ods include maintaining a steady stream of correspondence with the lawmaker, even when not demanding a specific favor; arranging recess visits to local establishments; and dealing frequently and skillfully with local newspapers and television. These tools are not new to established groups; what is new is the magnitude and sophistication of them.

Modern Techniques

A fact of modern lobbying is that home-district pressure frequently does not spring spontaneously from the public. The genuine grass-roots support often is enhanced by the highly technical orchestration of a special-interest group, the more subliminal stimulation of a professional public relations campaign, and occasionally the persuasion of an employer or union.

Still the oldest and favorite instrument of the organized grass-roots lobbying campaign remains the postage meter. Computer technology and high-speed, low-cost telegram services enabled interest groups in the 1970s and 1980s to target mailings where they would do the most good.

Some lobby experts maintain that grass-roots pressures might not change a lawmaker's mind, but concede that they do attract attention to issues. According to political scientists Roger H. Davidson and Walter Oleszek in the second edition of *Congress and Its Members*, "Legislators understand that lobby groups orchestrate 'spontaneous' outpourings of letters and postcards. Pressure mail is easily recognized, because each piece is nearly identical to all the others. Members may discount the content of such mail, but its sheer volume is sure to attract their attention as they think about the next election."

Richard A. Viguerie, a conservative widely recognized as the preeminent expert on mass mail, said that — contrary to his image as primarily a fund-raiser — most of his work was grass-roots lobbying. Viguerie said 90 percent of the 60 million-70 million pieces of mail his computers disgorged in 1982 for groups such as the National Right to Work Committee and the Conservative Caucus urged the recipient to do something other than contribute — sign a petition, write a letter to Congress, send a post card, or boycott a product.

In a departure from the general belief that personalized letter-writing campaigns are more effective, Viguerie used the technique of bombarding Congress with thousands of preprinted post cards or clip-out coupons. He admitted that members of Congress would recognize his campaigns as orchestrated and that they did not value the opinions expressed in a standardized post card as much as a thoughtful, individual letter. But neither could they ignore them, he argued.

His view was supported by the Burson-Marsteller study, which found that "orchestrated mail," while not so effective as spontaneous constituent letters, ranked "surprisingly high" as an influence on lawmakers.

Another grass-roots lobbying technique involves gaining attention through mass media campaigns — on the radio, television, or in newspapers and magazines. Thoughtful editorials in well-known or more obscure newspapers in members' districts often stimulate readers to write their congressman. John Shattuck, executive director of the American Civil Liberties Union, said that many lobbyists underestimated the importance of developing close relationships with newspaper editors and editorial writers, whose influence upon constituents, and thereby upon members, could be pivotal on controversial issues.

Attention also is purchased through paid advertising. According to Ornstein and Elder, "Nearly every day, *The Washington Post* — a popular outlet for lobbying appeals, because of its universal circulation among Washington politicians — has full or half-page ads placed by groups, either urging public and congressional support for or opposition to a particular legislative proposal, or promoting a general viewpoint on a broad public policy issue."

The technological age also offers the contemporary lobbyist a back door into the public print through "media distribution services." North American Precis Service, the largest of its kind, claimed it could "generate tons of letters to legislators" by getting clients' views placed in smaller newspapers and on radio and television stations. North American would package a company or trade group pitch as an editorial or light feature, with a title such as "Washington Wants to Know" or "Capitol Ideas." The firm's brochure promised the articles would be run verbatim in hundreds of outlets without being labeled as paid public relations. One North American brochure promised: "Our IBM 5120 computer will address your material to the editors who are most likely to print it."

Some newspapers, including the *Washington Post,* viewed such products as propaganda masquerading as news and barred them from their news or editorial columns. They refused to use editorial pieces written by public relations or media distribution firms. The president of North American defended his company's releases as always fair and accurate, aimed at "increasing public awareness of the truth so that you generate massive public support."

Campaign Support

Campaign contributions to members of Congress serve two important functions for lobbying organizations. Political support not only can induce a congressman to back the group's legislative interests but also can help to ensure that members friendly to the group's goals remain in office.

While corporations have been barred since 1907, and labor unions since 1943, from making direct contributions to campaigns for federal office, contributors have found numerous ways to get around the restrictions. Labor pioneered in setting up separate political arms, such as the AFL-CIO's Committee on Political Education, that collect voluntary contributions from union members and their families and use the money to help elect senators and representatives favorable to their cause. It also is legal for unions to endorse candidates.

Similarly, corporations can organize political action committees (PACs) to seek contributions from stockholders and executive and administrative personnel and their families. Corporate PACs have proliferated, especially after the Federal Election Commission SunPAC decision in 1975, and their influences have come to rival, if not surpass, those of labor. The SunPAC decision allowed business PACs to solicit employees and not just stockholders, vastly expanding their potential to raise money. *(Political Action Committees, p. 47)*

Twice a year union and corporate political action committees are allowed to seek anonymous contributions by mail from all employees, not just those to which they were initially restricted. The same general resources for political support and opposition are available to members of citizens' groups and, indeed, to a wide range of organizations seeking to exert political pressure on members of Congress.

In approaching the typical member, a pressure group has no need to tell him outright that future political support or opposition depends on how the member votes on a particular bill or whether, over a long period, the member acts favorably toward the group. The member understands this without being told. The member knows that when the vital interests of some group are at stake, a vote supporting those interests normally would win the group's friendship and future support, and a vote against them would mean the group's enmity and future opposition.

Lobbyists themselves frequently deny this is the intention of their campaign support. But lobbyists do admit that political support gives them access to the legislator that they otherwise might not have.

2

The Presidential Lobby

The president is the strongest source of pressure on Congress. No one else can subject the legislative branch of government to as much influence as the president and his helpers in the executive branch. No one else can organize the pressure as thoroughly or sustain it as long as the president.

How does he do it? The Constitution is tight-lipped. Presidents have had to find their own ways. Strong presidents have done so. Strong presidents have learned to lobby Congress directly, in person, or through staff. They have influenced Congress indirectly, by focusing public opinion. They have used government jobs, contracts, and other forms of patronage. They have threatened to veto bills, and — when all else failed — they have gone ahead and vetoed them. These are the main ways presidents pressure Congress.

The Constitution vests Congress with "all legislative powers" and vests the president with "the executive power." Despite this apparent separation, the president has become, over the years, a *maker* of laws in his own right. Bertram M. Gross, in *The Legislative Struggle: A Study in Social Combat*, goes as far as to call the president "the most important legislative leader in the government," adding that "except in wartime, Presidents are now judged more by the quality of the legislation they propose or succeed in getting enacted than by their records as executives."

The president's role as lawmaker begins with his constitutional duty to "from time to time give to the Congress Information of the State of the Union, and recommend to their Consideration such Measures as he shall judge necessary and expedient." To these bare bones Congress has attached other requirements. The president is required, for example, to send Congress an annual budget message, setting forth his plans for taxes and spending, and an economic report, giving his program for achieving "maximum employment, production and purchasing power," as outlined in the Employment Act of 1946.

The Constitution only hints at how a president is supposed to go about persuading Congress to pass his economic program, his tax and spending plan, and the other measures he deems necessary and expedient. "He may, on extraordinary Occasions, convene both Houses, or either of them." And "he shall nominate, and by and with the Advice and Consent of the Senate, shall appoint Ambassadors, other public Ministers and Consuls, Judges of the Supreme Court, and all other Officers of the United States, whose Appointments are not otherwise provided for, and which shall be established by Law: but the Congress may by Law vest the appointment of such inferior Officers, as they think proper, in the President alone, in the Courts of Law, or in the Heads of Departments."

Finally, the Constitution gives the president the power to "return . . . with his Objections" any bill Congress has passed but that he disapproves of. This is the veto power.

Over the decades, a sort of gentleman's understanding has evolved concerning what is proper and what is improper presidential salesmanship. The understanding is that direct pressure generally is acceptable, but spending money to solicit outside pressure on Congress is not.

A criminal statute adopted in 1919 appears to prohibit the executive branch from spending money to influence votes in Congress. Violation is punishable by a $500 fine, a year in jail, and removal from office. But the statute is so ambiguous that it never has resulted in an indictment or prosecution. Alleged violations have been tried in the press, in congressional hearings, and General Accounting Office reports, but never in a courtroom.

Weak presidents have discovered in the law's near silence an excuse for inactivity. Strong presidents have taken silence to mean they may do anything not expressly forbidden. But a strong president's success at pressuring Congress depends on many things, among which are: Congress's own strength, the popularity of the president and his program, whether the issue is foreign or domestic, and whether the White House and Congress are in the hands of different political parties.

It was House Speaker Henry Clay, not the president, who set the domestic agenda during the administrations of James Madison and James Monroe. Clay conceived and promoted his American Plan — a program of improvements at home and tariff protection against imports from abroad.

Woodrow Wilson was master of virtually all the arts of pressure — direct lobbying, public opinion, and patronage. But when Wilson failed to persuade the public of the need to join the League of Nations, the Senate rejected the League.

Between World War II and Vietnam, Congress kept presidents on a short leash at home but let them run far abroad. "The postwar Presidents, though Eisenhower and Kennedy markedly less than Truman, Johnson and Nixon, almost came to see the sharing of power with Congress in foreign policy as a derogation of the presidency. Congress in increasing self-abasement, almost came to love its impotence," wrote Arthur M. Schlesinger, Jr., in *The Imperial Presidency*.

No president has ever come to office more schooled in the ways of Congress than Lyndon B. Johnson. He had worked at the Capitol 32 years — as a secretary, member of the House, senator, Senate minority leader, majority leader, and vice president. With President Johnson cracking the whip in 1965, Congress passed the most sweeping domestic program since Franklin D. Roosevelt (FDR): aid to schools, voting rights, health care for the aged, rent supplements for the poor, and freer immigration. Yet Johnson knew that success was fleeting. "I have watched the Congress from either the inside or the outside, man and boy, for more than 40 years," he remarked early in 1965, "and I've never seen a Congress that didn't eventually take the measure of the president it was dealing with."

Unhappy with the war in Vietnam and its attendant inflation, the voters elected 47 more Republicans to the House in 1966. Johnson's decision not to seek reelection in 1968 was made public amid growing signs of uneasiness among Democratic politicians and party officials about supporting him for renomination at the Democratic National Convention.

Like Presidents Kennedy and Johnson, Richard Nixon had served in Congress before the White House. Unlike his predecessors, however, Nixon had a Congress controlled by the opposition party. Within 15 months of Nixon's inauguration, the Democratic Congress had rejected two of his nominees for the Supreme Court, both of them southerners. In 1971 Nixon set "Six Great Goals" for his administration: welfare reform, revenue sharing with the states and localities, comprehensive health insurance, clean air and water, government reorganization, and full employment. By the end of Nixon's first term, Congress had approved only revenue sharing.

In Nixon's second term, the Democratic Congress imposed the first congressional limits on a president's power to act in international emergencies. It passed the Congressional Budget and Impoundment Control Act of 1974 to limit the president's power to impound money appropriated by Congress. The uproar over the Watergate scandal finally forced Nixon to resign the presidency; he became the first president ever to do so.

Having a Congress of the president's own party is no guarantee of success, however. Although Jimmy Carter had a Democratic House and Senate, he was inept at pressuring Congress, either directly or through public opinion. Congress rejected, or drastically changed, many of Carter's big legislative proposals. Among Carter's most notable failures were proposals for a 10-cent-per-gallon gasoline tax as an energy conservation measure, controls on ballooning hospital costs, labor law changes, and tax revision. Nevertheless, Carter managed to score some significant legislative and foreign policy victories.

Nor does opposition control of Congress necessarily spell a president's defeat. In 1981 Ronald Reagan put together a coalition of Republicans and Southern Democrats to force his tax and spending plans through a House "controlled" by Democrats.

Presidential Lobby: More Open, Elaborate

Since the birth of the Republic, presidents have lobbied Congress, in person or through helpers. Careful of the form if not the substance of separate powers, early presidents kept their congressional lobbying discreet and their helpers few. In recent years, presidential lobbying has become more open and more elaborate.

George Washington visited the Senate to try to win its advice and consent to an Indian treaty. Washington expected to force quick action. He failed. After that, the first president stayed away from the Capitol, except to deliver annual messages. Instead, he sent Secretary of State Thomas Jefferson and Treasury Secretary Alexander Hamilton for private talks on foreign and fiscal matters. Hamilton became so influential that the House established its committee on Ways and Means to defend against him.

When Jefferson became president, he used a series of Virginia representatives, beginning with William B. Giles, as his eyes, ears, and hands in Congress.

In this century, Woodrow Wilson made his lobbying as discreet as possible. His chief congressional lobbyist was Postmaster General Albert Burleson, a Texas Democrat who had quit the House to take the cabinet job. With postmasterships and post offices at his disposal, Burleson had considerable influence over members of Congress.

At Burleson's suggestion, Wilson enlisted another Texas Democrat, John Nance Garner, to act as his confidential lobbyist *inside* the House. Garner was a member of the Ways and Means Committee and later was to become Speaker and vice president. The Wilson-Garner relationship was hidden from the House Democratic hierarchy. Supposedly on private business, Garner left Capitol Hill twice a week by streetcar, got off near the White House, entered through a side door, and was ushered into Wilson's private study where he reported to the president.

But Wilson knew how to apply pressure in person, too. In pursuit of tariff revision, he dropped by congressional committee meetings. In the Senate, every Democrat voted for the tariff bill.

Franklin Roosevelt used White House aides James Rowe, Thomas G. Corcoran, and Benjamin Cohen to exert pressure on Congress. As their official duties included drafting legislation, they were natural choices to lobby to get bills enacted. Postmaster General James A. Farley was also the Democratic national chairman. Farley used both the postal and the political power to influence votes in Congress. Like Roosevelt, Harry S Truman used White House assistants Clark Clifford and Charles Murphy in part-time legislative liaison.

By not publicly naming their congressional lobbyists, wrote Neil MacNeil in *Forge of Democracy*, "Wilson, Roosevelt and Truman . . . kept up a pretense of staying within the traditional strictures of the assumed independence of the President and the Congress. They felt the need for such intimate contact with the members of Congress, but they hesitated to offend the sensibilities of the House and Senate as institutions."

Full-time Liaison Officers

Beginning with Dwight D. Eisenhower, presidents have appointed full-time legislative liaison officers to their White House staff. In addition, all federal departments now have their own congressional liaison forces. The practice began in 1945, when the War Department created the office of assistant secretary for congressional liaison, centralizing congressional relations that had been handled separately by the military services.

Eisenhower named Bryce N. Harlow, long an employee of the House Armed Services Committee, as his top special assistant for congressional affairs, a post he held under various titles for eight years. The position no longer was anonymous, nor did Harlow have other White House assignments.

According to MacNeil, Harlow "normally operated from his White House office, answering and making telephone calls, perhaps as many as 125 a day." MacNeil's account of Harlow's liaison methods continues: "Only rarely did he slip up to the House of Representatives and usually then only to have a private lunch with Charles Halleck of Indiana, one of the Republican leaders. . . . Harlow kept the Republican party's congressional leaders informed of forthcoming Eisenhower legislative proposals and kept in touch with Democratic leaders. Frequently he escorted Speaker Sam Rayburn and Senate Majority Leader Lyndon Johnson into the White House late in the day for a highball and chat with the President. . . . Harlow tried to satisfy the requests of members and tried to persuade them to support the President's programs. 'In this game,' he said, 'it's what you've done lately that counts.' "

Kennedy-O'Brien Team

President John F. Kennedy sought to beef up the liaison function, appointing his long-time associate Lawrence F. O'Brien as chief lobbyist and giving O'Brien full authority to speak for him on legislative matters. O'Brien was given coequal rank with other top White House aides and was assigned assistants for both House and Senate. MacNeil reports that "to even the most influential senators who telephoned Kennedy in the first weeks of his presidency, the President had a stock reply: 'Have you discussed this with Larry O'Brien?' "

At the outset of the Kennedy administration, O'Brien organized a series of cocktail parties, all held in House committee rooms, where he sought to meet House members on a purely social basis. Later, O'Brien invited House members in groups of 50 for coffee at the White House. For committee chairmen, he set up private discussions with the president. At a dinner with the Democratic Study Group, a bloc of about 100 House liberals, O'Brien promised that the president would support them for reelection if they backed his legislative program. "The White House certainly remembers who its friends are," MacNeil reported of O'Brien, "and can be counted on to apply significant assistance in the campaign."

Clearing their activities with O'Brien, cabinet officials sought to cultivate congressional leaders. Defense Secretary Robert S. McNamara courted House Armed Services Committee chairman Carl Vinson, D-Ga. (1914-65), Vinson's Senate counterpart Richard B. Russell, D-Ga. (1933-71), and other key members of the House and Senate military committees. Treasury Secretary Douglas Dillon kept in close touch with House Ways and Means Committee chairman Wilbur D. Mills, D-Ark. (1939-77). Agriculture Secretary Orville L. Freeman consulted frequently with congressional leaders on the president's farm program. Other cabinet officers and their liaison staffs made similar contacts.

Kennedy and O'Brien made extensive use of the congressional liaison offices of the cabinet departments and executive agencies. When an administration bill was introduced in Congress, the department involved was given prime responsibility for getting the measure through subcommittee and committee. When the bill neared the House or Senate floor, O'Brien and his corps of White House lobbyists joined forces with the agency liaison teams. There were about 35 agency lobbyists working during the Kennedy-Johnson era although not all of them devoted full time to legislation.

The Kennedy tactics often were successful in removing major legislative obstacles, but the obstacles appeared so frequently that the president's program foundered in Congress. Some members, primarily the older, more conservative ones, resented the pressure treatment. As Meg Greenfield, a newspaper and magazine writer, reported in 1962: "The most widely shared and loudly voiced grievance that Congress has against administration practices concerns the unremitting attention it receives from those it describes simply and without affection as the 'young men.' They badger, to hear the members tell it. They hector. They even chase.... Legislators who still cherish the notion that they themselves will decide how to vote appear to have been at various times amused, confused and infuriated by the discombobulation of incoming messages.... 'Why are you calling me, son?' an august legislator asked an all but anonymous administration phoner not long ago.... To the White House counterclaim that pushing and prodding sometimes helps and never hurts, one congressman replies by citing the case of a young liaison man, the very sight of whom at the cloakroom door, he claims, is enough to cost the administration 25 votes. Under questioning, he lowered the figure to three, but this time he seemed serious."

Liaison Under Johnson

The liaison system Kennedy nurtured paid dividends during the Johnson administration. Loyal Democrats had picked up a working margin of seats in the 1964 election, and with O'Brien still supervising the liaison job, almost all of the old Kennedy measures sailed through Congress. Even when Johnson appointed O'Brien postmaster general, he continued as chief White House lobbyist, after Johnson himself.

O'Brien abided by one self-imposed

rule. He would not enter the public congressional galleries, either to listen to debate or watch the members vote. "He could read the debate and count the vote in the *Congressional Record* the next day," wrote MacNeil. "To appear in the gallery, however, might smack of an impropriety; it might seem that he was asserting an undue pressure on the members of Congress. O'Brien's sensitivity here was a trace, a faint trace, of the old constitutional separatism between the executive and legislative branches of the government. There were scarcely any others left. The rest had been eroded by the imperious demands of modern America."

Nixon and Ford

Although President Nixon sought to slow down the furious pace of legislation that had marked the Johnson years, he still relied on a large liaison staff to push key administration bills. As chief lobbyist, he named Bryce Harlow, who came back to the White House after eight years of lobbying for the Procter & Gamble Co. In Nixon's first two years, his lobby force lost critical battles over two Supreme Court nominations and over restrictions on the administration's Southeast Asia policy but won a notable victory on funds for deployment of a controversial antiballistic missile system.

Harlow served Nixon until April 1974, four months before Nixon's resignation. In addition to Harlow, during the Nixon years, much of the day-to-day congressional liaison was handled by William E. Timmons, who had served in both Senate and House offices.

When Timmons resigned as chief liaison officer, President Gerald R. Ford promoted Max L. Friedersdorf to the position. A former newspaper reporter, Friedersdorf had been an administrative assistant to Rep. Richard L. Roudebush, R-Ind. (1961-71), and a congressional relations officer with the Office of Economic Opportunity.

Problems for Carter

A newcomer to Washington, President Carter got off to a bad start by appointing another Georgian and an equally inexperienced hand, Frank B. Moore, as his chief congressional lobbyist. Moore quickly offended congressional sensibilities by failing to return phone calls, missing meetings, and neglecting to consult adequately about presidential appointments and programs. He broke with precedent by organizing his 20-man staff around issues rather than geographical areas. This hampered vote-trading. As a former Carter aide explained, a White House liaision officer "is no longer in a position to discuss a sewage treatment plant in the context of a foreign aid vote, because the liaison aide who handles foreign aid does not also handle environmental issues."

Six months after taking office, Carter reorganized his liaison team by geography and added several Washington veterans, including William H. Cable, a respected House staffer who was put in charge of lobbying the House. Moore also adopted some of Lawrence O'Brien's techniques for pushing major bills through Congress, including close coordination of White House and department lobbyists and personal intervention by the president before key votes. The White House also began using computers to analyze past votes and target supporters for the future.

These "task force" techniques were used to help persuade Congress to stop development of the B-1 bomber, ratify the Panama Canal treaty, and revise the civil service system.

After its shaky start, the Carter liaison team also learned to work through the Democratic leadership in the House and Senate. Carter himself met with the leaders every Tuesday. But according to most observers, Carter's team never recovered totally from its beginnings.

Max L. Friedersdorf worked on congressional relations under Presidents Richard Nixon, Gerald R. Ford, and Ronald Reagan.

Reagan

Attention to detail is one of the factors that set President Reagan's legislative liaison team, headed initially by Max Friedersdorf, apart from the Carter team that preceded it. Friedersdorf had worked on congressional relations under Nixon and Ford. His chief assistants, Powell E. Moore in the Senate and Kenneth M. Duberstein in the House, had substantial experience on Capitol Hill.

Reagan built a reputation for a winning way with Congress during his first years, thanks mainly to a few major showdowns on the budget, taxes, and the sale of the Airborne Warning and Control System (AWACS) radar planes to Saudi Arabia.

During 1981 Duberstein became known as an effective, discreet, and partisan go-between. When Friedersdorf stepped down from his post at the end of the year, Reagan turned the job over to Duberstein.

By mid-1984 the administration found itself straining in its dealings with Congress. White House strategists sometimes had to struggle to win a majority of votes in the GOP-held Senate while facing tougher odds in the Democratic-controlled House. Although the administration was able to win crucial votes on such issues as defense spending and foreign policy, many were by paper-thin margins only after Reagan reluctantly agreed to significant concessions.

The results of the 1982 midterm congressional elections did much to diminish the administration's lobbying leverage. A net loss that year of 26 House Republican seats robbed Reagan of a working majority he had welded together during his first two years in office and complicated the task of White House lobbyists. Another explanation, offered by White House aides, was that, in 1984, election-year partisanship created obstacles to Reagan's legislative agenda.

The December 1983 departure of the highly regarded Duberstein also was part of the reason for the administration's tougher sledding in Congress, according to Capitol Hill sources. Duberstein was replaced by M. B. Oglesby, Jr., a former White House aide who worked on the White House lobbying staff since the start of Reagan's first term. Oglesby — called "B" by friends and associates — was the chief House lobbyist under Duberstein and earned a reputation as a good vote-counter. But Oglesby brought a far different style to the job.

Duberstein "had a more personal, down-in-the-trenches, hand-to-hand combat type of approach," said Rep. Trent Lott, R-Miss., the House minority whip. "B is quieter, more methodical type worker, not as inclined to really confront a member in almost an argumentative way, which is the way Ken was sometimes. . . ."

The scrappy and salty-tongued Duberstein had a knack for building personal bridges to important potential adversaries. Oglesby was considered an effective lobbyist but was not so good a planner of overall strategy. In February 1985, Max Friedersdorf came back to the White House as "legislative strategy coordinator" and was expected to beef up the White House lobbying office in numbers and talent. His return was short-lived, however. When Friedersdorf left in August to take on another position within the administration, his responsibilities were assumed by Oglesby.

In February 1986, Reagan named William L. Ball III his chief liaison with Congress. From March 1985 until his appointment, Ball served as assistant secretary of state for legislative and intergovernmental affairs. From 1981 to 1985 he was an administrative assistant to Sen. John Tower, R-Texas (1961-85).

Despite some narrow victories and defeats, Reagan continues to enjoy a reputation as a successful president in dealing with Congress. "The public perception and the Washington perception is that he is still Jack the Giant Killer when it comes to Congress," said Stephen J. Wayne, a political science professor at the George Washington University.

According to his aides, Reagan genuinely enjoys the lobbying side of his job. He stands in stark contrast to Jimmy Carter, who left lobbying chores largely to others and suffered in his relations with Congress as a result.

In December 1985, following his landslide reelection victory, Reagan once again demonstrated the almost mystical powers of political persuasion that have been his hallmark as president. He was able to convince 54 House Republicans to switch their votes in favor of a rule that paved the way for passage of a major tax-overhaul bill.

To keep the tax bill alive, Reagan relied on the same vote-seeking skills that had served him so well on issues such as funding for the MX missile and his policies in Central America. In addition to a blitz of phone calls and White House visits with individual members, Reagan made a rare journey to Capitol Hill where he met for nearly an hour in a closed-door session with House Republicans.

Moving Congress by Going to the People

When even the most skillful direct pressure fails, presidents often turn to the public for help in moving Congress. Going over congressional heads to the people has always required cultivation of reporters and others responsible for gathering and transmitting the news. Today, radio and television permit a president to go over reporters' heads, too, in marshaling public opinion.

Among the early presidents, Andrew Jackson was the most skillful at public relations. Jackson arranged to have official documents leaked to his favorite newspapers. According to James E. Pollard in *The Presidents and the Press*, Jackson "knew what he wanted, he meant to have his way, and he was fortunate in finding journalists devoted to him and capable of carrying out his desires."

Abraham Lincoln found himself on the defensive with Congress in regard to his war policies. But he overcame congressional opposition with public support, generated by the stories he passed out to reporters and editors and by letters he wrote that found their way into print. The press also published Lincoln's eloquent speeches. While Lincoln "paid some heed to the sanctity of military secrets, he declined to worship at that shrine," wrote George Fort Milton in *The Use of Presidential Power*. "He knew that the people had ears, whether the walls had them or not, and took advantage of every appropriate occasion to tell his innermost thoughts."

Andrew Johnson was the first president to grant a formal interview to the press. He gave 12 exclusive interviews, most of them on his troubles with Congress over Reconstruction. But press coverage failed to generate enough public sympathy to save Johnson from impeachment by the House. He escaped conviction in the Senate by a single vote.

Theodore Roosevelt made himself easily available to reporters. Credited with having invented the "background" press conference, Roosevelt launched "trial balloons" to test public opinion before deciding on a course of action. Under Roosevelt, the White House began issuing regular news releases.

Roosevelt saw the White House as a "bully pulpit," to be used to mobilize public support. Eager to show the American flag abroad, Roosevelt sent the U.S. battleship fleet around the world, even though the Navy lacked funds to pay for the cruise. The public was so impressed with this display of American naval power that Congress lost no time in appropriating the necessary money.

Woodrow Wilson began the practice of holding regular and formal press conferences. Until the war in Europe took most of his time, Wilson met the press an average of twice a week. But Wilson was most effective with his appeals directly to the public. Several weeks after Wilson's inauguration, the new president issued a statement attacking the "extraordinary exertions" of special interest groups to change his tariff bill, according to *The Presidents and the Press*. "The newspapers are filled with paid advertisements," he said, "calculated to mislead the judgment of public men not only, but also the public opinion of the country itself."

While Wilson succeeded in having his way with the tariff, the technique failed him in 1919, when he conducted a whistle-stop tour of the country to drum up support for the League of Nations. He was followed by a "truth squad" of senators opposed to the League. In the end, the Senate rejected the Treaty of Versailles, which contained the Covenant of the League.

Like his distant relative Theodore, Franklin Roosevelt viewed the president as more than a chief executive. "The presidency is not merely an administrative office. That is the least of it," he said during the 1932 campaign. "It is pre-eminently a place of moral leadership."

FDR: Master of the Art

Probably no other president has used the news media so skillfully as FDR. He showered attention on White House reporters, holding 998 press conferences during his 147 months in office. According to Pollard, Roosevelt "was on an unprecedented footing with the working press. He knew its ways, he understood many of its problems and he more than held his own in his twice-weekly parry and thrust with the correspondents."

But it was in the radio that Roosevelt found a powerful new tool for shaping public opinion and pressuring Congress. At the end of his first week in office, Roosevelt went on the radio to urge support for his banking reforms. He addressed a joint session of Congress, too. His reforms were passed that very day.

Similar radio messages followed, and they became known as "fireside chats." As Arthur Schlesinger, Jr., put it, these radio talks were effective because they "conveyed Roosevelt's conception of himself as a man at ease in his own house talking frankly and intimately to neighbors as they sat in their living rooms."

According to Wilfred Binkley in the book *President and Congress*, Roosevelt "had only to glance toward a microphone or suggest that he might go on the air again and a whole congressional delegation would surrender. They had no relish for the flood of mail and telegrams they knew would swamp them after another fireside chat to the nation."

So Congress went on, in the spring of 1933, to approve a spate of Roosevelt proposals, pausing to change scarcely so much as a comma. At the time, the president's program was known as the "Roosevelt Revolution," but he said he preferred "New Deal." In Roosevelt's first 100 days, Congress approved the bank bill, a 25 percent cut in government spending, farm relief, public works, relief for the states, the Civilian Conservation Corps, and other important measures. Although the going got much tougher later on, Roosevelt still won passage of the Trade Agreements Act, Social Security, and the Public Utilities Holding Company Act.

Television Becomes Important

President Eisenhower permitted his news conferences to be filmed and then televised, after editing by the White House. President Kennedy permitted live telecasts of his news conferences. For the first time, the public saw the actual questions and answers as they occurred, unedited. While these TV encounters with the press helped make Kennedy popular, they were not sufficient to pressure Congress into passing his program.

President Johnson succeeded in getting both public and Congress to accept his Great Society program at home. Johnson was a master at moving members of Congress in person. Although he often appeared uncomfortable and unpolished on TV, Johnson, in his televised address to Congress on voting rights, proved that he could move the people, too.

The war in Vietnam eventually soured Johnson's public and congressional relations. In 1966 Congress showed that TV can be as powerful a weapon against a president as for him. When the administration asked for more money to conduct the war, the Senate Foreign Relations Committee turned the televised hearing into a full-scale debate on the war itself.

President Nixon tried to go over the heads of the Washington press corps, which he regarded as hostile, by holding press conferences outside of the capital. He also tried to generate public support through TV, with mixed results. His televised veto of a Labor-Health, Education, and Welfare appropriations bill in 1970 brought 55,000 telegrams down on the Democratic House, which upheld the veto.

But Nixon's TV appearances failed to erase Watergate from the public mind. On November 17, 1973, Nixon told a startled nation: "I am not a crook." Meanwhile, the Senate Watergate Committee's televised hearings and the House Judiciary Committee's televised impeachment proceedings undermined public support for Nixon. He resigned the presidency August 9, 1974.

President Ford took office promising

an "open administration." Indeed, at the end of 1975, the National Press Club praised him for conducting 24 news conferences in 19 months in office, compared with Nixon's 37 in 5½ years. But the club criticized Press Secretary Ron Nessen for being unprepared and devious in his briefings.

President Carter campaigned as a Washington outsider and continued to cultivate that populist image after he took office. Carter's inaugural walk with his wife, Rosalynn, up Pennsylvania Avenue, "town meetings," fireside chats, and bluejeans — all conveyed to the people through television — failed, however, to generate enough support in the country to move his program through Congress. "We used to be frightened to death that he would go over the top of Congress and appeal directly to the people," said Rep. Timothy E. Wirth, D-Colo., "but there's not enough cohesion in his program to do that. There's no reason to feel threatened."

An exception was the televised signing, in March 1979, of the peace treaty between Israel and Egypt, following the Camp David summit meeting, which Carter called in 1978. That ceremony played a part in persuading an otherwise stingy Congress to give foreign aid to Israel and Egypt.

President Reagan, a former actor, enjoyed early success with TV. He became known as "The Great Communicator" for his ability to project his ideas to audiences, both in person and via the electronic media.

In May 1981, Reagan made a televised address to a joint session of Congress to appeal for passage of his budget package, one that cut social spending and increased spending for defense. It was Reagan's first public appearance following the March 30 attempt on his life. A few days after his address, the Reagan budget easily passed the Democratic House. Speaker Thomas P. O'Neill, Jr., D-Mass., called the Reagan effort "the greatest selling job I've ever seen."

Theodore Roosevelt saw the presidency as a "bully pulpit," to be used to mobilize public opinion. He invented the "background" press conference, and during his administration the White House began issuing regular news releases.

High-profile speeches on Central America, and especially Nicaragua, became a staple of the Reagan administration. Reagan delivered at least one nationally televised speech asking for congressional support of his Central America policies annually from 1983 to 1986.

Reagan continued to rely on his strategy of appealing directly to the American people, despite the somewhat diminished effectiveness of that strategy over time. For example, in April 1985 Reagan made a televised address supporting a fiscal 1986 GOP Senate budget plan. The public response was mixed, contrasting sharply with the overwhelming support Reagan received following his 1981 budget speech. His plea for action failed to move the Senate to consensus.

Reagan generally did not perform so well in nationally televised press conferences as he did delivering speeches. He often made misstatements and appeared confused on the issues. Reagan's meetings with the press, as compared with his predecessors', were infrequent, and complaints arose about his inaccessibility. After four years in office Reagan had held 26 news conferences; Carter had held 59.

The good-natured persona that Reagan projected contributed to his personal popularity. His faculty for walking away from criticism apparently unaffected was matched by an ability to escape serious blame for setbacks and embarrassments that occurred during his administration. Rep. Patricia Schroeder, D-Colo., bestowed on Reagan the title of "the Teflon president." Blame, it seemed, would not stick to him. As Bruce Buchanan wrote in *The Citizen's Presidency: Standards of Choice and Judgment,* "It became an article of faith among journalists on the presidency beat that the public simply would not stand for harsh treatment of this president. . . . Consequently, Reagan's press has been noticeably less critical than Carter's was."

Another technique Reagan used to drum up public support for his policies was to dispatch top administration officials to congressional districts. Elizabeth Hanford Dole served as Reagan's first official liaison with the public before becoming secretary of transportation in February 1983.

Her stock in trade included invitations to White House briefings by the president, cabinet members, and staff for business and community leaders, farm groups, and others. Dole herself gave numerous speeches. And it became her office's job to arrange for presidential greetings, on film or tape, for a fledgling Hispanic radio service or a Teamsters' convention, for example. Her operation was but a piece of a broader effort to win public support for the president's program.

Patronage: Favors for Votes

Another means of exerting pressure on Congress is patronage — the president's power to fill government jobs, award government contracts, or do other political favors. Patronage can create a debt that is repaid by voting the president's way on legislation. At least it creates an atmosphere of friendly familiarity between the president and members of Congress.

"Broadly conceived, patronage involves not only federal and judicial positions, but also federal construction projects, location of government installations, offers of campaign support, access to strategic information, plane rides on Air Force One, White House meetings for important constituents of members, and countless other favors both large and small," wrote Roger H. Davidson and Walter J. Oleszek in *Congress and Its Members.* "Their factual or potential award enables presidents to amass political IOUs they can 'cash in' later for needed support in Congress."

In this century, civil service and postal reform has reduced the number of jobs the president has to fill. But award of government contracts and other favors remains a powerful lever in the hands of presidents.

How effective patronage is as a pressure tool is a matter of debate. Neil MacNeil reported that Sen. Everett M. Dirksen of Illinois (1951-69), a Republican leader in the 1960s, called patronage a "tremendous weapon," adding that "it develops a certain fidelity on the part of the recipient." But Rep. Paul J. Kilday, D-Texas (1939-61), said in 1961 that a member of Congress usually has 100 applications for every job. According to MacNeil, Kilday said: "You make 99 fellows mad at you and get one ingrate."

George Washington thought that government jobs should be filled by "those that seem to have the greatest fitness for public office." The framers of the Constitution, meanwhile, sought to protect members of Congress from the president's patronage power. The Constitution says: "No Senator or Representative shall, during the Time for which he was elected, be appointed to any civil Office under the Authority of the United States, which shall have been created, or the Emoluments thereof shall have been increased during such time; and no Person holding any Office under the United States, shall be a member of either House during his Continuence in Office."

"In other words," wrote Rep. DeAlva Stanwood Alexander, R-N.Y. (1897-1911), in 1916 in *History and Procedure of the House of Representatives,* "a legislator was not to be induced to create an office, or to increase the emoluments of one, in the hope of an appointment; nor was the Executive able to appoint him while he continued in Congress. But in practice these constitutional limitations neither preserved the legislator's independence nor restrained executive influence. In fact, the President's possession of an ever-increasing patronage has enabled him at times to absorb the legislative branch of Government."

While the Constitution forbids members of Congress to hold other federal jobs, it does not forbid appointment of his friends, family, and supporters. With the emergence of political parties in the first decade of government under the Constitution, party loyalists started demanding federal jobs.

Spoils System: Created, Perfected

The inauguration of Thomas Jefferson in 1801 marked the first change in political parties at the White House. The new president found himself surrounded by Federalist party officeholders appointed by Washington and John Adams. Jefferson replaced enough of the Federalists with Democratic-Republicans to ensure, he said, a more even distribution of power between the parties.

Jefferson initiated the "spoils system," which allows victors to appoint their own people to public office. But it was Andrew Jackson, 20 years later, who perfected and justified spoils. As Martin and Susan Tolchin wrote in *To the Victor: Political Patronage From the Clubhouse to the White House,* Jackson was "the first to articulate, legitimize, and translate the spoils system into the American experience." The spoils system engendered power struggles. Jackson had a House controlled by his own Democratic party and a Senate in the hands of the opposition Whigs. The president and Congress spent much of their time fighting over patronage.

In the Senate, Jackson was challenged by John Tyler and John C. Calhoun, who led the battle against confirming some of the president's appointees and conducted a formal inquiry into the extent of federal patronage. According to the Tolchins, Calhoun said that "patronage made government too big: if this practice continued, he warned, states' rights would be crushed under the force of an ever-expanding federal bureaucracy. His investigation revealed the shocking fact that the 60,294 employees of the federal government, together with their dependents and other pensioners, made up a payroll of more than 100,000 people dependent on the federal treasury."

Lincoln used patronage to promote a constitutional amendment abolishing slavery. Unsure whether enough states would ratify the amendment, Lincoln sought to hasten the admission of a new state, Nevada. The Nevada bill was bogged down in the House, when Lincoln learned that the votes of three members might be up for bargaining. When Assistant Secretary of War Charles A. Dana asked Lincoln what the members expected in return for their votes, Lincoln reportedly replied: "I don't know. It makes no difference. We must carry this vote. . . . Whatever promises you make, I will perform." Dana made a deal with the three representatives, and Nevada entered the Union. The new state then voted for the Thirteenth Amendment.

President William McKinley appointed members of Congress to commissions, thus breaching the constitutional prohibition against members holding other federal offices. McKinley appointed them to make peace with Spain, settle the Bering Sea controversy, set the boundary between Alaska and Canada, arrange a commerce treaty with Great Britain, and gather information on Hawaii. McKinley asked the Senate to confirm senators named to the Hawaiian commission, but it declined to do so.

Perhaps the most successful dispenser of patronage ever to hold the presidency was Wilson, who made patronage an important instrument of his party leadership. Although patronage jobs had been cut back severely under President Grover Cleveland, as part of his civil service reform, Wilson used what patronage was left him with maximum effect. According to the *New York Sun,* Wilson's use of patronage "was never better illustrated than last Saturday, when at four o'clock, it became apparent that the senators from the cotton-growing states of the South had effected a coalition with the Republican side to kill the war-revenue bill or suspend it until legislation was put into the measure for the relief of the cotton planters. Immediately a strong arm was extended from the White House which promptly throttled the movement within thirty minutes after the fact of the revolt became known to Postmaster General Burleson, with the immense post-office patronage of the country at his disposal. . . . When the test came, four hours later, three of the eight revolters faltered and the scheme collapsed."

FDR, Eisenhower, Kennedy, and Johnson

The next Democrat in the White House, Franklin Roosevelt, also made effective use of his patronage power. His patronage chief, Postmaster General Farley, asked patronage seekers such questions as "What was your preconvention position on the Roosevelt candidacy?" and "How did you vote on the economy bill?" If a member was asked to vote for a presidential measure against local pressures, the matter was put "on the frank basis of quid pro quo."

The Eisenhower administration used patronage more as a stick than a carrot. The president's patronage dispenser, Postmaster General Arthur Summerfield, frequently set up shop in the office of House minority leader Charles A. Halleck, R-Ind. (1935-69), and berated Republican representatives who broke party ranks. Insurgents were warned that key jobs such as postmasterships might be cut back unless they got behind the president's program. The president himself sought to broaden the spoils, however, by removing 134,000 classified jobs from the Civil Service.

Presidents Kennedy and Johnson both assigned the task of dispensing patronage to John Bailey, chairman of the Democratic National Committee. Although clever use of patronage swayed votes on several key bills, Kennedy preferred the pressure of direct lobbying. Johnson was a master at dispensing jobs and other favors. He invited members of Congress to the White House for tete-à-tetes, danced with the wives, telephoned them on their birthdays, and invited them to his Texas ranch.

Dissolution of Patronage Empire

Nixon presided over the dissolution of a large piece of the president's patronage empire when he signed a bill that converted the 141-year-old Post Office Department into the politically independent U.S. Postal Service. While the main reason Congress passed the bill in 1970 was to solve the postal system's money problems, the measure ended the power of politicians to appoint or promote postmasters and other postal workers.

While the president's power over government jobs has declined, his power over the award of federal contracts and the location of federal installations has remained strong. According to Nelson W. Polsby in *Congress and the Presidency*, a president can use this power "to reward and punish congressional friends and foes quite vigorously. . . . Small Business Administration and Area Redevelopment Administration loans to certain areas may get more and more difficult to obtain, as applications fail to qualify. Pilot programs and demonstration projects may be funneled here rather than there. Defense contracts and public works may be accelerated in some areas, retarded in others."

Distribution of contracts and installations became increasingly important as the federal budget grew after World War II. The greatest beneficiaries were members of the House and Senate Armed Services committees and Defense Appropriations subcommittees. In return for their support of military requests, they received defense plants and installations in their states and districts.

Meanwhile, presidents have shown varying degrees of skill at handling the small change of patronage. Carter did not enjoy socializing with members of Congress. *Congress and Its Members* recounted this story of a House Democrat: "When I came here, President Kennedy would have six or seven of us down to the White House every evening for drinks and conversation. Johnson did the same thing, and they created highly personal, highly involved relationships. With Carter, he has 140 people in for breakfast and a lecture." The Carter White House refused a request from House Speaker O'Neill for extra tickets to the Carter inaugural.

Reagan enjoyed swapping small talk and stories with members of Congress of both parties. Reagan had Speaker O'Neill to dinner, and the White House staff invited O'Neill to a surprise birthday party for the president.

Veto Threat: Ultimate Weapon

When surprise parties and tickets, Army bases and jobs, lobbying on the Hill and at the grass roots all fail to move Congress, a president may resort to his most powerful defensive weapon, the veto.

A president uses the veto not only to try to kill unpalatable bills but also to dramatize his policies and put Congress on notice that he is to be taken seriously. Short of a veto itself, a presidential threat to veto legislation is a powerful form of lobbying.

The Constitution says that any bill Congress passes must go to the president. The president must either sign it or send it back to Congress with his objections. If he does neither while Congress is in session, it becomes law without his signature. A pocket veto occurs if Congress adjourns and the president does not sign a bill within 10 days after receiving it.

A two-thirds vote of each house is required to override a veto. The Supreme Court ruled in 1919 that two-thirds of a quorum, rather than two-thirds of the total membership, is enough for an override.

The veto is powerful because a president usually can muster the support of at least one-third plus one member of a House or Senate quorum. Woodrow Wilson said the veto power makes the president "a third

Vetoes and Veto Overrides of Public and Private Bills . . .

From 1789 through October 28, 1986, presidents had vetoed a grand total of 2,444 bills, with all except 59 of the vetoes occurring in the years after the administration of President Lincoln. Of the vetoed bills, only 98 became law through action by Congress overriding the president's veto.

Until 1969 presidents usually vetoed more private bills than public bills. President Truman, for example, vetoed 83 public bills and 167 private bills. But President Nixon reversed the trend. He vetoed only 3 private bills during his years in office. Generally, a private bill names a particular individual or entity who is to receive relief from the federal government under the terms of the bill — payment of claims, a pension, citizenship, etc. A public bill relates to matters affecting the people as a whole and deals with individuals only by classifications or categories.

Before 1936 the distinction between public and private bills was hazy, with some bills now considered public designated as private and vice versa. After 1936, if a bill was listed in the bill status section of the *Digest of Public General Bills,* Congressional Quarterly categorized it as public; if not, it was classified as private. The *Digest* first was published by the Library of Congress for the 74th Congress, 2d Session (1936). By then, however, three years of Roosevelt's first term in office had elapsed. Consequently, a reliable breakdown of vetoes by public and private bills was not feasible.

The first table below (1789-1945) shows the number of private and public bills vetoed by each president through Franklin Roosevelt, the type of veto used, and the number of vetoes overridden. The second table (1945-86) lists total bills vetoed from 1945 through October 28, 1986. The table shows the number of public bills vetoed, the type of action taken, and the number of vetoes overridden.

1789-1945

		Public and Private Bills		
President	**All Bills Vetoed**	**Regular Vetoes**	**Pocket Vetoes**	**Vetoes Overridden**
George Washington	2	2	0	0
John Adams	0	0	0	0
Thomas Jefferson	0	0	0	0
James Madison	7	5	2	0
James Monroe	1	1	0	0
John Quincy Adams	0	0	0	0
Andrew Jackson	12	5	7	0
Martin Van Buren	1	0	1	0
William Henry Harrison	0	0	0	0
John Tyler	10	6	4	1
James K. Polk	3	2	1	0
Zachary Taylor	0	0	0	0
Millard Fillmore	0	0	0	0
Franklin Pierce	9	9	0	5

... From George Washington to Ronald Reagan, 1789-1986

President	All Bills Vetoed	Public and Private Bills: Regular Vetoes	Pocket Vetoes	Vetoes Overridden
James Buchanan	7	4	3	0
Abraham Lincoln	7	2	5	0
Andrew Johnson	29	21	8	15
Ulysses S. Grant	93[1]	45	48[1]	4
Rutherford B. Hayes	13	12	1	1
James A. Garfield	0	0	0	0
Chester A. Arthur	12	4	8	1
Grover Cleveland (1st term)	414	304	110	2
Benjamin Harrison	44	19	25	1
Grover Cleveland (2d term)	170	42	128	5
William McKinley	42	6	36	0
Theodore Roosevelt	82	42	40	1
William Howard Taft	39	30	9	1
Woodrow Wilson	44	33	11	6
Warren G. Harding	6	5	1	0
Calvin Coolidge	50	20	30	4
Herbert Hoover	37	21	16	3
Franklin D. Roosevelt	635	372	263	9

1945-86

President	All Bills Vetoed	Public Bills: Total Vetoed	Regular Vetoes	Pocket Vetoes	Vetoes Overridden
Harry S Truman	250	83	54	29	11[2]
Dwight D. Eisenhower	181	81	36	45	2
John F. Kennedy	21	9	4	5	0
Lyndon B. Johnson	30	13	6	7	0
Richard Nixon	43[3]	40	24	16[3]	5
Gerald R. Ford	66	63	46	17	12
Jimmy Carter	31	29	13	16	2
Ronald Reagan[4]	53	47	29	18	6

[1] Veto total listed for Grant does not include a pocket veto of a bill that apparently never was placed before him for his signature.

[2] Truman also had one private bill overridden, making a total of 12 Truman vetoes overridden.

[3] Includes Nixon pocket veto of a bill during the 1970 congressional Christmas recess that was later ruled invalid by the District Court for the District of Columbia and the U.S. Court of Appeals for the District of Columbia.

[4] Through October 28, 1986.

Source: *Presidential Vetoes, 1789-1976,* compiled by the Senate Library under the direction of J. S. Kimmitt, secretary, and Roger K. Haley, librarian (U.S. Government Printing Office, 1978) and the staff of the Senate Library.

branch of the legislature." From 1789 through October 28, 1986, presidents vetoed 2,444 bills, and Congress overrode only 98. *(Vetoes, box, p. 26)*

The concept of veto (literally, I forbid) originated in ancient Rome as a means of protecting the plebeians from injustice at the hands of the patricians. Roman tribunes, representing the people, were authorized to veto acts of the Senate, dominated by the patricians. English rulers were given absolute veto power, and in 1597 Queen Elizabeth I rejected more parliamentary bills than she accepted. The English veto, which cannot be overridden, is still nominally in effect but has not been used since 1707.

Early American presidents conceived of the veto as a device to be used rarely and then only against legislative encroachment on the prerogatives of another branch of government. Washington vetoed only two bills; Adams and Jefferson, none. Madison vetoed seven bills, in most cases citing constitutional grounds for doing so. Monroe vetoed one bill; John Quincy Adams, none.

Jackson's View of Veto

The concept of the veto underwent a marked change under Andrew Jackson, who vetoed 12 bills, mostly because he took issue with their content or purpose. Jackson's most noteworthy veto was of a bill to recharter the Bank of the United States, which Jackson considered a creature of special interests. Binkley described Jackson's veto message as "a landmark in the evolution of the presidency." Binkley says: "For the first time in American history, a veto message was used as an instrument of party warfare. Through it, the Democratic Party, as the Jacksonians were now denominated, dealt a telling blow to their opponents, the National Republicans. Though addressed to Congress, the veto message was an appeal to the nation. Not a single opportunity to discredit the old ruling class was dismissed."

President John Tyler's veto of a tariff bill in 1843 brought on the first attempt by Congress to impeach a president. An impeachment resolution, introduced in the House by Whig members, charged the president "with the high crime and misdemeanor of withholding his assent to laws indispensable to the just operation of the government." When the impeachment move failed, Henry Clay proposed a constitutional amendment to enable Congress to override the president's veto by a simple majority instead of the required two-thirds. The president's right of veto gave him power equal to that of almost two-thirds of Congress, Clay said, adding that such power would ultimately make the president "ruler of the nation."

Use of Veto After the Civil War

When, after the Civil War, Andrew Johnson vetoed a bill to protect the rights of freedmen, Congress passed the measure over his head — the first time Congress had overridden the president's veto on a major issue. The civil rights bill was only the first of a number of measures to be passed over Johnson's veto. Among others was the Tenure of Office Act, which led indirectly to Johnson's impeachment. When Johnson refused to abide by the provisions of the act, which prohibited the president from removing appointed officials from office until their successors had been confirmed, the House initiated impeachment.

During the rest of the nineteenth century, presidents used the veto mainly to prevent corruption through the passage of private bills. Grover Cleveland vetoed 584 bills (346 directly and 238 by pocket veto), including 301 private pension bills, which previous presidents had signed routinely. While meant to discourage fraudulent claims, Cleveland's veto incurred the wrath of veterans' groups.

Cleveland's veto record stood until

Franklin Roosevelt, who disapproved 635 bills, 372 directly and 263 by pocket vetoes. Nine Roosevelt vetoes were overridden.

Under Roosevelt, vetoes increased both in absolute numbers and in relation to the number of bills passed. This, according to Professors Binkley and Malcolm C. Moos in *A Grammar of American Politics: The National Government,* reflected the growing complexity of America, which in turn was reflected in legislation. While Cleveland focused his vetoes on private pensions, Roosevelt took on the full range of issues. Until Roosevelt, no president had vetoed a revenue bill, and it was assumed that precedent exempted tax bills from the veto. Roosevelt first vetoed a revenue bill during World War II.

Truman and Eisenhower continued to make extensive use of the veto. Truman used it to safeguard organized labor against industry and agriculture. When, during the coal and rail strikes of 1946, Congress passed a bill restricting strikes, Truman vetoed it, and Congress sustained the veto. The votes to sustain came mainly from members representing big cities. In 1947, Truman vetoed the Taft-Hartley Labor Act, claiming it was unfair to labor. By then, however, Republicans were in control of Congress and the veto was overridden.

Eisenhower used the veto and the veto threat to defeat or limit social programs favored by the Democrats, who controlled Congress during six of his eight years in office. To fight liberal measures, Eisenhower put together a coalition of the Republican minority and conservative Southern Democrats. In 1959, for example, he vetoed two housing bills and another to promote rural electricity. Congress was unable to override either veto. That same year, Eisenhower used the threat of veto to defeat Democratic proposals for school aid, area redevelopment, a higher minimum wage, and health care for the aged.

Kennedy and Johnson seldom had to

use the veto or threaten it. They were activist presidents whose main interest lay in getting their programs through a Congress controlled by their own party. But in 1965 Johnson vetoed a military construction authorization bill that required advance congressional review of presidential decisions to close military bases.

Like Eisenhower, Nixon and Ford used the veto and its threat to prevent enactment of Democratic programs. Nixon often justified his vetoes on grounds that the bills were inflationary. When Congress passed a Labor-Health, Education, and Welfare appropriations bill that exceeded his request by $1.1 billion, Nixon vetoed it on national radio and TV. The Democratic House sustained the veto. Congress also sustained him on his vetoes of bills authorizing funds for the war on poverty and for manpower training and public service jobs.

But in 1973 Congress approved legislation to limit the president's power to commit armed forces abroad without congressional approval. Nixon vetoed the bill but Congress overrode him.

Ford vetoed 17 major bills in 1975 alone and was sustained in all but 4 of those. Seven of the 17 bills concerned energy and the economy. Not one of these vetoes was overridden. In 1975 both houses passed a consumer protection bill. The measure never went to conference, because Ford threatened to veto it.

Carter was the first president since Truman to have a veto overridden by a Congress in the hands of his own party. In 1980 he disapproved a debt limit bill that included a section killing an import fee he had imposed on foreign oil. Only a handful of senators and representatives, all Democrats, voted to sustain the veto. Later that year, Congress voted overwhelmingly to override Carter's veto of a bill to increase salaries of doctors at veterans hospitals.

Carter enjoyed a couple of notable triumphs. In 1977 he threatened to veto the public works appropriations bill because it contained money for dams and other water projects that Carter said were wasteful. Congress passed the bill anyway, and Carter made good on his threat. Defying its own leadership, both Democratic and Republican, the House voted to sustain the president. The vote was 223-190, which was 53 short of the two-thirds needed to override. The House in 1978 also sustained Carter's veto of a weapons procurement bill that authorized funding for a nuclear-powered aircraft carrier that he opposed.

As of October 28, 1986, President Reagan had vetoed 53 bills, including 6 private bills. Congress made 11 override attempts; 6 were successful. Reagan, for the first time since the 72d Congress (1931-33) and the days of Herbert Hoover, faced a Congress split between the parties. The Republicans controlled the Senate; the Democrats, the House.

Reagan often used or threatened to use the veto on budget-related matters. He vetoed a continuing appropriations bill in November 1981 on grounds that it was "budget busting." Instead of trying to override the veto, Congress regrouped and sent Reagan a bill he would sign.

Wielding his veto power twice in two days, Reagan vetoed two versions of the same supplemental appropriations bill in mid-1982. Congress sustained both vetoes. In September Congress handed Reagan his first big budget defeat when it overrode his veto of a supplemental bill. The president wanted more for defense and less for social programs than the bill provided, but his attempts to portray the measure as a "budget-buster" backfired as Congress insisted on its right to help set spending priorities.

In 1984 Congress overrode Reagan's veto of a bill to continue federal funding for state university water research institutes. Arguing that states should finance those programs, the president had proposed ending federal financial support in his budget proposals for fiscal 1982 through 1985. Congress, however, kept the program alive through year-to-year appropriations, then reauthorized the program over Reagan's veto.

Bipartisan efforts to restore administration budget cuts for public broadcasting failed twice in 1984, when Reagan vetoed bills that would have authorized more than three times his funding request. In both cases the president said the increases could not be justified in light of the need to exercise spending restraint to lower the federal budget deficit.

Citing the nation's "chronic budgetary crisis," Reagan in November 1985 vetoed an appropriations bill for the Treasury Department, U.S. Postal Service, Executive Office of the President, and various other agencies. He said the bill contained more than he had requested, most of it for a federal postal subsidy he had sought to end. While a presidential veto was "an instrument to be used with care," he said he would not hesitate to employ it "until the Congress comes to grips with the problem of the large budget deficit." Congress did not attempt an override.

The president and Congress also sparred in the area of foreign policy. In November 1983 Reagan pocket-vetoed a measure that would have continued a requirement that the president certify twice each year that El Salvador was making sufficient progress on human rights and other issues to warrant receiving U.S. aid. The veto infuriated Democrats in Congress, many of whom had used the semiannual certification reports to challenge the Reagan administration's support of the Salvadoran government.

Reagan barely averted a major foreign policy defeat in June 1986 when the Senate upheld a White House plan to sell weapons to Saudi Arabia. On a 34-66 vote, the Senate sustained Reagan's veto of a measure that would have blocked the sale from going forward. The 34 votes were the absolute minimum needed to uphold the president's action.

In one of the most stunning blows to Reagan's presidency, Congress in October 1986 overrode the president's veto of a measure imposing economic sanctions against South Africa. The vote was the first override of a presidential veto on a major foreign policy issue since 1973, when Congress enacted into law the War Powers resolution.

3

Lobbying and the Law

Although lobbying is protected by the First Amendment guarantees of freedom of speech and the right of citizens to petition the government for a redress of grievances, abuses led to periodic efforts by Congress to regulate lobbying.

In 1876 the House adopted a resolution requiring lobbyists to register during the 44th Congress with the clerk of the House, but the bill never became law. Beginning with the 62d Congress in 1911, federal lobbying legislation continued to be considered in practically every session. Yet by early 1987 only one comprehensive lobbying regulation law and a handful of more specialized measures had been enacted. In many cases, congressional investigations of lobby corruption, in response to the public outcry over corruption, took the place of tightening the rules.

Lobby Regulations

The principal method of regulation was disclosure rather than actual control. In four laws, lobbyists were required to identify themselves, who they represented, and their legislative interests. In one law, lobbyists also were required to report how much they and their employers spent on lobbying. But definitions were unclear, enforcement minimal. As a result, the few existing disclosure laws produced only limited information, and their effects were questionable.

One reason for the relative lack of limitations on lobbies was the difficulty of imposing effective restrictions without infringing on the constitutional rights of free speech, press, assembly, and petition. Other reasons included a fear that restrictions would hamper legitimate lobbies without reaching more serious lobby abuses, the consolidated and highly effective opposition of lobbies, and the desire of some members to keep open avenues to a future lobbying career. Congress succeeded in enacting two major lobbying laws, the Foreign Agents Registration Act of 1938 and the Federal Regulation of Lobbying Act of 1946.

The Foreign Agents Registration Act was enacted in 1938 amid reports of Fascist and Nazi propaganda circulating in the United States before World War II. It was amended frequently after that, and its history was as much a part of this country's struggle with internal security as it was a part of efforts to regulate lobbying.

The one existing omnibus lobbying law, the Federal Regulation of Lobbying Act, was enacted as part of the 1946 Legislative Reorganization Act. Its vague language and subsequent court interpretations combined to reduce seriously the effectiveness of the law's spending and lobbying disclosure provisions.

The political spending of pressure groups also was the object of numerous campaign finance bills enacted over the years by Congress. The ability to promise electoral support or opposition gave pressure groups one of the most effective devices in their attempts to influence Congress on legislation.

Precisely for this reason, Congress attempted on several occasions to limit campaign contributions made by corporations, organizations, and individuals in connection with federal elections. The limitations were intended to prevent those with great financial resources from using them to dominate the selection of members of Congress and thereby its legislative decisions. *(Political Action Committees, p. 47)*

Following are brief discussions of the lobby laws arranged in chronological order.

Utilities Holding Company Act

Section 12 (i) of the Public Utilities Holding Company Act of 1935 required anyone employed or retained by a registered holding company or a subsidiary to file certain information with the Securities and Exchange Commission (SEC) before attempting to influence Congress, the Federal Power Commission, or the SEC itself, on any legislative or administrative matter affecting any registered companies. Information required to be filed included a statement of the subject matter in which the individual was interested, the nature of the individual's employment, and the nature of the individual's compensation.

Merchant Marine Act

Section 807 of the Merchant Marine Act of 1936 required any persons employed by or representing firms affected by various federal shipping laws to file certain information with the secretary of commerce before attempting to influence Congress, the Commerce Department, and certain federal shipping agencies on shipping legislation or administrative decisions. The information included a statement of the subject matter in which the person was interested, the nature of the person's employment, and the amount of the person's compensation.

Foreign Agents Registration Act

The Foreign Agents Registration Act of 1938, as amended, required registration with the Justice Department of anyone in the United States representing a foreign government or principal. Exceptions were allowed for purely commercial groups and certain other categories. The act brought to public view many groups, individuals, and associations that, while not necessarily engaged in lobbying Congress directly, carried on propaganda activities that might ultimately affect congressional legislation and national policy.

The Foreign Agents Registration Act was amended frequently following its passage in 1938 — for example, in 1939, 1942, 1946, 1950, 1956, 1961, and 1966 — without changing its broad purposes. From 1950 on, the Justice Department followed the practice of reporting annually to Congress, in the form of a booklet listing registrants under the act and their receipts and the names of the foreign principals of registrants.

The 1966 amendments sought to clarify and strengthen the act by imposing stricter disclosure requirements for foreign lobbyists, by adding to the scope of activities for which individuals must register, by requiring them to disclose their status as agents when contacting members of Congress and other government officials, and by prohibiting contingent fees for contracts (where the fee was based upon the success of political activities) and campaign contributions on behalf of foreign interests.

In 1974 the Justice Department toughened its enforcement policy toward the activities of foreign agents. The department adopted a General Accounting Office (GAO) suggestion and began to make use of the Section 5 inspection clause of the act, which encouraged more detailed and accurate reports. Increased litigation resulted.

Federal Regulation of Lobbying Act

The Federal Regulation of Lobbying Act was passed as part of the Legislative Reorganization Act of 1946. The lobbying provisions prompted little debate at the time and, despite frequent attempts to change the law since, it has not been subsequently amended.

The 1946 act did not in any way directly restrict the lobbyists' activities. It simply required any person who was hired by someone else for the principal purpose of lobbying Congress to register with the secretary of the Senate and clerk of the House and to file certain quarterly financial reports so that the lobbyist's activities would be known to Congress and the public. Organizations that solicited or received money for the principal purpose of lobbying Congress did not necessarily have to register, but they did have to file quarterly spending reports with the clerk detailing how much they spent to influence legislation.

In 1954 the Supreme Court in *United States v. Harriss* upheld the constitutionality of the 1946 lobbying law but narrowly interpreted its key aspects. Opportunities for evading the loosely written law increased after that, and some critics described the statute as "more loophole than law."

One loophole opened by the decision involved collection or receipt of money. As interpreted by the court, the law did not cover groups or individuals that spent money to influence legislation, unless they also solicited, collected, or received money for that purpose.

Another loophole involved the term "principal purpose." A number of organizations argued that because influencing Congress was not the principal purpose for which they collected or received money, they were not covered by the law regardless of what kind of activities they carried on.

IRS Tax Ruling

The Internal Revenue Service (IRS) clarified the kind of business activities the agency regarded as non-tax-deductible "grass-roots" lobbying in a ruling issued March 20, 1978.

Section 162 of the Internal Revenue Code distinguished between "direct" lobbying, the costs of which were deductible by business organizations, and "indirect" or grass-roots lobbying expenses that were not deductible.

The IRS said in the rulings, "No deduction is allowable for expenses incurred by a corporation in preparing and placing advertisements in major state newspapers and regional magazines setting forth objections to proposed legislation of direct interest to the corporation." The gist was that costs of direct communication with a legislative body were deductible, but not the costs of informing others of a corporation's views.

The IRS also said a trade association could deduct the costs of urging its members to contact representatives and senators on legislation of direct interest to the group, but it could not deduct the cost of informing prospective members or of asking its members to urge their employees or customers to communicate with Congress.

The court held, in addition, that an organization or individual was not covered unless the method used to influence Congress contemplated some direct contact with members. The significance of this interpretation was that individuals or groups whose activities were confined to influencing the public on legislation or issues — grass-roots lobbying — were not subject to the 1946 law.

The decision left vague precisely what kind of contacts with Congress constituted lobbying subject to the law's reporting and registration requirements. The law specifically exempted testimony before a congressional committee, and in 1950, in *United States v. Slaughter,* a lower federal court held that this exemption applied also to those helping to prepare the testimony. Other direct contacts presumably were covered, but a gray area soon emerged, with some groups contending that their contacts with members of Congress were informational and could not be considered subject to the law.

Another weakness was that the law applied only to attempts to influence Congress, not administrative agencies or the executive branch, which originated much legislation enacted by Congress and which put into effect many regulations similar to legislation.

The law also left it up to each group or lobbyists to determine what portion of total expenditures were to be reported as spending for lobbying. As a result, some organizations whose Washington office budgets ran into the hundreds of thousands of dollars reported only very small amounts spent on lobbying, contending that the remainder was spent for general public information purposes, research, and other matters. Other organizations, interpreting the law quite differently, reported a much larger percentage of their total budgets as being for lobbying. The result was that some groups gained reputations as "big lobby spenders" when, in fact, they simply were reporting more fully than other groups spending just as much.

Finally, reinforcing all the other weaknesses was the lack of enforcement. The 1946 law did not designate anyone to investigate the truthfulness of lobbying registrations and reports or to seek enforcement. The House clerk and Senate secretary were not directed or empowered to investigate reports they received or to compel anyone to register. Since violations were made a crime, the Justice Department had power to prosecute offenders but no mandate was given the department to investigate reports. In fact, the Justice Department eventually adopted a policy of investigating only when it received complaints, and its prosecutions were rare.

Efforts to enact a lobby disclosure statute that covered all significant lobbying of Congress — something no one claimed the existing 1946 act did — were pursued throughout the 94th, 95th, and 96th Congresses. Both the House and Senate passed a new bill in 1976, but conferees were unable to resolve differences between the two versions before Congress adjourned. Although similar bills were introduced almost each year after that, including one the House passed in 1978, no new lobbying disclosure law had been enacted by the end of 1986.

Opposition from lobbyists for many different interests doomed the legislation. Disclosure of organized grass-roots campaigns turned out to be the hardest-fought obstacle to new lobbying legislation.

Lobbying Investigations

Over the years investigations of lobbying practices stemmed from a wide range of motives, and these studies sought to achieve nearly as broad a range of objectives. Lobby investigations were used to respond to intense public concern about lobbying, to gather information on the workings of existing regulatory legislation, and to help prepare the way for, and to shape, proposed new regulatory legislation.

Since 1913 most sessions of Congress have been marked by investigations of lobbying activities in general or of specific alleged abuses. Following are summary accounts of selected major lobbying investigations.

Business Lobbying, 1913

The first thorough investigation of lobbying was undertaken by the Senate in 1913 in reaction to President Woodrow Wilson's charges of a massive grass-roots lobbying effort against his tariff program. Wilson was enraged by alleged lobbying activity of the National Association of Manufacturers (NAM) and other protectionist groups on the Underwood tariff bill. He denounced what he called an "insidious" lobby that sought to bring on a new tide of protectionism.

"I think the public ought to know," Wilson said, "that extraordinary exertions are being made by the lobby in Washington to gain recognition for certain alterations in the tariff bill. . . . Washington has seldom seen so numerous, so industrious, or so insidious a lobby. . . . There is every evidence that money without limit is being spent to sustain this lobby. . . . The government ought to be relieved from this intolerable burden and the constant interruption to the calm progress of debate."

The Senate hearings disclosed that large amounts had been spent for entertainment and for other lobbying purposes both by the interests seeking high tariff duties and by those interested in low duties, such as the sugar refiners. Following the hearings, a lobby registration bill was introduced, but farm, labor, and other special interests warded off a vote on it.

Also in 1913, Col. Martin M. Mulhall, lobbyist for NAM, published a sensational account of his activities in a front-page article in the *New York World.* Among other disclosures, Mulhall said he had paid "between $1,500 and $2,000" to help Rep. James T. McDermott, D-Ill. (1907-14, 1915-17), for legislative favors.

A four-month inquiry by a select House committee found that many of Mulhall's allegations were exaggerated. The panel established that Mulhall had set up his own office in the Capitol, had paid the chief House page $50 a month for inside information, had received advance information on pending legislation from McDermott and House Republican leader John W. Dwight, N.Y. (1902-13), and had influenced the appointment of members to House committees and subcommittees. Six of seven House members implicated by Mulhall were exonerated, but the panel recommended that McDermott be "strongly censured." The House adopted the panel's recommendations. Although McDermott was not expelled from the House, he resigned in 1914 and was reelected that same year to another two-year term.

Tax and Utilities Lobbying, 1927

Interest in lobbying activities was rekindled in the 1920s after the American Legion and other veterans' groups obtained passage of a bonus bill over the veto of President Calvin Coolidge.

In 1927 an investigating committee under Sen. Thaddeus H. Caraway, D-Ark. (1921-31), conducted extensive public hearings on lobbying efforts. One of the immediate reasons was the pressure being applied to the Ways and Means Committee for repeal of the federal estate tax.

The American Taxpayers League brought more than 200 witnesses, including one governor and many state legislators, to Washington to testify. All travel expenses were paid and some of the witnesses received additional compensation.

The second activity to which Congress

objected at the time was the establishment of Washington headquarters by the Joint Committee of National Utility Associations to block a proposed Senate investigation of utility financing. The joint committee succeeded in having the investigation transferred to the Federal Trade Commission (FTC), but that agency took its assignment seriously and gave the utility situation a thorough going-over.

At the end of the investigation, the Caraway committee recommended a sweeping registration bill. It defined lobbying as "...any effort in influencing Congress upon any matter coming before it, whether it be by distributing literature, appearing before committees of Congress, or seeking to interview members of either the House or Senate." A lobbyist was defined as "... one who shall engage, for pay, to attempt to influence legislation, or to prevent legislation by the national Congress." The Senate passed the bill unanimously but a House committee pigeonholed it.

Despite failure of the Caraway bill, the Senate Judiciary Committee's report on the measure contributed greatly to the public's knowledge of lobbying. The panel asserted that about 90 percent of the 300 to 400 lobbying associations listed in the Washington telephone directory were "fakes" whose aim was to bilk unwary clients.

These organizations, according to the committee report, included groups that purported to represent scientific, agricultural, religious, temperance, and antiprohibition interests. "In fact," the panel said, "every activity of the human mind has been capitalized by some grafter." The committee estimated that $99 of every $100 paid to these groups "go into the pockets of the promoters." Caraway himself disclosed that one of the lobbyists had collected $60,000 in one year from business interests by simply writing them every time a bill favorable to business was passed and claiming sole credit for its passage.

Naval Armaments, 1929

The next congressional probe of lobbying came in 1929, when a Senate Naval Affairs Subcommittee looked into the activities of William B. Shearer, who represented shipping, electrical, metals, machinery, and similar concerns interested in blocking limitation of naval armaments and in obtaining larger appropriations for Navy ships. The path to Shearer's exposure had been paved when he filed a suit in the New York courts to recover $257,655, which he said was owed to him by the New York Shipbuilding Co. Shearer claimed the money was due for lobbying services he had performed in Washington and at the Geneva naval limitation conference of 1927.

Testimony showed that shipbuilding interests sent Shearer to Geneva, where he did everything he could to torpedo an agreement. Following the conference, at which no agreement was reached, Shearer had led industry lobbying efforts for bigger naval appropriations and for merchant marine subsidies. His other activities included preparing pro-Navy articles for the Hearst newspaper chain, writing articles for the 1928 Republican presidential campaign, in which he characterized peace advocates as traitors, and writing speeches for the American Legion and like-minded lobby groups.

Utilities Lobbies, 1935

A decade of congressional concern over the influence exerted by private utilities led to a stormy probe of that industry's lobbying activities in 1935. Although Congress nine years earlier had instructed the Federal Trade Commission to investigate utility lobbying, a two-year FTC probe had been largely inconclusive.

Intensive lobbying that threatened to emasculate an administration bill to regulate utility holding companies prompted President Roosevelt to send Congress a special message describing the holding companies as "private empires within the nation" and denouncing their lobbying techniques. The bill's congressional supporters demanded an investigation to determine how far the power interests' lobbying had gone.

A special Senate investigative panel was set up under the chairmanship of Hugo L. Black, D-Ala. (1927-37), an administration stalwart who later became an associate justice of the Supreme Court. Following a sometimes raucous hearing, Black concluded that the utilities had spent about $4 million to defeat the bill and had engaged in massive propagandizing to convince the public that it was an iniquitous invasion of private rights and a sharp turn toward socialism. Black's panel also stated that the utilities had financed thousands of phony telegrams to Congress, using names picked at random from telephone books.

Amid a furor over the telegrams, Congress passed the Public Utilities Holding Company Act, which required reports to federal agencies on some utility lobbying activities. The Senate and House also passed lobbyist registration bills. A compromise was agreed upon but the House rejected the agreement and final adjournment came before a new agreement could be reached. The measure's defeat was attributed to the combined efforts of hundreds of lobbyists.

Munitions Lobby, 1935

Another Senate investigation during 1935 looked into activities of the munitions lobby. The Special Committee Investigating the Munitions Industry, headed by Gerald P. Nye, R-N.C. (1925-45), disclosed bribery and arms deals in Latin America and Great Britain, prompting sharp responses from leaders there.

Further Studies, 1938 and 1945

The Temporary National Economic Committee, which Congress set up at President Roosevelt's request under the chairmanship of Sen. C. Joseph O'Mahoney, D-Wyo. (1934-53, 1954-61), included lobbying among its subjects of study in 1938.

The Joint Committee on the Organization of Congress, established in 1945, studied lobbying activities along with other matters pertaining to Congress. On the basis of the committee's recommendations, Congress in 1946 passed the Legislative Reorganization Act, including the Federal Regulation of Lobbying Act.

Omnibus Lobbying Probe, 1950

A House Select Committee on Lobbying Activities headed by Frank M. Buchanan, D-Pa. (1946-51), investigated the lobbying activities of a wide range of organizations in 1950. The probe had been prompted largely by President Truman's assertion that the 80th Congress was "the most thoroughly surrounded . . . with lobbies in the whole history of this great country of ours."

Truman said: "There were more lobbyists in Washington, there was more money spent by lobbyists in Washington, than ever before in the history of the Congress of the United States. It's disgraceful. . . ." Most of the publicity centered on the Committee for Constitutional Government's efforts to distribute low-cost or free "right-wing" books and pamphlets designed to influence the public.

The House investigating committee requested detailed information from 200 corporations, labor unions, and farm groups to determine more accurately the amount of money spent to influence legislation. Replies from 152 corporations showed a total of $32 million spent for this purpose from January 1, 1947, through May 31, 1950. More than 100 of these corporations had not filed reports under the 1946 Federal Regulation of Lobbying Act. Reports of the 37 that did showed expenditures of $776,000, which was less than 3 percent of the amount reported by respondents to the committee questionnaire. In releasing the survey results, Chairman Buchanan noted that it covered activities of only 152 of the country's 500,000 corporations. "I firmly believe," he said, "that the business of influencing legislation is a billion-dollar industry."

The House committee recommended strengthening the 1946 lobbying law but no action was taken.

Omnibus Lobbying Probe, 1956

In 1956 a major lobbying inquiry was conducted by the Senate Special Committee to Investigate Political Activities, Lobbying, and Campaign Contributions. The inquiry was initiated against a background of an alleged campaign contribution to Francis H. Case, R-S.D. (1951-62), in connection with voting on a natural gas bill. The panel was chaired by John L. McClellan, D-Ark. (1943-77).

Following a long investigation, McClellan on May 31, 1957, introduced a new lobbying registration bill designed to replace the 1946 act. The bill proposed to tighten the existing law by making the comptroller general responsible for enforcing it (there was no administrator under the 1946 act); by eliminating a loophole that required registration of only those lobbyists whose principal purpose was lobbying; by extending the coverage to anyone who spent $50,000 or more a year on grass-roots lobbying; and by eliminating an exemption that made the law inapplicable to persons who merely testified on proposed legislation.

The bill was opposed vigorously by the Chamber of Commerce of the United States and was criticized on certain points by the National Association of Manufacturers, the Association of American Railroads, and the American Medical Association, although the latter endorsed the measure as a whole. The bill did not reach the floor and died with the close of the 85th Congress.

Retired Military Lobbyists, 1959

In 1959 the House Armed Services Subcommittee on Special Investigations held three months of hearings on the employment of former Army, Navy, and Air Force officers by defense contractors, and on the influence of the retired officers in obtaining government contracts for their new employers. The subcommittee found that more than 1,400 retired officers with the rank of major or higher — including 261 of general or flag rank — were employed by the top 100 defense contractors.

In its report in 1960, the subcommittee said that "The coincidence of contracts and personal contacts with firms represented by retired officers and retired civilian officials sometimes raises serious doubts as to the objectivity of these [contract] decisions." Congress largely accepted subcommittee recommendations for tighter restrictions on sales to the government by former or retired personnel.

Foreign Lobbyists, 1962

Lobbying in connection with the Sugar Act of 1962 led the Senate Foreign Relations Committee to launch an investigation of foreign lobbies and the extent to which they attempted to influence U.S. policies. At the request of Foreign Relations Committee chairman J. William Fulbright, D-Ark. (1945-74), and Sen. Paul H. Douglas, D-Ill. (1949-67), the Finance Committee, which had jurisdiction over the sugar bill, had queried sugar lobbyists on their arrangements with their employers, mostly foreign countries. A compendium of the answers, made public June 26, 1962, showed that some payments to sugar lobbyists were made on the basis of the size of the sugar quotas granted by Congress.

Hearings conducted some months later by the Foreign Relations Committee produced evidence that some lobbyists also lobbied their own clients. Fulbright disclosed, for example, that Michael B. Deane, a Washington public relations man hired by the Dominican Sugar Commission, apparently had given the commission exaggerated, sometimes inaccurate reports.

Deane admitted that he had reported falsely that the president had invited him to the White House and that he had talked with the secretary of agriculture. Deane said he occasionally gave himself "too much credit," but "one tends to do that a little bit when they have a client who is outside of Washington." Similar testimony was elicited from other sugar lobbyists.

The Fulbright probe continued well into 1963 and, at its conclusion, Fulbright introduced a bill to tighten registration requirements under the 1938 Foreign Agents Registration Act. The bill passed the Senate in 1964 but died in the House. It was revived in the 89th Congress and enacted in 1966.

'Koreagate,' 1978

On October 24, 1976, the *Washington Post* disclosed that the Justice Department was probing reports that South Korean agents dispensed between $500,000 and $1 million a year in cash and gifts to members of Congress to help maintain "a favorable legislative climate" for South Korea.

Tongsun Park, a Washington-based Korean businessman and socialite, was named as the central operative. Park fled to London shortly after the story appeared. He stayed there until August 1977, then went to Korea. He later returned to the United States to testify at House and Senate hearings on Korean influence-peddling.

By 1978 the House and Senate ethics committees had ended their probes without recommending any severe disciplinary action against colleagues linked to the scandal. The House investigation, which began in early 1977 with reports that as many as 115 members of Congress had taken illegal gifts from South Korean agents, ended in October 1978 with the House voting its mildest form of punishment, a "reprimand," for three California Democrats: John J. McFall (1957-78), Edward R. Roybal (1963-), and Charles H. Wilson (1963-81).

Two former representatives were prosecuted for taking large sums of money from Tongsun Park: Richard T. Hanna, D-Calif. (1963-74), who pleaded guilty to a reduced charge and went to prison; and Otto E. Passman, D-La. (1947-77), who was acquitted in 1979.

The Senate Ethics Committee concluded its Korean investigation in October 1978 with a report that recommended no disciplinary action against any incumbent or former senator.

A third committee investigating U.S.-Korean relations concluded that the South Korean government sought to bribe U.S. officials, buy influence among journalists and military procurement contracts to win support for what the panel called the "authoritarian" government of President Park Chung Hee. In its final report, released in November 1978, the House International Relations Subcommittee on International Organizations said that the South Korean government's illegal activities went beyond its legal and extra-legal lobbying efforts. The 450-page report, which outlined the history of U.S.-Korean relations, indicated that the South Koreans frequently pursued policies antithetical to U.S. interests. The most notable of those incidents involved South Korean efforts to develop nuclear weapons, a campaign the subcommittee said was abandoned by 1975.

Deaver Case, 1986

A special prosecutor was named in May 1986 to probe allegations that Michael K. Deaver violated conflict-of-interest laws by lobbying White House officials after he resigned as President Reagan's deputy chief of staff in May 1985. Whitney North Sey-

Deaver Case Prompts Congressional Efforts ...

Whether or not Michael K. Deaver violated federal ethics laws, the controversy surrounding his lobbying activities after leaving the White House fueled efforts in the 99th Congress to toughen conflict-of-interest strictures on former government employees. None of the proposals, however, received final congressional action before adjournment.

The 1978 Ethics in Government Act bars mid- to high-level officials from representing anyone before their former agency for one year after leaving government. The law permanently bars officials from representing anyone in connection with an issue they had direct involvement with while in government. Since enactment of the law, efforts to tighten the restrictions had focused on Defense Department procurement officials.

Closing the 'Revolving Door'

Taking aim at what they called a conflict of interest costing taxpayers billions of dollars, congressional critics of Pentagon purchasing wanted to close the "revolving door" through which workers leave as government employees and return employed by government contractors. These members said that some federal workers, in hope of landing high-paying jobs with contractors they worked with, could be lax in enforcing rigid quality control or contract auditing. This too cozy relationship between contractors and federal agencies, they said, could drive up costs.

The House Armed Services Committee June 13, 1985, approved a bill (HR 2554) that would bar a defense contractor from hiring certain Pentagon managers for two years after the employees left the Defense Department, if those workers had approved or monitored the firm's contracts. The bill would exempt certain senior Pentagon positions from the hiring ban. The House Judiciary Committee approved a tougher version of HR 2554 on March 11, 1986.

Other revolving-door measures were introduced in the 99th Congress. S 409 and HR 1201 would prohibit high-level federal employees who worked in procurement from taking jobs with federal contractors for five years. A less stringent proposal (S 385) would prohibit a contractor from hiring a government worker for two years after leaving the government if the employee worked with that contractor during the previous three years. Sen. Carl Levin, D-Mich., sponsored a bill (S 815) that would prohibit high-level procurement officials in all government agencies — not just the Defense Department — from taking jobs for two years with contractors with whom they dealt while working for the government.

Thurmond Bill

About the same time that Deaver's case became public, Sen. Strom Thurmond, R-S.C., chairman of the Judiciary Committee, introduced a bill (S 2334) to bar senior administration officials forever from working for foreign governments. The bill also would bar all government employees, including members of Congress, from lobbying any part

. . . To Toughen Conflict-of-Interest Legislation

of the government for one year after leaving office, or lobbying on behalf of a foreign government for two years.

Thurmond said Deaver's case was not the reason for his bill. Rather, he was upset by reports that former U.S. trade officials could have divulged to foreign employers U.S. strategy in negotiations to renew the Multifiber Arrangement governing textile trade agreements between countries.

An unusual alliance of conservative Republicans and First Amendment activists joined forces to soften the impact of the lobbying restriction bill. Conservatives Orrin G. Hatch, R-Utah, Paul Laxalt, R-Nev., and Jeremiah Denton, R-Ala., working in concert with the American Civil Liberties Union (ACLU), challenged the sweeping nature of Thurmond's bill. Hatch said S 2334 would affect 40,000 employees and could stifle the interest of competent persons to work for the government. He also echoed the ACLU's contention that the measure could pose a conflict with Bill of Rights protections of free speech and citizens' ability to petition the government.

Thurmond grudgingly accepted a scaled-back measure proposed by Hatch in order to win bipartisan committee approval. The panel approved the measure June 26 with only Charles McC. Mathias, Jr., R-Md., opposed.

As approved, S 2334 would bar senior government officials and members of Congress from working for a foreign government for three years and from lobbying any part of the government for 18 months. The bill would also bar all government officials at the $61,000 salary level or higher from lobbying on behalf of a foreign entity for two years after leaving office and from lobbying their own agencies for one year. Unlike current law, which covered only senior officials in the executive branch, the new ban would apply to judiciary and legislative branch employees, as well. Committee staff members said that would affect about 10,000 government employees in all. The bill would become effective six months after enactment. It included stiffer penalties for "willful" violations, increasing the maximum prison sentence from two to five years and adding forfeiture of any financial gains to a maximum $250,000 fine.

The bill also added new disclosure rules for government employees who go to work for foreign entities, requiring lobbyists to itemize periodically with their former agencies the money they were paid, the government contacts they make, and the names of any employees who assisted in lobbying.

House Proposals

On August 7, 1986, the House Judiciary Subcommittee on Administrative Law approved a measure (HR 5426) that would bar high-level government officials and members of Congress from lobbying for foreign governments for four years after leaving office.

The subcommittee also held hearings on a bill (HR 3733) that would bar top-level officials from either representing or advising foreign governments or companies for 10 years after leaving government.

mour, Jr., was appointed after the Justice Department determined that an independent counsel for Deaver's case was warranted under the Ethics in Government Act.

Deaver left the administration to run a public relations firm that represented Canada, South Korea, Mexico, Saudi Arabia, and Caribbean sugar producers, among others. Deaver's activities were controversial because, in addition to his professional connection to the administration, he was a longtime personal friend of President and Nancy Reagan. Upon leaving the White House, Deaver kept his White House pass and continued to receive a copy of Reagan's daily schedule. He also played tennis on the White House courts.

The Deaver case spurred new conflict-of-interest legislation in the 99th Congress, focusing particular attention on government officials — and members of Congress — who go to work for foreign governments. *(Conflict-of-Interest Legislation, box, p. 42)*

GAO Report. On May 12, 1986, the General Accounting Office reported that Deaver appeared to have violated conflict-of-interest laws by representing Canada on acid rain shortly after he helped to determine administration policy on the issue as a White House aide. After a five-month investigation that involved interviews with about 10 White House officials, the GAO concluded that Deaver could have violated four sections of the ethics law governing postemployment conflict of interest:

- A lifetime ban for any executive branch employee on lobbying a "particular matter involving a specific party" if the official "participated personally and substantially" in the issue while in office.

The GAO said Deaver participated in 15 White House discussions on acid rain in preparation for the March 1985 summit meeting between President Reagan and Prime Minister Brian Mulroney of Canada and became a supporter of the decision to appoint a special envoy for acid rain. Deaver discussed with national security adviser Robert C. McFarlane two potential nominees for the job, former interior secretary William P. Clark and former transportation secretary Drew Lewis, who eventually got the volunteer position.

- A two-year lobbying prohibition for federal officials on specific matters that fell under the official's responsibility in the last year of federal service.

The GAO said Deaver's attorney reported that Deaver shared "overall responsibility" for the U.S.-Canadian summit, but that other White House officials had specific responsibility for the acid rain issue. "Given the apparently broad scope of Mr. Deaver's White House duties," the GAO reported, "it may be that the issue of whether the United States should agree to appoint a special envoy for acid rain was a matter that was 'actually pending' under his official responsibility within the year prior to his resignation."

- A two-year ban for a specific group of top-level civilian and military officials against representing, counseling, assisting, or advising on an issue in which the official "participated personally and substantially."

Five months after he left the White House, Deaver accompanied Canadian officials to the River Club in New York City, where he met with Lewis, the GAO said. Lewis told GAO that the group discussed the content and timing of a special envoy report, with the Canadians pressing the administration for a funding commitment to control acid rain. Deaver did not discuss the content of the report, but merely the timing of its release. But GAO said Deaver's very presence at that meeting appeared to constitute lobbying an officer of the United States.

- A one-year ban on senior government officials lobbying their former agency or department.

The question was whether the special envoy was a State Department official or a

White House official. Deaver maintained that Lewis was attached to the State Department, where Deaver was free to make contacts. But GAO concluded that Lewis worked mainly out of the White House and reported directly to the president.

The role of employer, according to the GAO, appeared to have been served by the White House Office and the Office of Policy Development. The Office of Government Ethics ruled in 1983 that these two offices together are considered a separate "agency" in the Executive Office of the President. Deaver, as a former member of the White House Office, was barred from contacts with anyone in that office or in the Office of Policy Development. If Lewis was part of the latter office, Deaver violated the law by seeing him in New York City, the GAO said.

On January 8, 1986, the special envoys of Canada and the United States issued a joint report that included a recommendation that the U.S. government implement a five-year, $5 billion demonstration program to control acid rain. On March 19, Reagan reversed a longstanding policy and agreed to this recommendation.

GAO deputy counsel James F. Hinchman said there was "enough basis" for believing that the postemployment laws were violated to justify referring the case to the Justice Department. The department, however, was already conducting a preliminary investigation into Deaver's lobbying activities. An FBI probe was triggered April 24 by a letter from five Democratic members of the Senate Judiciary Committee, who asked Attorney General Edwin Meese III to determine if sufficient grounds existed to ask a special federal court to appoint an independent counsel to look into Deaver's activities. Deaver himself joined the call for a special prosecutor, saying in an April 28 letter to Meese that it was the only way to clear his name.

Deaver Testimony. Reacting to the

Allegations arose in 1986 that Michael K. Deaver violated conflict-of-interest laws by lobbying White House officials after he resigned as President Reagan's deputy chief of staff.

mounting publicity against him, Deaver defended his occupation and his reputed influence with the Reagans in private testimony May 16, 1986, before the House Energy and Commerce Subcommittee on Oversight and Investigations. The subcommittee, headed by John D. Dingell, D-Mich., questioned Deaver's work for the Canadian government on acid rain, as well as other lobbying efforts on behalf of foreign trading partners of the United States.

In his statement to the subcommittee, Deaver said he had stayed "within the law at all times" and "faithfully adhered" to the

Foreign Agents Registration Act. Deaver said that he had been attacked "virtually without restraint or qualification" by critics who believed it was improper for a former presidential adviser to represent a foreign government before the U.S. government. But Congress "never has even suggested the impropriety of, much less prohibited by legislation, what these critics now assert," Deaver said. "I submit that if there is a dispute over what the nation's policy with respect to this issue should be, then such criticism should be directed to Congress, not to individual citizens."

Subcommittee Staff Report. The House Energy subcommittee August 12 unanimously adopted a scathing report alleging Deaver could have committed "perjury" and "obstruction of justice." The subcommittee voted 17-0 to turn evidence of Deaver's possible criminal violations over to the special prosecutor.

The report, prepared by the majority and minority staff members, said Deaver "knowingly and willfully" made false statements when he testified before the subcommittee. The report alleged that Deaver failed to tell members about a conversation in 1985 with a national security adviser on getting tax breaks for Puerto Rico, did not tell them about contacts with two U.S. ambassadors on behalf of clients, and misrepresented his dealings with the administration's budget director on behalf of a defense contractor. The report concluded that Deaver "may have violated federal statutes relating to perjury, false statements and obstruction of a congressional investigation."

The subcommittee's action effectively requested that the independent counsel decide if Deaver committed the federal offense of perjury in his sworn testimony before the panel. Dingell stressed that Seymour would have to judge whether prosecution on that charge was warranted. Resolution of the Deaver case was still pending as of November 1986.

4

Political Action Committees

To some, political action committees (PACs) represent a healthy way for individuals and groups to participate financially in the political process. To others, they are an insidious outgrowth of Watergate-inspired legislation. But all sides agree that PACs are an increasingly important force in the financing of congressional races.

The term "PAC" is not precisely defined in the 1971 Federal Election Campaign Act (FECA), the law that provides the basic ground rules for financing federal election campaigns. FECA does define a nonparty political committee as any committee, club, association, or other group of members that either has receipts or expenditures in a calendar year of at least $1,000, or operates a separate, segregated fund to raise or disburse money used in federal campaigns. Committees that fit this definition have come to be known as PACs.

Because corporations and labor unions are prohibited by federal law from using corporate and union treasury funds for political contributions, PACs have become a tightly regulated vehicle for political involvement by business and unions. Campaign contributions by political action committees must come from voluntary gifts to the PACs. But corporate and union funds may be used to administer PACs and solicit money for them.

Most PACs are affiliated with corporations or labor unions. But there are a large number of PACs affiliated with trade, membership, and health organizations and a growing number of independent, nonconnected PACs set up by groups interested in a particular cause, such as abortion, farm subsidies, and the environment.

In 1974 there were 608 PACs. The number grew to 2,000 in 1979. By the end of 1984, it had more than doubled.

Impetus for PACs

Labor unions began forming PACs about fifty years ago to maximize their influence in the political process. But the real impetus for PAC formation did not come until the 1970s when the federal campaign finance laws were overhauled. Crucial were the 1974 amendments to the FECA, which clamped a $1,000 limit on the amount an individual could contribute to a House or Senate candidate in a primary or general election.

PACs were permitted to give $5,000 per candidate per election, with no limit on how much the candidate could receive in combined PAC contributions.

Overnight the political landscape was changed. Before 1974 there was little need

Members Set Up Political Action Committees . . .

More than two dozen members of Congress have joined thousands of businesses, unions, and trade associations in setting up political action committees (PACs) to contribute to congressional campaigns. Officially, the fund-raising vehicles associated with House and Senate members are classified in the same way as the corporate, labor, and trade association fund-raising committees — as "multi-candidate PACs" entitled to give money to office-seekers. But the PACs associated with congressmen are more commonly known as "leadership PACs" because many of their originators harbor ambitions for such positions as president, House Speaker, or committee chair.

If a member has designs on a leadership job and wants to earn the good will of his colleagues, campaign finance law in effect encourages him to set up a PAC. The law allows a PAC to contribute up to $5,000 per election cycle to a candidate, whereas an individual may give only $1,000 from his personal funds. A member with a PAC also may use its moneys to travel to political events around the country.

Some members are frank about the link between their PACs and their leadership ambitions. Presidential prospects, however, are prone to deny any connection between their PACs and their White House ambitions, saying their PACs merely aim to boost party allies or promote their philosophies. What they do not say is that setting up a PAC allows them to delay forming an official campaign committee, something federal law requires an active presidential candidate to do. A few members' PACs do focus mainly on helping ideological or partisan allies win elections.

The largest PAC linked to a member of Congress is the National Congressional Club, run by associates of Sen. Jesse Helms, R-N.C., to aid conservative candidates. Through the end of June 1986, it had raised and spent nearly $2.5 million. The club is somewhat in its won league because it has ties to an entire network of Raleigh-based firms involved in an array of political activities.

After the club, the five most active leadership PACs are connected with present or former members often mentioned as contenders for the presidency. The list is led by Campaign America, which raised nearly $1.5 million in the first half of 1986 on the strength of its influential sponsor, Senate majority leader Robert Dole, R-Kan. These committees compete for funds not only against each other, but also against PACs formed by noncongressional presidential possibles.

Some of these PACs provide assistance to candidates based more on their partisan label than on their philosophical bent. For instance, the PAC associated with Dole, who had a big personal stake in continued GOP Senate control in the 100th Congress, planned to give to all Republican Senate incumbents and to the GOP candidates for open Senate seats in the 1986 election. Other leadership PACs put more weight on ideology in their giving. Although the criteria for giving may vary from PAC to PAC, the committees' large budgets and the relatively small number of key races makes it likely that leadership PACs will contribute to many of the same candidates. This "canceling-out" of influence, however, does not negate another important benefit of having a leadership PAC: the travel money it provides.

. . . To Contribute to Congressional Campaigns

Being able to make appearances and improve name recognition across the country is crucial to any potential presidential candidate, but the means with which to get around are limited. Taxpayers' dollars provided to members for official business may not be used for strictly political travel. And while influential members often have large surpluses in their personal campaign accounts, their contributors usually give with the expectation that the money will go toward the members' congressional reelection, not for extracurricular politicking. By forming PACs, members are able to avoid these obstacles. Their fund-raising appeals clearly spell out that the money will be used by the lawmakers to campaign for other candidates or to pitch their political gospel to a wider audience.

Because federal election law requires an active presidential contender to make a declaration and form a campaign committee, members who sponsor PACs deny that their travels are connected with their rumored White House ambitions.

Though members' PACs have found a variety of ways and reasons to spend their money, the source of their revenues is not so diverse. Some PACs rely heavily on small contributions from individuals, mostly solicited by direct mail; some on large donations from wealthy supporters. But most members' PACs receive the majority of their financing from other political action committees. Some target their fund-raising efforts on those PACs that have an interest in the member's field of expertise.

Many contributors, however, do not seem much concerned that the money given to a member's PAC may make its way to candidates who are not necessarily sympathetic to the original contributors' interests. The universal explanation of members' PAC directors for why liberal interests give money that could wind up going to conservatives (or vice versa) is, "they trust our judgment." But there is evidence that this trust is not universal. For example, Dole's PAC, which gives to all Republican Senate incumbents without regard to ideological stripe, was willing to accept contributions earmarked for a particular candidate from PACs that worried their money could wind up in the wrong hands.

One industry group, the National Forest Products Association PAC, announced in May 1986 that it would not give money to leadership PACs and would donate money only to candidates "who have an understanding of and support for forest products industry positions on legislation affecting our industry."

A barrage of criticism has been leveled at leadership PACs by campaign-finance watchdogs. Common Cause is a strong critic of PACs in general, but its position on leadership PACs is even more severe. Common Cause chairman Archibald Cox called for the prohibition of PACs associated with members of or prospective candidates for Congress. Common Cause alleges that members' PAC contributions to other congressional campaigns could provide the givers with undue influence, not only in leadership elections, but also in votes on legislative issues. By the PAC opponents' reasoning, it is difficult for a member to avoid the gaze of a colleague whose PAC had taken a healthy interest in his election.

for political action committees outside the labor movement. Individuals — whether business executives or wealthy political philanthropists — could give unlimited amounts to the candidates of their choice. But the 1974 legislation ended this era of unbridled giving and forced wealthy individuals, corporations, and other organizations to seek new outlets to remain financially involved in the political process.

Legislative Background

The legislative groundwork for the PAC boom of the 1970s was laid by the 1971 act. When the decade began, the political activities of corporations and unions were tightly restricted.

Corporate gifts of money to federal candidates had been prohibited since 1907 by the Tillman Act. In 1925 the ban was extended by the Federal Corrupt Practices Act to cover corporate contributions of "anything of value." Labor unions were prohibited by the Smith-Connally Act of 1943 and the Taft-Hartley Act of 1947 from making contributions to federal candidates from their members' dues.

The 1971 act modified these bans by allowing the use of corporate funds and union treasury money for "the establishment, administration and solicitation of contributions to a separate, segregated fund to be utilized for a political purpose." Administrative units of those funds became known commonly as PACs.

But the 1971 act did not modify the ban on political contributions by government contractors. This resulted in many corporations holding back from forming PACs. Labor unions, many of which had government manpower contracts, also became concerned that they would be affected and led a move to have the law changed to permit government contractors to establish and administer PACs. That change was incorporated into the 1974 amendments to the FECA.

SunPAC Decision

Labor's efforts, however, had unexpected consequences. While the easing of the prohibition against government manpower contractors forming PACs removed a headache for organized labor, it also opened the door to the formation of corporate PACs.

Yet in the wake of Watergate many corporations remained skittish about what they were permitted to do. Not until November 1975, when the Federal Election Commission (FEC) released its landmark ruling in the case involving the Sun Oil Co.'s political committee, SunPAC, did many businesses feel comfortable about establishing PACs.

The FEC decision was in response to a request from Sun Oil for permission to use its general treasury funds to create, administer, and solicit voluntary contributions to its political action committee. The company also sought permission to solicit its stockholders and all employees for PAC contributions and to establish a separate "political giving program" among corporate employees that could be financed through a payroll deduction plan. Sun Oil indicated that employees would be allowed to designate the recipients of their contributions.

By a 4-2 vote, the bipartisan commission issued an advisory opinion approving the requests, although the FEC emphasized that SunPAC had to abide by guidelines ensuring that the solicitation of employees was totally voluntary. Dissenting commissioners objected to the scope of SunPAC solicitations. They argued that because federal law permitted unions to solicit only their members, SunPAC should be restricted to soliciting only its stockholders. Labor was incensed by the ruling, since it greatly enlarged the potential source of funds available to corporate PACs. The unions pressed hard to have the FEC decision overturned, and they succeeded in the 1976 FECA amendments in having the range of corporate solicitation restricted from all employees to a company's management personnel and its stockholders. Corporations and unions were given the right to solicit the other's group twice a year by mail.

The 1976 amendments also permitted union PACs to use the same method of soliciting campaign contributions as the company PACs used, such as a payroll deduction plan. And the law sought to restrict the proliferation of PACs by maintaining that all political action committees established by one company or international union would be treated as a single committee for contribution purposes.

The PAC contributions of a company or an international union would be limited to no more than $5,000 overall to the same candidate in any election no matter how many PACs the company or union formed.

In the short run, the 1976 amendments were a victory for labor, because they curbed some of the benefits for corporate PACs authorized by the FEC's SunPAC decision. But the legislation did nothing to undercut the primary effect of the SunPAC ruling: abetting the formation of PACs within the business community. Moreover, the law explicitly permitted trade associations, membership organizations, cooperatives, and corporations without stock to establish PACs.

Controls on Political Spending

A story is told in Washington about a veteran U.S. House member engaged in a campaign debate with a young, reform-minded challenger. "You see my opponent's $500 silk suit," the challenger barks. "You know who paid for it? The special interest corporations! You see his wife's mink coat? You know who paid for it? The special interest labor unions!" With that, the challenger stalks off to his seat. The old-timer then ambles to the podium and says: "I have to agree with my young friend. In fact, he forgot to mention my two $20,000 Cadillacs sitting in my driveway at home. You know how I paid for them? With special interest money, and lots of it. My question to you is: Do you want a congressman who's bought and paid for, or do you want to start all over again with a new one?"

The story is apocryphal, but its point is not. Money and politics are inextricably linked, mainly because of the large amounts needed to run for federal office.

Until the 1970s, campaign finance, American style, was freewheeling, a shadowy area with virtually toothless legislation covering the disclosure of campaign contributions and expenditures. But in the early 1970s the pendulum began to swing sharply in the other direction. Spiraling media costs provided the first impetus for reform. Watergate accelerated the movement. By the mid-1970s, three major pieces of campaign finance legislation had been passed, transforming the practically unregulated "industry" into one with strict controls.

By the late 1970s, however, the push for reform clearly was weakening. Criticism was growing that the law was an overreaction to Watergate that stifled contributors, candidates, and political parties alike. Whereas throughout the 1970s the impetus for campaign finance legislation came from the political left, during the early 1980s the conservatives had the power in Congress to seize the initiative. By the mid-1980s liberal reforms such as congressional public financing and political action committee spending curbs were being considered side by side with conservative alternatives such as loosening restrictions on party giving.

Campaign Spending Controversy

One of the major difficulties politicians have faced in molding campaign finance legislation has been an absence of consensus.

No national system of campaign finance exists that covers all political races. The legislation of the 1970s dramatically overhauled presidential elections, establishing a system of partial public financing for the nominating process and virtually complete federal funding for the general election. But Congress never extended public financing to its own contests; money used to run federal political campaigns comes from four sources: the candidates' own personal funds, the political parties, individual donations, and contributions from political action committees. Races at the state and local levels are a mixture of the public and private financing systems.

Reformers have sought to curb campaign spending by limiting and regulating campaign expenditures and donations made to candidates as well as by informing voters of the amounts and sources of the donations, and the amounts, purposes, and payees of the expenditures. Disclosure was intended to reveal which candidates, if any, were unduly indebted to interest groups, in time to forewarn the voters. But more than a century of legislative attempts to regulate campaign financing resulted in much controversy and minimal control.

Until the 1970s, the basic federal law regulating campaign spending and requiring public disclosure was the Corrupt Practices Act of 1925. The act set a statutory maximum of $25,000 in expenditures for a Senate campaign and $10,000 for a House race, but it was not enforced. Watergate, though, changed all that. The scandal became the code word in the 1970s for government corruption. Although there were many aspects to the scandal, money in politics was at its roots.

Included in Watergate's catalog of misdeeds were specific violations of campaign spending laws, violations of other criminal laws facilitated by the availability of virtually unlimited campaign contributions, and still other instances where campaign funds were used in a manner that strongly suggested influence peddling.

Faced with escalating media costs, Congress had begun to move on campaign finance legislation even before the June 1972 break-in at the Democratic national headquarters in Washington, D.C. In 1971 it worked hard to pass two separate pieces of legislation: the Federal Election Campaign Act of 1971, which for the first time set a ceiling on the amount federal candidates could spend on media advertising and required full disclosure of campaign contributions and expenditures; and the Revenue Act of 1971, a tax checkoff bill to allow taxpayers to contribute to a general public campaign fund for eligible presidential and vice presidential candidates.

But Watergate focused public attention on campaign spending at all levels of government and produced a mood in Congress that even the most reluctant legislators found difficult to resist. In the aftermath of the scandal came the most significant overhaul in campaign finance legislation in the nation's history. Major legislation passed in 1974 and 1976, coming on the heels of the 1971 legislation, radically altered the system of financing federal elections.

Almost two and a half years after it passed the FECA of 1971 — a factor in breaking open the Watergate scandal — Congress, reacting to presidential campaign abuses, enacted another landmark campaign reform bill that substantially overhauled the existing system of financing election campaigns. Technically, the 1974 law was a set of amendments to the 1971 legislation, but in fact it was the most comprehensive campaign spending measure ever passed.

The new law established the first spending limits ever for candidates in presidential primary and general elections and in primary campaigns for the House and Senate. It set new expenditure ceilings for general election campaigns for Congress to replace the limits established by the 1925 Federal Corrupt Practices Act that were never effectively enforced and were repealed in the 1971 law.

The 1974 law also introduced the first use of public money to pay for political campaign costs by providing for optional public financing in presidential general election campaigns and establishing federal matching grants to cover up to one-half of the costs of presidential primary campaigns. It also repealed the media spending limitations introduced in the 1971 FECA and established the Federal Election Commission.

As soon as the 1974 law took effect, it was challenged in court. The plaintiffs argued that the law's new limits on campaign contributions and expenditures curbed the freedom of contributors and candidates to express themselves in the political marketplace and that the public financing provisions discriminated against minor parties and lesser-known candidates in favor of the major parties and better-known candidates.

The case went to the Supreme Court, which handed down its historic *Buckley v. Valeo* decision on January 30, 1976. In its decision, the court upheld the provisions of the statute that:

- Set limits on how much individuals and political committees could contribute to candidates.
- Provided for the public financing of presidential primary and general election campaigns.
- Required the disclosure of campaign contributions of more than $10 and campaign expenditures on behalf of the candidate of more than $100.

But the court overturned other features of the law, ruling that the campaign spending limits were unconstitutional violations of the First Amendment guarantee of free expression. For presidential candidates who accepted federal matching funds, however, the ceiling on expenditures remained intact. The court also struck down the method for selecting members of the FEC.

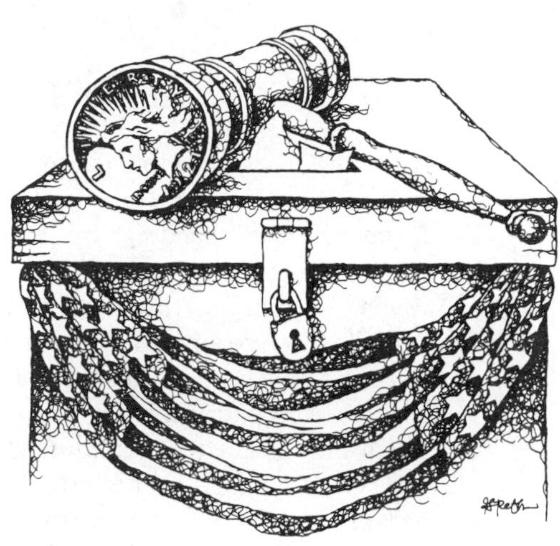

Responding to the Supreme Court decision, the 1976 amendments to FECA reconstituted the watchdog commission and revised some contribution limits. Throughout the late 1970s reformers sought to curb campaign spending by pressing for the extension fo public financing to congressional races. But the post-Watergate mood in Congress was less amenable to major campaign finance reforms. Legislative drives in 1977, 1978, and 1979 all failed. In late 1979 legislation was passed by Congress that reduced paperwork requirements for candidates and political committees and encouraged more volunteer as well as grass-roots activity.

The controversy over campaign finance continued into the 1980s, with countless reform bills introduced each year.

Initiatives for More Change

In the wake of the 1982 election, Congress took a serious look at federal election laws and in particular at the role of money in campaigns. Although both the House and

Supreme Court Strikes Down Limits . . .

Clearing the way for continued expansion of the power of political action committees (PACs), the Supreme Court March 18, 1985, ruled that Congress cannot limit independent spending by PACs on behalf of publicly funded presidential candidates.

By a 7-2 margin, the court struck down as unconstitutional a provision of the Federal Election Campaign Act Amendments (PL 93-443) that limited to $1,000 the amount a PAC may spend independently to promote or prevent the election of publicly funded presidential candidates. The court said the spending limit infringed on freedom of speech and association guaranteed by the First Amendment.

The court's ruling did not affect a separate provision of the campaign law that limits the amounts PACs may *contribute* to candidates, as opposed to spending independently on their behalf. Those limits are $5,000 per candidate per election for congressional races, and $5,000 per presidential candidate in primary elections. No contributions are permitted to presidential candidates who accept public funding for general elections.

The PAC Case

The campaign funding decision marked the second time the court has invalidated the PAC spending limit, which has never actually been enforced. In 1982, the court by 4-4 upheld a lower court decision that the spending ceiling was unconstitutional. But that ruling had no force as precedent because of the tie vote. The court's decision in *Federal Election Commission (FEC) v. National Conservative Political Action Committee (NCPAC), Democratic Party of the United States and Democratic National Committee v. NCPAC* affirmed a 1983 ruling by a three-judge federal court.

The cases were initiated by the FEC and by the Democrats, who had hoped to forestall heavy pro-Reagan spending by conservative PACs in the 1984 election. But the three-judge panel ruled against them, and the Supreme Court refused to accelerate its consideration of that decision, leaving the limit unenforced during the 1984 campaign.

Spending and Speech

The court's decision in *FEC v. NCPAC* was grounded in the majority's view that "the expenditures at issue in this case produce speech at the core of the First Amendment," which Congress cannot limit without weighty justification. The ruling was a logical extension of the court's 1976 decision in *Buckley v. Valeo*, which upheld limits on campaign contributions as justified to prevent corruption, but struck down limits on campaign spending by a candidate or an individual. The $1,000 limit abridged not only the freedom of speech, but also the protected First Amendment freedom of association, the court held.

"NCPAC and FCM [Fund for a Conservative Majority] are mechanisms by which large numbers of individuals of modest means can join together in organizations which serve to amplify the voice of their adherents," William H. Rehnquist wrote, noting that

. . . On Independent PAC Outlays

each of these organizations received contributions in the 1979-80 period from more than 100,000 people. NCPAC's contributions averaged $75 each; those to FCM, $25 each. "To say that their collective action in pooling their resources to amplify their voices is not entitled to full First Amendment protection would subordinate the voices of those of modest means as opposed to those sufficiently wealthy to be able to buy expensive media ads with their own resources," Rehnquist continued.

The majority found no evidence that PAC contributions posed a threat of corruption. "The fact that candidates and elected officials may alter or reaffirm their own positions on issues in response to political messages paid for by the PACs can hardly be called corruption," wrote Rehnquist, "for one of the essential features of democracy is the presentation to the electorate of varying points of view." And, the court said, "even were we to determine that the large pooling of financial resources by NCPAC and FCM did pose a potential for corruption or the appearance of corruption," the $1,000 limit is "a fatally overbroad response to that evil. It is not limited to multimillion dollar war chests; its terms apply equally to informal discussion groups that solicit neighborhood contributions to publicize their views about a particular presidential candidate."

The Dissent

Justices Byron R. White and Thurgood Marshall dissented, viewing these PAC expenditures as campaign contributions that Congress could limit without directly burdening the freedom of speech. "The First Amendment protects the right to speak, not the right to spend, and limitations on the amount of money that can be spent are not the same as restrictions on speaking," wrote White. "I cannot accept the cynic's 'money talks' as a proposition of constitutional law." He added, "If the elected members of the legislature, who are surely in the best position to know, conclude that large-scale expenditures are a significant threat to the integrity and fairness of the electoral process, we should not second-guess that judgment."

Congress wanted no contributions to publicly funded presidential contenders, White said. "It is nonsensical to allow the purposes of this limitation to be entirely defeated by allowing the sort of 'independent' expenditures at issue here, and the First Amendment does not require us to do so." With this decision, he warned, the court continued its "dismemberment of congressional efforts to regulate campaign financing." Once again, he concluded, "the court has . . . transformed a coherent regulatory scheme into a nonsensical loophole-ridden patchwork."

In a separate dissenting opinion, Justice Marshall said he saw no constitutional distinction between campaign contributions and campaign spending, and found limits on both well justified by the interest in preventing corruption. "It simply belies reality," he wrote, "to say that a campaign will not reward massive financial assistance provided in the only way that is legally available. . . . An eager supporter will be able to discern a candidate's needs and desires; similarly, a willing candidate will notice the supporter's efforts."

Senate held extensive hearings on the issue in 1983, neither chamber took floor action on the proposed legislation before the 98th Congress adjourned.

There was general agreement among members of the 98th Congress involved in the debate that the existing law performed a valuable function by requiring disclosure of campaign contributions and expenditures. But there were widely varying opinions on the limits the election law placed on receiving and spending campaign funds and on how the law might be improved. But partisan conflicts and the controversy surrounding public campaign financing made quick legislative action impossible. PACs and most other groups involved with campaign finance were convinced that there would be little movement in 1983, so they did not do much lobbying on the issue.

Central to any campaign finance debate were the contribution limits. In 1984 an individual could give no more than $1,000 to a federal candidate in any primary, runoff, or general election. An individual also could not exceed an aggregate $25,000 in contributions per year to all federal campaigns. A PAC could not give more than $5,000 to a candidate per election.

These limits were set in 1974. Ten years later inflation had lowered the ceilings by more than 50 percent. One result of this, observers contended, was increasing independent expenditures. No limit existed on independent spending. The only restriction was that an independent spender have no contact with the candidate he sought to aid. Independent expenditures surged in the 1980 election season. Low contribution limits also increased the importance of personal wealth. With individual contributions by outsiders severely limited, the person of independent means becomes a more potent candidate.

HR 2490 sought to curb campaign spending by placing a cap on the amount of money a candidate could accept from PACs and on the amount he could spend of his own personal wealth. It was introduced in the 98th Congress by a bipartisan coalition led by Rep. David R. Obey, D-Wis.

The bill was backed by Common Cause, the only group to undertake vigorous lobbying on campaign finance in 1983. After "declaring war" on PACs in February of that year, the public interest lobby worked hard to develop grass-roots support for campaign finance changes.

Instead of providing public financing or limiting PACs, the Republican leadership wanted to loosen restrictions on party spending that were embedded in existing election law. The GOP proposal was grounded in the belief that money in congressional campaigns was a necessary and desirable element. Supporters also believed that an enhanced role for the parties would help curb the influence of campaign contributions from special interests.

The Republican plan was embodied in S 1350, introduced by Sen. Paul Laxalt, Nev., and HR 3081, sponsored by Rep. Bill Frenzel, Minn. But the Republican approach faced strong opposition from Democrats, who feared that it would further the GOP's already sizable financial advantage over them. The Repubican National Committee collected $79.8 million in 1982, far outdistancing the $15.5 million taken in by the Democratic National Committee. The Democrats said they would like to close that gap before loosening the bonds on party spending.

Others had more philosophical reservations about the legislation. "The proposal has a tendency to encourage dependency on political parties," said Illinois Democratic senator Alan J. Dixon, who had introduced a bill (S 85) offering public funding for senatorial candidates. "I would prefer things that encourage independent, individual members."

"I don't want my party . . . to wind up

having the same kind of leverage over me . . . as you can have by implication with a lot of other groups around here," Obey said.

Obey and 90 other members of Congress introduced in late 1983 a compromise proposal designed, according to its sponsors, to "break the logjam on campaign finance reform." The bill retained the PAC-limiting language of HR 2490 but dropped public financing provisions in favor of giving tax credits for campaign contributions.

Boren and Boschwitz Proposals

After months of fits and starts, the Senate the week of August 11, 1986, came to the brink of passing sweeping campaign finance reforms designed to loosen the binds of special interest groups on congressional office seekers. But in the partisan drive to gain the higher ground on the sensitive election-year issue, Republicans and Democrats played a high-stakes game of "political chicken" and eventually dodged a final decision.

Senators in the 99th Congress went on record twice in favor of strict new controls on campaign fund-raising, but in the end failed to pass legislation to that effect. On a 69-30 vote, the Senate approved a measure by David L. Boren, D-Okla., to limit the amount of money that PACs can give congressional candidates. Then, on a 58-42 roll call, the Senate approved a GOP countermeasure by Rudy Boschwitz, Minn., to stifle PAC contributions to political parties and force party operations to disclose all hidden sources of their funds. Both amendments were attached to an unrelated bill (S 655) that had been stripped of its other provisions in 1985. A last-minute effort to bring S 655 to a final vote — thus sending the PAC-limiting measure to the House — was stymied by partisan maneuvering and tactical infighting.

Majority Leader Robert Dole, R-Kan., a vocal opponent of the bill, appeared willing to allow a final vote after both amendments were approved. Boren, despite the reluctance of some Democrats, was ready to take up the offer. But Boschwitz, who had devised his amendment partly to embarrass Democrats whose national party apparatus relies most heavily on PAC donations, ultimately nixed the idea of passing the bill as a political gambit.

Boren had been the primary instigator in the Senate to limit PAC contributions to congressional campaigns. Though he attracted bipartisan support — including Barry Goldwater, R-Ariz., and John C. Stennis, D-Miss. — for the most part he conducted a lonely crusade to force Senate action. He introduced a bill (S 1806) in October 1985 and forced temporary Senate action on the measure when he offered it as an amendment to S 655. But the anticipated showdown dissipated after both sides said they were uncertain how the votes were lining up. Dole promised Boren future action on his bill, including hearings in the Senate Rules Committee and a subsequent floor vote, and Republicans and Democrats then joined in an overwhelming 7-84 vote against killing the Boren bill.

The crux of Boren's attack on PACs was creation of a limit on how much each Senate and House candidate could accept from all PACs, and the setting of new limits on how much each could receive from one PAC, in any two-year election cycle. The cap on receipts from PACs overall would be $100,000 for House candidates and between $175,000 and $750,000 for Senate candidates, depending on the populations in their states. The limits would be increased to allow for contested primaries and runoff elections.

The Boren measure also would reduce from $5,000 to $3,000 the cap on what a PAC could give to one candidate per election. It would at the same time increase the limit on what an individual contributor could give a candidate from $1,000 to $1,500 per election.

In addition, Boren would close a loophole in campaign finance law that allows a PAC to exceed current limits by "bundling" further donations from individuals and passing those on to candidates in the PAC's name.

Besides limiting PAC contributions to candidates, Boren's bill attacked the practice of using PAC money to campaign against one candidate without the money being covered by an opponent's campaign spending limits. Boren would require that such advertising announce that it was not subject to campaign contribution limits. It would also require broadcasters to give equal time to the subjects of "negative" ads.

Boschwitz became the point man for Republican opposition to the Boren plan when Dole appointed him to head a special GOP task force to come up with an alternative. Boschwitz came back with a countermeasure to prohibit PAC contributions to national political parties, which included the partisan campaign committees run by leaders of the House and Senate. Boschwitz' amendment also would require political parties to disclose the so-called "soft money" they accept from corporations, unions, and other donors that currently goes unreported.

Soft money is used for general "party-building" purposes, such as paying for campaign headquarters or bolstering the coffers of state party organizations, rather than for a particular candidate's campaign. The practice allows wealthy donors to exceed limits on individual contributions and allows party organizations to provide indirect support for candidates with money that would be illegal if given directly to a candidate.

Boschwitz' amendment was assailed as a blatantly partisan attempt to embarrass Democrats, who traditionally rely more heavily on PAC contributions to party organizations than do Republicans, who get most of their donations from individuals.

In the 1984 congressional elections, national Democratic Party organizations, such as the Democratic Senatorial Campaign Committee and the Democratic Congressional Campaign Committee, received $6.5 million in contributions from PACs, compared with $58.3 million from individuals, according to the Federal Election Commission. On the other hand, Republican organizations, including the National Republican Senatorial Committee and the National Republican Congressional Committee, received only $1.7 million from PACs, compared with $262 million from individual contributors.

Boschwitz acknowledged that his amendment was crafted with a political strategy in mind. The amendment and the rules governing the two votes were designed to give Republicans a way to vote successively for the Boren amendment and the Boschwitz alternative, working on the assumption that the Democratic-controlled House would probably not want to act on a bill that contained both measures.

While the vote on the Boren amendment drew broad bipartisan support, the tally on Boschwitz' proposal proceeded almost strictly along party lines, until the outcome in the Republicans' favor was assured and a handful of Democrats joined with Boschwitz. Final action was not taken on S 655 before Congress adjourned.

Boschwitz described the issue of campaign finance as too politically charged for Congress to handle objectively. He called for a bipartisan commission to come back in 1987 with recommendations for campaign finance reform; a bill (S 528) to that effect was approved by the Senate Governmental Affairs Committee August 12, 1986.

Washington Pilgrimage: In Search of PAC Dollars

Long before election day, congressional candidates set out to become familiar with one of Washington's corridors of power — the political action committee community. For months, congressional contenders from all across the country troop to the capital to canvass for PAC contributions that they hope would help pave the way to electoral victory.

This pilgrimage in search of PAC dollars has become an integral part of congressional campaigns in recent years, as challengers and open-seat contenders have come to view PACs as vital to their political welfare. Consultants and professional fundraisers have helped promote the pilgrimage by peddling opportunities for access to the PAC community. Those access-providers are finding an increasing number of candidates eager for their services.

Candidates make their journeys in the face of daunting odds. Most PACs have been showing decidedly pro-incumbent tendencies for years. What little money PACs do invest in nonincumbents often is funneled to a small coterie of top-flight contenders who are strongly favored to win. PAC managers who support failed candidates know they will have to explain their losses to a hostile board of directors; as a result, they are extremely risk-averse.

But if candidates realize the problems they face in trying to tap the Washington PAC community, one would not know it from the way they behave. The number of candidates making the Washington pilgrimage seems to be growing with each election cycle, as they eagerly compete for a slice of the PAC pie. Candidates not only are showing up in Washington in increasing numbers; they are showing up earlier and earlier with each passing campaign. Far from being a biennial event, the Washington pilgrimage often begins immediately after election day for a contest two years down the road.

Washington is not the only place to which candidates travel in search of PAC money. Houston and Los Angeles are prominent among the other cities that are emerging as important PAC centers. But Washington still is regarded as the symbolic and financial capital of the PAC world.

There is little mystery about the major reason candidates come to Washington to visit PACs: They come in search of cash. But there are other potential benefits from such journeys that may not be as apparent. The PAC pilgrimage affords candidates an opportunity to test their political appeal before a critical, seasoned audience. It also gives them valuable practice at trying to raise funds — practice that could pay off when they return home. Some candidates feel that a trip to Washington can help them convince PAC managers they are serious about their race.

Candidates also may gain an intangible sense of purpose and excitement from visiting the capital that fires their imaginations — and their campaigns.

PAC managers, too, can benefit from the pilgrimage. It often provides the only chance they get to develop a firsthand feel for contenders they have known only through press clippings, poll numbers, and other analysts' remarks. By meeting personally with a particular candidate, PAC managers say, they stand a better chance of keeping track of that contender's campaign. With a field of hundreds of candidates for federal office, that is no easy task.

Chances for Success

A variety of factors conspires to determine the success that candidates have when they approach Washington's PAC community, but a surprising number of those factors are already decided before candidates arrive in Washington.

At a fundamental level, candidates strengthen their case if they are committed to waging a campaign before they come looking for money. A potentially strong contender arguably should not be penalized for visiting a PAC director in the course of making up his mind whether to run. But in practice, it often works out that way.

Many challengers also misuse time and resources trying to get money from organizations that have a strong record of support for the incumbents the challengers hope to unseat.

Many PAC managers also have a tendency to avoid candidates who are involved in crowded or difficult primaries. Most PACs are leery of losing out in an intraparty battle; they steer clear of a candidate until he emerges as the likely nominee. There is, however, an important exception to that rule. Directors of ideologically oriented PACs are much more likely than their corporate or labor colleagues to enter a primary if they find a clear philosophical ally.

Perhaps the most decisive event in a candidate's PAC pilgrimage takes place behind the PAC manager's door. There, a congressional hopeful faces the same kind of pressure to make a favorable impression that is felt by an anxious applicant interviewing a potential employer. A good performance at that meeting can help a candidate establish credibility and spread interest in his campaign throughout the PAC community. A bad showing can effectively shut a candidate out of PAC money.

PAC managers agree that political naiveté on the part of the candidates is a recurrent problem that damages their chances of establishing credibility. Too often, contenders cite broad partisan trends and offer shallow political complaints in lieu of offering a fully developed case for their candidacy. What helps a candidate build credibility, PAC managers say, are poll results, a realistic budget, an assessment of an opponent's vulnerabilities, and names of prominent political and financial supporters back home.

A successful PAC pilgrimage seldom ends with a single visit. By supplying a steady barrage of updated poll results, press releases and newspaper clippings, a candidate can keep the PAC community abreast of his progress and reinforce PAC interest in the campaign. PAC fund raising has become, as one consultant put it, "almost a constant public relations job."

Great Expectations

Those who counsel candidates about PAC fund raising often urge them to temper their expectations about what their PAC pilgrimage will bring. Challengers and open-seat contenders who think a PAC visit pays big monetary dividends up front are in for a big shock.

Some candidates apparently are unaware of the proincumbent bias most political action committees maintain; others misunderstand the limits that govern the legal amount a PAC can contribute to any one contender's campaign. Still others fail to make a distinction between the different kinds of aid offered a candidate by different kinds of political committees. Most corporate and labor PACs make financial contributions as well as so-called "in-kind" contributions — assistance of an organizational or technical nature. For the ideological PACs, however, in-kind contributions usually are the rule.

The PAC Community

If candidates often overestimate the amount of money they will receive from their Washington forays, they often underestimate how much their requests for money are influenced by communication within the PAC community. The conversation between one PAC director and another about a candidate may be crucial to that candidate's receiving PAC support.

By landing a PAC's endorsement, a candidate assures himself access to that grapevine. Through regular meetings, "meet-and-greet" sessions with candidates, and other informal contact, members of the Washington PAC community share their lists, rating contenders who are strong and

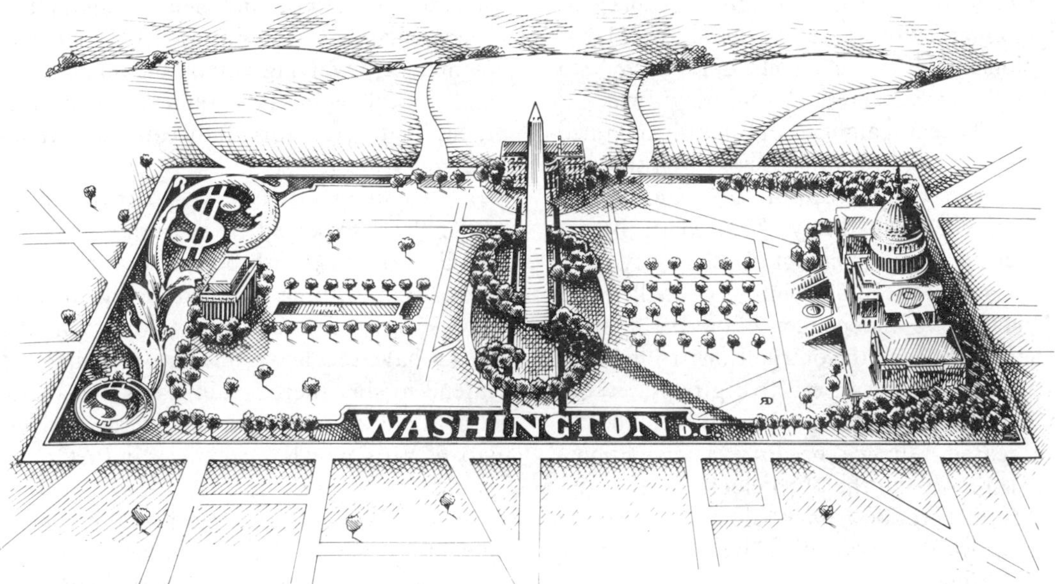

incumbents who are in trouble.

Some PAC directors urge candidates to use their endorsement as a way of courting other PAC support. Support for a candidate also can spread throughout the PAC community via the national parties, which have become an increasingly vital link between PACs and campaigns. PAC managers of all stripes say both national party organizations generally provide good intelligence about challengers and open-seat candidates — as well as helping coach contenders about how to win support from political committees. The national parties' attitude toward a challenger often helps PAC managers decide whether or not to recommend committing support.

Candidates who do not find themselves on PAC support lists should not abandon hope. An increasing number of contenders are taking advantage of a defensive strategy toward the PAC community — even if their offensive ploys fall short. Courting political action committees that are unlikely to give to a challenger's campaign can prove profitable — if the challenger can convince the PAC to remain neutral or scale back support for the incumbent. The process has been dubbed "negative fund raising."

While there is little argument that the Washington pilgrimage has become an institution in congressional campaigns, not everyone agrees that this is a positive development. A significant number of PAC directors feel that many candidates place too much emphasis on Washington — when they should be tending to PACs' local constituencies back home.

1984 Elections: PAC Gifts to Incumbents

Democrat Robert A. Borski's 1984 reelection campaign to his Philadelphia House seat illustrates a trend that became even more pronounced in 1984 — the tendency of incumbents to depend on special interest groups to finance their races. Nearly two-thirds of the more than $303,000 Borski's campaign received came from political action committees representing an array of interests ranging from labor unions, real estate agents, and doctors to dairy farmers and a Houston law firm.

The campaign was a significant turnabout from 1982, when Borski won the seat by defeating Republican incumbent Charles F. Dougherty. That year, Borski received only 28 percent of his money from PACs and scored points by challenging Dougherty's independence on the ground that he accepted contributions from business and other conservative groups.

In addition to pointing up incumbents' increased reliance on PAC contributions, final reports on the 1984 elections from the Federal Election Commission also show little change in two other trends of recent campaigns. Almost without exception, incumbents far outpaced their challengers in campaign contributions and spending levels, and PACs continued to favor incumbents by a significant margin.

But at the same time the FEC reported that growth of the campaign money supply — which had skyrocketed in recent years — slowed considerably. Even the growth of PAC spending fell off, though not as precipitously.

Spending Spree Slows

House and Senate candidates spent $374.1 million in 1984 compared with $342.4 million in 1982, an increase of 9.3 percent. That contrasts with a 43 percent jump in spending between 1980 and 1982 and a 23 percent rise between 1978 and 1980. PAC contributions also increased during the 1984 political season at a slower rate than in previous years. Overall, PACs dispensed $104.9 million to House and Senate candidates, a 25 percent increase over 1982. That compares with a 51 percent increase between 1980 and 1982.

Political analysts offered several reasons for the reduced growth in PAC contributions and overall fund-raising and spending by House and Senate candidates. They included fewer seriously contested campaigns involving vulnerable incumbents and a decline in the number of open-seat races that often turn into expensive fund-raising contests.

The lower rate of PAC contributions in 1984 "was expected in the sense that the PAC world has mushroomed and that most large organizations that are going to form PACs have formed them. Many of the PACs have reached a level of financing and intend to stay there," said Larry J. Sabato, a political science professor at the University of Virginia who specializes in PACs and campaign finance.

The problem at some PACs has been dwindling memberships for the sponsoring organization, hampering fund-raising efforts and lowering the pool of money that can be doled out to political candidates.

Other PACs, however, stand out as glaring exceptions to the pattern of slower growth rates in their total contribution levels. For example, in 1980 the PAC operated by the National Association of Letter Carriers contributed $44,715 to House and Senate candidates. In 1984, the postal union's PAC delivered enough cash — $1.2 million — to make it the ninth largest PAC contributor to congressional candidates. Officials of the group said President Reagan's attempts to reduce health and retirement benefits for federal and postal employees motivated its members.

Are Costs Moderating?

Some observers believe the costs of campaigning are moderating and may continue to level off.

Michael J. Malbin, a political scholar at the American Enterprise Institute, noted that recent large increases in campaign costs have been the result of modern — and expensive — techniques such as extensive polling and the use of specialized political consultants. Now that virtually all congres-

Top 15 PACs in 1984

Following is a list of the leading 15 political action committees (PACs), based on direct contributions to congressional candidates in the 1984 election cycle.

	Political Action Committee	Amount
1.	Realtors Political Action Committee (National Association of Realtors)	$2,429,552
2.	American Medical Association Political Action Committee	1,839,464
3.	BUILD-PAC (National Association of Home Builders)	1,625,539
4.	National Education Association Political Action Committee	1,574,003
5.	UAW V-CAP (United Auto Workers Volunteer Community Action Program)	1,405,107
6.	Seafarers Political Activity Donation (Seafarers International Union)	1,322,410
7.	Machinists Non-Partisan Political League (International Association of Machinists and Aerospace Workers)	1,306,497
8.	Active Ballot Club (United Food and Commercial Workers International Union)	1,271,974
9.	Committee on Letter Carriers Political Education (National Association of Letter Carriers)	1,234,603
10.	National Association of Retired Federal Employees Political Action Committee	1,099,243
11.	Committee for Thorough Agricultural Political Education of Associated Milk Producers Inc.	1,087,658
12.	Automobile and Truck Dealers Election Action Committee (National Automobile Dealers Association)	1,057,165
13.	Public Employees Organized to Promote Legislative Equality (American Federation of State, County and Municipal Employees)	905,806
14.	National Association of Life Underwriters Political Action Committee	900,200
15.	BANKPAC (American Bankers Association)	882,850

NOTE: The data are based on a two-year election cycle and only include direct contributions to candidates for the House and Senate.

SOURCE: Federal Election Commission

sional candidates have adopted such methods, there is no strong reason for spending levels to continue escalating. Some of the costs connected with high-technology campaigning are even coming down. In 1980 the use of personal computers in campaigns was an expensive luxury. By 1984, computers were much more affordable.

Overall spending in the 1983-84 election cycle might have been even lower were it not for a few lavishly expensive Senate races, notably in North Carolina, Texas, and West Virginia. Senate candidates in 1984 spent 23 percent more than their counterparts in 1982. House candidates, however, spent 0.2 percent less in 1984 than they did two years earlier.

Even if campaign costs level off, that offers little solace to challengers who continue to take a back seat to incumbents when it comes to raising and spending money. Incumbents running in the 1984 House and Senate elections raised 59 percent — $207.6 million — out of a total $353.6 million collected by all candidates who ran in the November general election. Challengers raised 22 percent — $77.7 million — while candidates in open races accounted for the remaining $68.1 million.

PACs Favor Incumbents

Political action committees also continued to heap an increasing share of their cash on incumbents, and incumbents relied more heavily than before on PAC contributions as a share of total receipts.

During the 1983-84 cycle, incumbents received 72 percent of the money dispensed by PACs. Challengers received only 16 percent, and the rest went to open-seat candidates. By comparison, incumbents received 66 percent of all PAC contributions in 1982 and 61 percent two years earlier.

The average House incumbent received 43 percent of his campaign funds from PACs compared with 20 percent for challengers and 21 percent for candidates in open races. The average Senate incumbent collected 24 percent from PACs. Challengers received 16 percent and open-seat candidates gathered 9 percent.

In both chambers, Democratic incumbents attracted significantly more PAC contributions than Republicans. In the House, for example, PAC contributions accounted for 46 percent of the average Democrat's campaign treasury compared with 37 percent for GOP incumbents.

Critics Concerned

The statistics on PAC contributions worry critics of the campaign finance system, who question whether legislators can escape the influence of so much special-interest money when it comes to voting on Capitol Hill.

Members of Congress "are growing more and more dependent on PAC money and less and less free to respond to the needs of their constituents," said Fred Wertheimer, president of Common Cause. "This system must change — and change soon — if we expect representative government to survive."

Many political scientists who specialize in campaign financing reject the charge that PAC money strongly influences the way members of Congress vote. "What is offered as evidence of the power of PACs in legislative politics often is anecdotal and frequently is based on simple correlations between PAC spending and legislative outcomes — correlations that are incapable of determining the true cause and effect," argued Herbert E. Alexander, founder and director of the Citizens' Research Foundation, a private organization that monitors campaign financing. Gary C. Jacobson, professor of political science at the University of California, San Diego, agreed. Even though it would be "bizarre to expect *no* relationship between contributions and behavior," Jacobson wrote in 1980, "any simple cross-sectional comparison of contributions and roll call votes is necessarily inconclusive" because it is impossible to determine specifically why a lawmaker votes for or against a bill.

Political scientists tend to agree that pressure from constituents influences lawmakers more than PAC contributions do. "I don't think many votes are changed by contributions," said Malbin. "On the whole, groups tend to give to [members of Congress] who agree with them because they have a past record of agreeing with them, and most votes tend to form fairly consistent patterns. . . . On general issues, you cannot afford to deviate from that historic pattern [because] it'll kill you in the next election." The basic forces that influence votes in Congress are "party, ideology and, above all, the needs and views of the constituency," said Sabato. "Votes always matter more than money to politicians. Votes are the only thing that re-elects them. Money is a means to an end. Votes are an end."

The public disclosure requirements mandated by federal law also may play an important role in mitigating the "buying and selling" of candidates. "Disclosure acts as a check on members of Congress," Malbin said. "When a member casts a vote, he or she has to do so with the knowledge that an organization such as Common Cause or a potential future opponent can look at the records and try to make some connection."

FEC chairman John Warren McGarry went so far as to say that because of the disclosure requirements, "there's nobody running for [federal] office who is blatantly ignoring election law."

Sen. Slade Gorton, R-Wash., pointed out that "through PACs, more people than ever before are participating in political activities." Gorton, however, conceded that PACs could have a damaging effect: "When encouraging and coordinating member participation in the political process, PACs are at their finest. But by building central war chests to allow lobbyists to assert direct political influence through large campaign contributions, PACs raise questions about the responsiveness of our political system." Gorton prefers requiring PACs to permit contributors to earmark money for particular candidates. Some PACs permit such earmarking, but the practice remains rare.

Groups such as Common Cause continue to clamor for changes in campaign finance laws. They want to decrease the role of PACs and permit challengers to be more financially competitive with incumbents. But the principal vehicle for doing so — public financing — has attracted little support in Congress. Critics blame the limited interest legislators have shown in revising campaign finance laws on the fact that incumbents usually benefit from the current system.

5

Congressional Rating Game

Each year members of Congress are "rated" by a variety of interest groups. The scores are based on what the groups saw as key legislative votes for the year. Usually, the ratings are widely circulated and frequently cited in campaigns and press reports. Yet they have been accused at one time or another of being biased, fickle, or misleading.

While ratings often are used as a political shorthand to depict politicians as, for example, "liberal" or "probusiness" or "proenvironment," what they actually show is a good deal more limited. They measure how often a lawmaker voted the way the interest groups wanted on an imperfect, subjectively selected sample of votes. Another problem with ratings is that interest groups' interests change over time, making comparisons from year to year difficult, if not impossible.

Partisan bias also is a common complaint about ratings. It was especially true of 1981, when President Reagan's economic program polarized the interest groups as much as it did Congress.

Following are sketches of four groups — Americans for Democratic Action (ADA), the American Federation of Labor and Congress of Industrial Organizations (AFL-CIO), the Chamber of Commerce of the United States (CCUS), and the American Conservative Union (ACU) — and names of the members of Congress who scored highest and lowest for 1985 on the groups' score cards.

Americans for Democratic Action

Since 1947, ADA ratings have been a standard, if sometimes disputed, measure of the term *liberal.* Early ADA ratings focused on lawmakers' support of New Deal-like programs and gradually grew to include support for a noninterventionist foreign policy.

Senate Votes

In the Senate, ADA selected 20 votes on which to base its ratings — 14 on domestic issues and 6 on foreign and military policy issues.

Positions on domestic issues that ADA supported included:

• Liberalized benefits for the long-term unemployed.

• Restoration of funding for Head Start, developmental disability and handicapped education programs, and guaranteed student loan and other education and training programs.

• Restoration of funding for the Summer Youth Employment Program at the fiscal 1985 level.

• Restoration of $4.6 billion in Medicare and Medicaid funding for fiscal 1986-88.

• A 15 percent minimum tax on corporate earnings over $50,000, with resulting revenues used to lower the federal deficit.

• Retaining the ban on the interstate sale of handguns.

• A new $30 million demonstration program to pay the medical expenses of victims of hazardous-waste dumping.

Defense and foreign policy positions backed by ADA included:

• Deletion of $2.1 billion for production of 21 MX missiles and a prohibition on the use of any defense authorization funds for production or deployment of MX missiles.

• Reduced funding for research on antimissile defenses.

• Economic sanctions against South Africa because of its policy of apartheid.

ADA opposed:

• Passage of the budget resolution, which included elimination of Social Security cost-of-living adjustments (COLAs) in 1986, termination of 13 domestic programs, and a hold on defense spending to the rate of inflation.

• Funding for procurement of binary chemical weapons.

• Authorizing funds for humanitarian assistance to Nicaraguan rebels.

• Repeal of the "Clark amendment" prohibiting U.S. military aid to antigovernment rebels in Angola.

• Giving the president line-item veto power on appropriations bills.

• Barring federal courts from considering cases involving prayer in public schools.

• A "seasonal worker" program to allow foreign workers into the country for up to nine months each year for agricultural work.

• The Gramm-Rudman-Hollings mandatory deficit-reduction plan.

• Barring the use in the District of Columbia of federal or District funds to pay for abortions.

House Votes

A number of the 20 House votes selected by ADA were on issues used to determine Senate ratings. In addition, ADA supported:

• The Democratic alternative to the Reagan budget.

• Reduced funding for U.S. Army Corps of Engineers' water projects.

• Congress's option to defer future military aid to the Philippines if significant political, economic, and military reforms were not achieved and if U.S. aid was used to violate the human rights of Filipinos.

• Denying federal farm assistance to any farmer with 10 or more field hand employees who fails to provide drinking water and sanitation facilities for his employees.

• Establishment of a commission to oversee a study of the federal work force to determine whether differences in pay and classification have arisen because of discrimination on the basis of sex, race, or national origin.

• Requiring employers of at least 50 full-time employees to give 90 days' notice of any plant shutdown or layoff involving at least 100 workers or 30 percent of the work force.

Positions opposed by ADA included:

• Authorizing $1.5 billion for procurement of 21 MX missiles.

• Funding for production of the Trident II missile.

• Amending the military legal code to make peacetime espionage punishable by death.

• A spending freeze on Clean Water Act programs at fiscal 1985 levels and limiting increases in fiscal 1987-90 to the level of inflation.

- Reduced funding for new public housing.
- Elimination of COLAs to federal reimbursements to schools providing school lunch and child nutrition programs, except the WIC program for needy pregnant women, infants, and children.
- The Republican tax reform plan.

ADA Study Findings

Senate

High Scorers. Five Northern Democrats scored 100 percent: Alan Cranston, Calif.; Gary Hart, Colo.; Tom Harkin, Iowa; Paul S. Sarbanes, Md.; and Howard M. Metzenbaum, Ohio.

The highest-scoring Southern Democrat was David Pryor, Ark., with 80 percent, followed by Dale Bumpers, Ark., 70 percent, and Albert Gore, Jr., Tenn., with 65 percent.

Lowell P. Weicker, Jr., Conn., and Charles McC. Mathias, Jr., Md., tied for the highest score among Republicans, both with 70 percent. The next highest score was received by Arlen Specter, Pa., with 55 percent.

Low Scorers. Eighteen Republicans received scores of zero. Among Southern Democrats, Russell B. Long, La., was the lowest scorer with 20 percent. Next were Howell Heflin, Ala., and John C. Stennis, Miss., both with 25 percent, and Sam Nunn, Ga., who scored 30 percent.

Lowest scoring Northern Democrats were Nebraska senators Edward Zorinsky and J. James Exon, with 25 percent apiece.

House

High Scorers. Twenty Democrats, including one Southern Democrat, Mickey Leland, Texas, scored 100 percent.

Other high-scoring Southern Democrats were William Lehman, Fla., with 95 percent, and Harold E. Ford, Tenn., with 90 percent.

Highest scoring Republicans were Silvio O. Conte, Mass., with 75 percent, followed by Christopher H. Smith, N.J., 65 percent; Jim Leach, Iowa, and Bill Green, N.Y., both with 60 percent.

Low Scorers. Seventeen Republicans received zero scores.

Among Southern Democrats, three representatives received low scores of 10 percent: Bill Nichols, Ala.; Marvin Leath, Texas; and Dan Daniel, Va.

Northern Democrat Beverly B. Byron, Md., also scored 10 percent, followed by Roy Dyson, Md., 30 percent, and Richard H. Stallings, Idaho, 35 percent.

American Federation of Labor and Congress of Industrial Organizations

The umbrella group for organized labor, which has rated members of Congress since 1955, claims its ratings represent "votes for or against the interests of workers." Twenty-one Senate and 17 House votes were used in this group's 1985 ratings.

Senate Votes

Positions in the Senate supported by the AFL-CIO included:

- Liberalized benefits for the long-term unemployed.
- Federal subsidies for Amtrak.
- Restoration of funds for Head Start, developmental disability and handicapped education programs, and guaranteed student loan and other education and training programs.
- Restoration of postal subsidies for charitable and religious organizations, small newspapers, and libraries.
- Restoration of the full Social Security COLA for fiscal 1986.
- Restoration of $4.6 billion in Medicare and Medicaid funding for fiscal 1986-88.
- A 15 percent minimum tax on corporate earnings over $50,000, with revenues used to lower the federal deficit.
- Economic sanctions against South Africa because of its policy of apartheid.
- A new $30 million demonstration program to pay the medical expenses of victims of hazardous-waste dumping.
- Restoration of funding for general revenue sharing.
- Import quotas on textiles and apparel.

The AFL-CIO opposed:

- Passage of the budget resolution, which included elimination of Social Security COLAs in 1986, termination of 13 domestic programs, and a hold on defense spending to the rate of inflation.
- Exemption of military construction projects from the Davis-Bacon Act, which regulates hourly wages for construction workers on federal projects.
- Giving the president line-item veto power on appropriations bills.
- A seasonal worker program to allow foreign workers into the country for up to nine months each year for agricultural work.
- The Gramm-Rudman-Hollings mandatory deficit-reduction plan.
- Exemption of government-generated commercial agricultural exports from cargo preference requirements.
- Deleting all but termination expenses for the Economic Development Administration.
- Requirement that federal energy assistance be counted as income in determining eligibility for food stamps.
- Deleting all funding for the National Endowment for Democracy.

House Votes

In determining House scores, the AFL-CIO used several votes that were similar to Senate issues. In addition, the organization supported:

- The Democratic alternative to the Reagan budget.
- Funding to establish an American Conservation Corps to put unemployed youths to work on conservation projects.
- Allowing compulsory union dues to be used for political activities.
- Expanded benefit and eligibility levels for food stamps.
- Denying federal farm assistance to any farmer with 10 or more field hand employees who fails to provide drinking water and sanitation facilities for his employees.
- Establishment of a commission to oversee a study of the federal work force to determine whether differences in pay and classification have arisen because of discrimination on the basis of sex, race, or national origin.
- Requiring that plant owners consult with employees before closing a plant and that workers be given 90 days' notice of any plant shutdown or layoff involving at least 100 workers or 30 percent of the work force.
- Funding for the "superfund" hazardous-waste cleanup program through increased taxes on chemical feedstocks, petroleum and hazardous-waste disposal, and

general revenues, rather than through a "value-added" tax.

• Allowing persons injured by release of toxic substances to sue in federal court.

The AFL-CIO opposed:

• The Republican budget plan.

AFL-CIO Study Findings

Senate

High Scorers. Three Northern Democrats received perfect scores: Sarbanes, Md.; Daniel Patrick Moynihan, N.Y.; and Metzenbaum, Ohio.

Lawton Chiles, Fla., topped Southern Democrats with a score of 89 percent. He was followed by Tennessee senators Gore and Jim Sasser, both scoring 86 percent; Wendell H. Ford, Ky., with 81 percent; and J. Bennett Johnston, La., with 80 percent.

Mathias, Md., ranked highest among Republicans with 84 percent, followed by Specter and John Heinz, both of Pa., scoring 71 and 67 percent, respectively.

Low Scorers. Four Republicans received zero scores: William L. Armstrong, Colo.; Steven D. Symms, Idaho; Don Nickles, Okla.; and Phil Gramm, Texas.

Lowest scoring Southern Democrats were Nunn, Ga., with 43 percent, and David L. Boren, Okla., 47 percent.

Zorinsky, Neb., scored lowest among Northern Democrats with 38 percent, followed by William Proxmire, Wis., and Exon, Neb., both with 43 percent.

House

High Scorers. Fifty-four representatives, including one Republican and two Southern Democrats, received perfect scores. The Southern Democrats who received perfect scores were Lehman and Claude Pepper, both of Fla.

Conte, Mass., was the lone Republican to receive a perfect score. Smith, N.J., ranked second with 88 percent, while New York representatives Benjamin A. Gilman and Frank Horton tied for third with 82 percent.

Low Scorers. Twenty-three Republicans received zero scores. The lowest-scoring Southern Democrats were Leath, Texas, and G. V. "Sonny" Montgomery, Miss., both with 18 percent, followed by Jim Chapman, Texas, 20 percent. The lowest-scoring Northern Democrats were Stallings, Idaho, 44 percent; and Byron, Md., and Timothy J. Penny, Minn., 47 percent.

Chamber of Commerce of the United States

CCUS, the nation's biggest business lobby, chose 29 Senate and 22 House votes, many of which included deficit-reduction measures.

Senate Votes

In the Senate, the Chamber supported:

• Release of more than $7 billion from the Highway Trust Fund to the states for work on Interstate highways.

• The Senate Republican-White House 1986 budget.

• Passage of the budget resolution, which included elimination of Social Security COLAs in 1986, termination of 13 domestic programs, and a hold on defense spending to the rate of inflation.

• Exemption of military construction projects from the Davis-Bacon Act, which regulates hourly wages for construction workers on federal projects.

• Giving the president line-item veto power on appropriations bills.

• Awarding of attorneys' fees to individuals, small businesses, and some local governments who prevail in legal disputes with the U.S. government.

• Revising the immigration laws to grant legal status to millions of illegal aliens and penalize employers who knowingly hire illegals.

- Reduced spending for the superfund hazardous-waste cleanup program.
- The mandatory Gramm-Rudman-Hollings deficit-reduction plan.
- A 5 percent reduction in discretionary funding for the Departments of Labor, Health and Human Services, and Education.
- A one-year freeze in target prices and a 5 percent annual reduction for wheat, feed grains, cotton, and rice.
- A reduction in the dairy price-support rate.

CCUS opposed:

- Taxation of limited personal use of cars used 75 percent or more of the time for business, and requiring the keeping of detailed "contemporaneous" logs of business and personal use of automobiles and other equipment to qualify for business tax deductions.
- The federal supplemental unemployment compensation program.
- Retention of existing Social Security COLAs.
- Restoration of $4.6 billion in Medicare and Medicaid funding for fiscal 1986-88.
- A 15 percent minimum tax on corporate earnings over $50,000, with resulting revenues used to lower the federal deficit.
- A new demonstration program to pay for medical expenses of victims of hazardous-waste dumping.
- A 20 percent minimum alternative tax on corporations.
- Budget reconciliation legislation in which spending increases are offset by tax increases.
- Funding for Amtrak.
- Deletion of funding for the National Endowment for Democracy.

House Votes

The Chamber chose similar issues in the House and also supported:

- A 5 percent reduction in supplemental funding for discretionary programs.
- A 4 percent reduction in discretionary funding for the Departments of Commerce, Justice, State, and the Judiciary.
- A demonstration of local "pretreatment" of industrial wastes.
- A fiscal 1986 spending freeze on Clean Water Act programs.
- Striking a wheat and feed grain referendum provision from the farm bill.
- The budget reconciliation plan that would eliminate new federal programs and increased spending; remove transportation trust funds from the budget; and reduce proposed salary increases for federal civilian employees.

The Chamber opposed the following issues:

- Allowing non-State Department personnel to serve on the U.S. permanent delegation to the Coordinating Committee for Export Controls.
- Economic sanctions against South Africa because of its policy of apartheid.
- Establishment of a commission to oversee a study of the federal work force to determine whether differences in pay and classification have arisen because of discrimination on the basis of sex, race, or national origin.
- Requiring that plant owners consult with employees before closing a plant and that workers be given 90 days' notice of any plant shutdown or layoff involving at least 100 workers or 30 percent of the work force.
- Allowing persons injured by release of toxic substances to sue in federal court.
- The Ways and Means Committee tax reform plan.

CCUS Study Findings

Senate

High Scorers. Two Republicans, John P. East, N.C., and Paul Laxalt, Nev., received perfect scores. Other high-scoring Republicans were Malcolm Wallop, Wyo., and Strom Thurmond, S.C., both with 97 percent.

Highest-scoring Southern Democrat was Nunn, Ga., with 59 percent, followed by Ernest F. Hollings, S.C., 55 percent, and Boren, Okla., 54 percent.

Zorinsky, Neb., topped Northern Democrats with 70 percent. Proxmire, Wis., ranked second with 48 percent.

Low Scorers. Hart, Colo., was the lowest-scoring Democrat with 18 percent. Other low-scoring Northern Democrats, each with 21 percent, were Cranston, Calif.; Quentin N. Burdick, N.D.; and Robert C. Byrd, W.Va.

Johnston, La., was the lowest-scoring Southern Democrat with 28 percent, followed by Chiles, Fla., 31 percent; Sasser, Tenn., 38 percent; and Long, La., 39 percent.

House

High Scorers. Four Republicans received perfect scores: Ed Zschau, Calif.; Bill Archer and Steve Bartlett, both from Texas; and Howard C. Nielson, Utah.

Chapman, Texas, scored highest among Southern Democrats with 92 percent, followed by Earl Hutto, Fla., and Charles W. Stenholm, Texas, both scoring 86 percent.

The highest scoring Northern Democrat was Les AuCoin, Ore., with 64 percent. The next highest scorers, each with 59 percent, were Andrew Jacobs, Jr., Ind.; Byron, Md.; and Ron Wyden, Ore.

Low Scorers. Joseph P. Addabbo, N.Y., scored lowest among Northern Democrats with 9 percent. Other low-scoring Democrats, each with 10 percent, were Cardiss Collins, Ill.; Charles B. Rangel, N.Y.; and Les Aspin, Wis.

Leland, Texas, was the lowest-scoring Southern Democrat with 10 percent. Dante B. Fascell, Fla., was second with 11 percent.

American Conservative Union

ACU, founded in 1964, seeks "to mobilize resources of responsible conservative thought across the country and further the general cause of conservatism." ACU chose 21 Senate and 19 House votes.

Senate Votes

In the Senate, ACU supported:

- Confirmation of Edwin Meese III to be attorney general.
- Authorizing $1.5 billion for 21 MX missiles.
- Funding for humanitarian and military assistance to Nicaraguan rebels.
- Reduced funding for mass transit.
- Passage of the budget resolution, which included elimination of Social Security COLAs in 1986, termination of 13 domestic programs, and a hold on defense spending to the rate of inflation.
- Repeal of the "Clark amendment" prohibiting U.S. military aid to antigovernment rebels in Angola.
- Revision of the Gun Control Act of 1968 to remove the ban on interstate sales of rifles, shotguns, and handguns.

- Giving the president line-item veto power on appropriations bills.
- Barring federal courts from considering cases involving prayer in public schools.
- Deleting all but termination expenses for the Economic Development Administration.
- Barring the use in the District of Columbia of federal or District funds to pay for abortions.
- Funding of $50 million for UNITA, the anticommunist rebel forces in Angola.
- Exclusion of Defense Department programs from automatic cuts specified in the Gramm-Rudman-Hollings deficit-reduction law if the president certifies such cuts would substantially impair national defense.
- The Gramm-Rudman-Hollings deficit-reduction plan.

The ACU opposed:

- Deletion of funding for binary chemical weapons.
- Barring antisatellite (ASAT) weapon tests against a target in space, unless the Soviet Union tests an ASAT or the president certifies the test is necessary for national security reasons.
- Reduced funding for the strategic defense initiative.
- Economic sanctions against South Africa because of its policy of apartheid.
- Reauthorization of the "superfund" hazardous-waste cleanup program.
- Requirement that federal energy assistance be counted as income in determining eligibility for food stamps.

House Votes

The group chose a number of comparable House issues. In addition, ACU supported:

- Prohibition of nonfood economic aid to Mozambique until the president certified to Congress that the number of foreign military advisers and troops in that country did not exceed 55.
- A rescission of $6 billion in funding for the Synfuels Corporation.
- Striking the wheat and feed grain farmer referendum provision from the farm bill.

The group opposed:

- Reauthorization of the Clean Water Act, authorizing $12 billion in federal grants over fiscal 1986-90 for construction of sewage treatment plants and $9 billion over 1986-94 in revolving loan funds.
- Establishment of a commission to oversee a study of the federal work force to determine whether differences in pay and classification have arisen because of discrimination on the basis of sex, race, or national origin.
- The budget reconciliation plan that would eliminate new federal programs and increased spending; remove transportation trust funds from the budget; and reduce proposed salary increases for federal civilian employees.
- Requiring that employers of 50 or more full-time employees give 90 days' notice of any plant shutdown or layoff involving at least 100 workers or 30 percent of the work force.
- Limits on imports of textiles, apparel, and shoes.

ACU Study Findings

Senate

High Scorers. Six Republicans received perfect scores: James A. McClure and Symms, Idaho; Chic Hecht, Nev.; Jesse Helms and East, N.C.; and Jake Garn, Utah.

Heflin, Ala., scored highest among Southern Democrats with 74 percent; Long, La., was second with 70 percent, followed by Stennis, Miss., 67 percent.

Nebraska senators Exon and Zorinsky ranked highest among Northern Democrats with scores of 59 and 55 percent, respectively.

Low Scorers. Three Northern Democrats received zero scores: Hart, Colo.; Sarbanes, Md.; and Metzenbaum, Ohio.

House

High Scorers. Eight Republicans received perfect scores: Bob Stump, Ariz.; Dan Burton, Ind.; Archer, Joe L. Barton, Beau Boulter, Larry Combest, and Thomas D. DeLay, all from Texas; and Dick Cheney, Wyo.

Stenholm, Texas, was the highest-scoring Southern Democrat, scoring 90 percent, followed by Buddy Roemer, La., 81 percent.

Maryland Reps. Dyson and Byron tied for the highest score among Northern Democrats, with 65 percent. They were followed by Samuel S. Stratton, N.Y., who scored 55 percent.

Low Scorers. Twenty-four Democrats, including three Southern Democrats, received zero scores. The Southern Democrats receiving zero scores were Ford, Tenn.; Henry B. Gonzalez, Texas; and Leland, Texas.

Other low-scoring Southern Democrats were Bill Alexander, Ark., Lehman, Fla., and Walter B. Jones, N.C., each scoring 5 percent.

The lowest-scoring Republican was Stewart B. McKinney, Conn., with 13 percent. He was followed by Conte, Mass., with 14 percent; James M. Jeffords, Vt., 16 percent; and Cooper Evans, Iowa, 24 percent.

Case Studies

Arab, Israel Lobbies

For close to 30 years the world has periodically held its breath while Arab-Israeli antagonists have brought the Middle East to the precipice of war. Five times the enemies have plunged over that precipice, leaving countless dead, maimed, or homeless.

The Arab-Israeli conflict is not restricted to the Middle East, however. Washington has become a key battleground, where expert is pitted against expert in poorly matched efforts to persuade, cajole, or coerce support from the White House or Congress. The battle for the U.S. government's friendship is the brass ring in the competition, and both sides employ skilled lobbyists to present their cases to the policy makers in Washington.

Issues in the Arab-Israeli conflict have become complicated. No longer are American government officials concerned solely with the military and political dimensions. The high cost of weapons for Israel and the booming currency reserves of the oil-producing states have raised economic and trade implications as well. It is no longer adequate for the lobbying groups to concentrate on emotional or political aspects. Dealing with issues such as the establishment of a free trade area with Israel, or emergency economic aid to Israel, or the signing of a strategic cooperation agreement between the United States and Israel requires the ability to understand econometric models and international trade theories, as well as the expertise to assess the performance of an F-16 jet. In all of these areas, the Arab and Israel lobbies have attempted to press their cases, with a certain degree of success on both sides.

The pro-Israel lobby, headed by the American Israel Public Affairs Committee (AIPAC), has risen from relative obscurity to become one of the more effective lobbying organizations in Washington. It has served to enhance the relationship between the two countries and has tried to quell criticism of Israeli policies that from time to time has emanated from Congress, the administration, or the press.

The Arab lobby on the other hand has not tried to foster good relations with any particular Arab country but has sought to strengthen U.S. ties to pro-Western Arab governments. It also has concentrated on trying to persuade policy makers to change U.S. policies toward Israel. This has resulted in a very limited amount of success. Congress remains firmly committed to a close relationship between the United States and Israel; it has consistently appropriated more than presidents have requested for aid to the Jewish state. Although the Arab lobby might have looked for solace at the strains in the U.S.-Israeli relationship in the early part of the Reagan administration, by the second Reagan term it must have reeled because the relationship between the two countries could not have been stronger. The Arab lobby's hopes faded that Secretary of State George P. Shultz would be able to convince the president to distance the United States from Israel. Instead, Reagan became even more sympathetic to Israel's problems and increasingly distrustful of the Arab regimes. This in part was due to U.S. involvement in Lebanon and the lack of cooperation Shultz felt he was getting from Arab governments possessing close ties to the United States.

Both sides of the conflict realize the importance of U.S. policy and the role public opinion plays in American policy formation. In essence, the struggle is as much for the hearts and minds of the American public as it is for the policy makers' support.

The Israel Lobby

As with almost any successful lobby, the Israel lobby's strength lies in the breadth and intensity of its membership. Studies indicate America's six million Jews differ from the public at large in their higher average level of education, social status, philanthropic activity, and political involvement.

"Two thousand years of painful experiences have forced us into round-the-clock political activity," said Thomas A. Dine, executive director of the principal pro-Israel lobbying organization, AIPAC. Said Hyman Bookbinder, Washington representative of the American Jewish Committee: "What we have going for us, and that's really the essence of the Jewish lobby, is an organized, committed, concerned Jewish community in America."

The focal point of this community, where Israel is concerned, is AIPAC, which evolved in 1954 out of the American Zionist Council. The group, which had a staff of about 30 and a budget of $1.3 million in 1980, grew to where in 1985 it had a staff of 75 and a budget of $5.7 million — all of it from American donors, according to AIPAC officials. None of the money was tax deductible because AIPAC is a registered lobbying organization. In addition, AIPAC has opened regional offices in New York, San Francisco, Los Angeles, and Austin. It also has a high visibility on campuses, with 150 campus liaisons and members at 425 colleges and universities nationwide. In Washington, AIPAC occupies offices within walking distance of the Capitol, guarded by a security camera. In 1977 the home of AIPAC's director was damaged by an explosion that was never explained.

While other Jewish groups have multiple interests, AIPAC's sole concern has been to nurture the U.S. alliance with Israel and to prevent American alliances with Arab nations from jeopardizing Israel's security. AIPAC has been careful to frame all of its issues in terms of the U.S. national interest and to keep an official distance from the Israeli Embassy, though informally the relationship is close.

In forming coalitions with other groups, AIPAC has drawn criticism from some in the Jewish community for being narrowly focused. Dine addressed this issue in an April 1985 speech to AIPAC's Policy Conference, saying that "AIPAC has but one mission: to preserve and advance the U.S.-Israeli relationship. We take no position on the ongoing battle between left and right, between conservatives and liberals. . . ." He defended AIPAC's decision to remain apolitical on issues outside those that relate to Israel. If it did otherwise, he said, it "would compromise the support we [AIPAC] have." Dine said he takes pride in the support Israel receives from members of

both political parties and adherents of varied ideologies. To demonstrate the range of support, Dine noted that AIPAC ". . . sponsored joint programs with the NAACP [National Association for the Advancement of Colored People] and with the Conservative Opportunity Society." He added that AIPAC's student intern program "has attracted applicants who are black and who are Christian fundamentalists."

AIPAC and other Jewish organizations are acutely sensitive about accusations that they have a "dual loyalty." This became an issue during the 1981 debate over the sale of Airborne Warning and Control System (AWACS) radar planes to Saudi Arabia. Many Jewish leaders felt their loyalty was called into question when the Reagan administration argued that a foreign power should not dictate U.S. policy. Those leaders believed the administration and other proponents of the sale were accusing the pro-Israel lobby of placing Israeli interests ahead of those of the United States. This was an especially sore point with Jewish organizations whose leaders could remember the anti-Semitic attacks charging that Jews could not be trusted in the government of any country, or that there was an international Jewish conspiracy to control governments. These slurs have made the pro-Israel lobby very sensitive to any questioning of their support for the United States.

Leaders of most other American Jewish organizations sit on AIPAC's executive committee. This ensures that the group's reports on congressional action and its calls for grass-roots pressure go far beyond AIPAC's own 51,000 members.

AIPAC does not rate or endorse political candidates, but it does distribute to its members records of how lawmakers vote on issues of importance to Israel. It also keeps the politically active Jewish community informed of issues before Congress. Almost every lawmaker has prominent constituents (and probably campaign contributors) who expect him to speak out in support of Israel.

Stories about AIPAC customarily identify its most dramatic successes as the rapid roundup of 76 Senate signatures on a letter endorsing aid to Israel in 1975 — a letter designed to counter the Ford administration's "reassessment" of Mideast policy

— and more recently its successful effort to get 97 senators and an overwhelming number of House members to delay sale of sophisticated arms to Jordan until meaningful progress took place in Arab-Israeli peace negotiations. AIPAC's greatest failures are usually seen as the 54-44 Senate vote in 1978 approving the Carter administration's sale of F-15 fighter jets to Saudi Arabia, and AIPAC's inability to block the sale of AWACS to Saudi Arabia in 1981.

AIPAC stalwarts reject the "failure" label for the 1978 and 1981 votes, noting that Congress had never blocked an arms sale and that the close calls have made presidents gun-shy about taking on Israel's supporters. AIPAC's real successes, they say, are relatively prosaic events such as the continuing growth of U.S. aid to Israel (at least $3 billion in fiscal 1986, the largest amount for any ally) in times of tight foreign-aid budgets.

Since September 1980 AIPAC has been headed by Thomas Dine, whose government experience includes a stint as the Peace Corps' congressional liaison and work for four liberal Senate Democrats. He is known for his technical savvy on military questions (he once directed national security issues for the Senate Budget Committee) and for a markedly gentler lobbying touch than his tough-talking AIPAC predecessor, Morris J. Amitay.

"I think AIPAC is a little more restrained under Tom Dine than under Morrie Amitay — a little more inclined to argue an issue less emotionally," said a Senate aide. A House aide agreed, saying that for Amitay "every item was the end of the world. In some quarters, he outwore his welcome."

Wide-Ranging Jewish Support

Many of the major Jewish organizations represented on AIPAC's board also belong to another group important to the Israel lobby, the New York-based Conference of Presidents of Major American Jewish Organizations. This is a coordinating body for debate on matters relating to Jews in other countries, especially in Israel and the Soviet Union. Thirty-four member groups and six observers participate, including groups primarily concerned with community relations, fraternal, Zionist, religious, and philanthropic activities. The Conference of Presidents was founded in 1955, just prior to the Suez Canal crisis, to present a unified voice from the American Jewish community to the U.S. government. Its presidency is rotated among the member organizations.

Unlike AIPAC, most of these groups live on tax-deductible donations and cannot legally devote a major portion of their resources to direct lobbying of Congress. They can, however, disseminate information and alert Jews when Congress needs persuading. The organizations have wide-ranging concerns and frequently disagree deeply on religious or political questions. But support for Israel is a common and constant priority.

According to one former chairman, the conference has two main purposes: to air disputes among Jewish groups and to educate American officials about pro-Israel policies.

Forum. The conference's primary function is to thrash out disagreements among Jewish groups in private — so adversaries cannot capitalize on them — and find a consensus where possible. This was especially difficult during Menachem Begin's Likud party control of the government from 1977 to 1984. Many American Jews feel more comfortable with Israel's Labor party, and there were boisterous disputes over how firmly to defend the hard-line Likud policies to American audiences.

This tension again became acute during Israel's 1981-85 war in Lebanon. Deeply concerned about U.S. public opinion and Israel's security, the American Jewish community became divided over the war and at times it clashed with the Israeli government over policies. A case in point was the reaction to the Reagan initiative of 1982. Although the Begin government rejected it out of hand, B'nai B'rith and the American Jewish Committee found positive points in the president's proposal. In addition, these and other Jewish groups were especially vocal in their call for an investigation into any indirect involvement by Israel in the massacre at the Sabra and Shatila refugee camps in September 1982.

Division over the future of the occupied territories is as pronounced in the American Jewish community as it is in Israel. But there is consensus that Israel's security cannot be compromised, and that Israel should be able to make a decision freely, without U.S. pressure. The American Jewish community also has been steadfast in its support for continued U.S. aid to Israel.

Interpreter. The conference's other major function is to help interpret Israel's views to American government officials and American views to Israel.

A few member organizations of the presidents' conference, such as the American Jewish Committee (AJC), American Jewish Congress, B'nai B'rith, and the Union of American Hebrew Congregations, have their own Washington representatives — Hyman Bookbinder of the AJC being the best known.

The 50,000-member AJC emphasizes civil liberties and social concerns, but Israel is always near the top of its agenda. In 1981, for instance, AJC lobbied against budget cuts and for extension of the Voting Rights Act. But the only issue on which it urged a mass mailing to members of Congress was on Reagan's proposed AWACS sale to Saudi Arabia.

Zionist Groups. Also important in building public empathy with Israel is a network of Zionist groups, originally organized to work for the creation of Israel and now active in supporting it. These include the Zionist Organization of America, the Zionist Labor Alliance, and Hadassah (the Women's Zionist Organization of America), said to be the largest women's association in the world.

These groups promote various projects, ranging from Hebrew classes and hospital work to pro-Israel films and trips to Israel for politicians and scholars. One of them, the American section of the World Zionist Organization, must file foreign agent reports with the U.S. Justice Department because it is based in Jerusalem.

Reward and Punishment

Pro-Israel members of Congress and groups that lobby for Israel are helped by the fact that many of their constituents not only write letters but donate freely at campaign time. A candidate out front on Israel can count on rewards. Sen. Bob Packwood, R-Ore., for example, raised a substantial portion of his 1980 campaign war chest at gatherings held in Jewish neighborhoods around the country.

Fund-raisers for Republicans and Democrats said there is no organized, central source of "Jewish money," but most politicians known as backers of Israel have an informal network of supporters they can count on to raise money nationwide. Also, there has been created a number of political action committees (PACs) whose sole purpose is to give campaign money in key election contests to individuals who support close U.S.-Israel ties. In 1984, 70 such PACs gave $3.6 million to candidates. It is uncertain what impact their donations have had.

Along with this support goes the knowledge that it may dry up if a member changes his voting pattern. Sen. Charles McC. Mathias, Jr., R-Md., writing about ethnic lobbies in *Foreign Affairs* magazine, said that while most members of Congress genuinely supported Israel "congressional conviction has been measurably reinforced by the knowledge that political sanctions will be applied to any who fail to deliver."

In 1982 the pro-Israel PACs were instrumental in defeating Rep. Paul Findley, R-Ill., a defender of Arab policies and an advocate of distancing the United States from Israel. They also helped to defeat senators Charles Percy, R-Ill., and Roger W. Jepsen, R-Iowa.

The campaign reward-and-punishment mechanism that backs up Israel's cause is not infallible. Strong Jewish support failed to save Israel backer Frank Church, D-Idaho, in his 1980 Senate reelection effort.

Again in 1984 they were unsuccessful in preventing the defeat of Rep. Clarence D. Long, D-Md., a vocal and important Israel supporter. As chairman of the House Appropriations Subcommittee on Foreign Operations, he was often a leader in congressional drives to boost aid to Israel.

The Arab Lobby

The American Arab community can point to a sizable shift in U.S. public opinion in the last decade or so. The energy crisis and increased concern about Soviet influence and activity in the Middle East have made U.S. leaders more open to the Arab world. A few articulate leaders in the Middle East, primarily the late president Anwar al-Sadat of Egypt, helped to modify the Western stereotype of the Arabs.

But lobbying by the Arab side has lagged far behind that of Israel, despite the putative advantages of petrodollars and oil power. The principal Arab-American organization is the National Association of Arab Americans (NAAA). The NAAA is openly modeled on AIPAC, from its pro-America oratory down to the graphics in some of its publications.

NAAA's priorities include the creation of a homeland for the Palestinians (though NAAA, unlike some Palestinian groups, publicly acknowledges Israel's right to exist), closer military and economic ties between the United States and Arab nations, and a loosening of the ties with Israel. All are couched in the language of American patriotism.

"Our most successful avenue of approach to Arab-Americans is that it's good for America if we have an active Arab-American effort. Otherwise, our Mideast policy gets distorted," said David J. Sadd, who became executive director in October 1980.

NAAA's ambition is to mobilize an Arab-American constituency, an essential step if the organization is to rise above accusations that it is a front for Arab embassies and wield some political clout. Since the organization began in 1972, NAAA founders have predicted that the awakening of an Arab-American political force was just around the corner. But NAAA is still waiting to turn the corner.

NAAA Membership, Financing

Although Sadd claimed that his organization sometimes reached an audience of one million Arab-Americans through Arab newspapers, NAAA's mailing list contains only 100,000 names, and most of those are people who have never written back. The group has sought to convert its mailing list into contributing members. This has resulted in a contributor list of only 13,000 names.

NAAA has not been able to generate the domestic financial support that would allow it to trumpet its independent status. Sadd said that although details of NAAA financing are "a trade secret" he could say that its budget, which stood at around $500,000 in 1981, had grown fourfold while the staff increased from 7 in 1981 to about 30 in 1985.

Most of the money, association officials confirmed, came from advertising revenue of a publication called the *Middle East Business Survey*. The *Survey* is a glossy compilation of advertisements, sold for up to $5,000 a page, with brief articles on Arab business prospects sandwiched in between. The advertisers are primarily Arab governments, the Palestine Liberation Organization (PLO), and corporations doing business in the region.

Naturally, Israel's friends cite this as evidence that NAAA is a tool of foreign governments. Some of NAAA's friends also are unhappy about it. "I've always felt it compromised their independence," said one NAAA founder, Richard Shadyac, a Washington area lawyer whose clients include Kuwait and Libya.

NAAA's problems are inherent in the nature of the Arab immigrant community in the United States. NAAA estimates the U.S. Arab population at about 2.8 million — a diverse and fractious community largely of Lebanese, Syrian, Palestinian, and Egyptian heritage, and Moslem, Maronite Christian, Orthodox Christian, Coptic, and Druze faiths. The greatest concentrations of Arab-Americans are located in Michigan, New York, California, Texas, Ohio, Pennsylvania, New Jersey, and Illinois. Most of them came to America as immigrants before World War II. They were mostly poor, children of farmers, and semi-literate. They came from colonial domination and thus had no practiced political involvement.

Nowadays these people and their children tend to be well assimilated into American society. Moreover, many of them, according to Arab leaders, are small-scale, independent entrepreneurs who are fearful of political participation. "A lot of their customers are Jewish, and if they know you are speaking out on the Mideast, they'll walk," said John P. Richardson, a former NAAA lobbyist.

A second wave of Arab immigrants that came after 1948 was made up more of professional people who were educated and strongly nationalistic. But many of them have avoided the American political process.

"Despite American citizenship, a lot of them have tended to view the U.S. government as the arch-villain," said one person familiar with Arab lobbying efforts. "Involvement with the U.S. government is often regarded by other Palestinians as collaboration. . . . That is changing, but it has been an obstacle, historically."

Probably the greatest inhibiting factor to NAAA's efforts has been the war in Lebanon. Alixa Naff of NAAA estimated that 80 percent of Arab-Americans are of Lebanese background. Many of them find it hard to sympathize with the Palestinians or Syrians wreaking war on that land, or the Saudis and others who sponsor warring factions.

NAAA has tried to have an American focus and to rise above the divisions in the Arab world through a "pan-Arab" approach, but it cannot satisfy all factions. Robert A. Basil, former chairman of the rival American Lebanese League, which claims 5,000 members and advocates a "pro-West, democratic, sovereign Lebanon," is harshly critical of NAAA.

"They have essentially no constituency in the United States," Basil declared. "How in the hell can NAAA have a constituency among the Lebanese when they support Syria, which is shelling Lebanese villages, and Saudi Arabia and Kuwait, which fund the PLO?"

Shadyac, son of a Lebanese father, dismisses Basil's group as a "rightist" organization but partially shares his criticism of the NAAA: "It seems to me they're afraid to tell the Palestinians to stop interfering in the domestic affairs of Lebanon."

Despite these divisions, both Shadyac and Sadd remain optimistic about what Shadyac calls "a great awakening of Arab-Americans to the political realities of the

U.S. system," and about increasing public attention to their views.

During a mid-1981 interview Sadd was interrupted twice for phone interviews about Israel's raid on Beirut, once by a black radio network and once by CBS Radio. "We never used to hear from these guys," he said. "Now they call us all the time." But generally on the Arab side, one lobbyist said, "You feast on crumbs."

Little Support at Polls

Arab-Americans have had little visible success to date in backing their lobbying with support at the ballot box. A classic instance was Shadyac's 1980 effort to organize a committee of Arab-Americans for Jimmy Carter. Shadyac said that, at the invitation of Carter campaign officials, he planned a registration drive that would both help Carter and invigorate the Arab votership.

Shadyac backed Carter because he felt a president in his second term would feel freer to take politically risky steps such as opening a dialogue with the PLO. But in July of the campaign year the president's brother, Billy Carter, stepped into a messy controversy over his relationship with Libya. The Carter campaign, taking note of Shadyac's unrelated — and legal — lobbying for Libya, disavowed the Arab-American committee.

Shadyac now says bitterly, "The rightist Lebanese combined with the Zionist lobby, and they prevailed upon the Carter administration to drop the movement. . . . The Zionists cannot allow the White House to be anything but 100 percent kosher."

In the 1984 election the results were mixed, but a little more promising. Jesse Jackson, in his bid for the Democratic nomination, chose James Zogby, then executive director of the American Arab Anti-Discrimination Committee (ADC), to be vice chairman of the campaign and act as liaison to the Arab-American community. For the Reagan-Bush campaign the involvement was more pronounced. Joseph Baroody was chosen to head Arab-Americans for Reagan-Bush. Sadd points out in *Foreign Policy* magazine that "Nearly nine percent of the recruitment of ethnic volunteers for Reagan-Bush resulted directly from Arab American involvement. . . ." Fund raising by NAAA-PAC, founded in 1984, fell far short of the money raised by NAAA's pro-Israel counterparts. For the 1984 election NAAA-PAC donated only $20,000 to some 46 candidates, almost evenly divided among Democrats and Republicans. The involvement of Arab-Americans in the 1984 campaign proved to be controversial. For example, during the primaries the Mondale campaign returned to the ADC $5,000 to be passed along to five contributors. This brought vociferous denunciations from Arab-Americans, with some calling for an investigation by the U.S. Civil Rights Commission. A Mondale spokesman said the contributions were returned to the five individuals because "the original purpose of the meeting never took place. The view that ensued was an anti-Semitic diatribe."

A new Arab-American Institute is seeking to elect more Arab-Americans to office through a political action committee. There were four Arab-Americans in the 99th Congress — senators James Abdnor, R-S.D., and George J. Mitchell, D-Maine, and representatives Mary Rose Oakar, D-Ohio, and Nick J. Rahall II, D-W.Va.

The bipartisan institute's leaders are Zogby, the former ADC aide who joined Jesse Jackson's 1984 bid for president, and George Salem of the Reagan-Bush campaign.

The NAAA conducted its own campaign effort in 1984. In Baltimore, for example, it sponsored billboards attacking Rep. Clarence Long for his pro-Israel stance. Whether the billboard campaign helped Long's GOP challenger, Helen Delich Bentley, defeat him in the November election is debatable, but Arab-American political strategists were overjoyed.

In the 1986 races these groups targeted for defeat pro-Israel senators such as Alan Cranston, D-Calif., and Arlen Specter, R-Pa.

But Arab-Americans also face frustrations. In 1984 Specter, who is Jewish, met with more than 20 NAAA members from Pennsylvania during the group's conference. Quickly, the meeting took on a testy tone as Specter outlined his support for Israel while his visitors challenged his position. Afterward, one participant, NAAA president Robert Joseph, conceded that little could be done to change Specter's mind. "Unless we had the muscle, the money, and the candidate to actually beat him in an election, there is very little we can do," he said.

Meanwhile, Arab-American activists have undertaken several other efforts aimed at influencing U.S. policy. One is the ADC, headed by former senator James Abourezk, D-S.D. (1973-79). The group planned to organize Arab-Americans and sympathizers — such as black groups and liberal churches — to fight what they consider to be discriminatory treatment of Arabs in the press and by the government.

In two or possibly three separate incidents in 1985, the ADC fell victim to violence. On October 11 the ADC's office in Santa Ana, Calif., was bombed and its regional director, Alex Odeh, was killed. Also in October, a bomb was found outside the ADC office in Boston and two police officers were injured while detonating the device. Finally, in late November, the national headquarters in Washington was heavily damaged by a fire of "suspicious origin."

Business Backing

Although lacking a widespread, outspoken constituency, the Arab side has other advantages. One is the influence of American businesses, which export an estimated $5.6 billion a year to Saudi Arabia alone and depend on its oil.

Executives of oil companies, banks, construction companies, and other international operators have access to members of Congress and cabinet officers and use it to argue for friendlier relations with the Arabs. But they have been leery of pressing the Arab case in a more overt way.

Andrew I. Kilgore, a consultant for American businesses in the Mideast and former U.S. ambassador to Qatar, ticked off several of the reasons: Arabs were not major customers until oil prices soared in the mid-1970s, multinational oil companies had little interest in strengthening Arab governments that might exert more authority over the oil companies, and lobbying on behalf of Arab nations might offend Jewish officers and stockholders.

A lobbyist for one Arab country noted that Arab nations were slow to realize the leverage they had over American business. He said he advised his client to favor U.S. contractors from states that were represented by lawmakers "willing to listen to both sides."

Some awkward efforts to promote U.S. good will toward the Arabs — such as an attempt by construction executive J. R. Fluor to endow an Arab-oriented studies center at the University of Southern California — produced only bad publicity.

NAAA's Sadd recently compiled a chart of campaign contributions from the political action committees of companies with Arab customers. "To date there has not been a correlation between Mideast voting records and contributions from PACs of companies doing business there," Sadd said disapprovingly.

Sadd said NAAA planned to begin rating members of Congress by their votes and advising business PACs on where they should contribute.

Frederick G. Dutton, a lawyer representing the Saudi government, said he had observed a growing willingness of businesses to lobby on the Mideast. "In 1978 you had a few businessmen who were willing to see a member of Congress privately and in confidence," he said. "Now . . . it's much more up front and out in the open. . . . You're developing a constituency of economic interests that is tending to erode the monopoly the Israeli lobby has had for several decades."

One sign of that was the American Businessmen's Group of Riyadh, made up of Saudi-based officials of more than 100 U.S. companies, which circulated a memo calling for a concerted effort to help Reagan sell the AWACS deal. "It is time for the 'silent majority' to speak up and be counted, or lose this battle and our business by default," the memo said. Some observers point to the controversial sale as a watershed event because it involved corporations in lobbying for Arab interests.

Foreign Agents

Arab nations historically have shown a penchant for hiring political insiders to help watch over their interests in the United States. Former senator J. William Fulbright, D-Ark. (1945-74), represented Saudi Arabia and the United Arab Emirates until late 1980. Michael Moynihan, brother of Sen. Daniel Patrick Moynihan, D-N.Y., did public relations work for the Saudis until 1979. Jimmy Carter's brother Billy registered as an agent for Libya in 1980.

Dutton, an assistant secretary of state for legislative affairs in the Johnson and Kennedy administrations, received a $200,000 retainer from the Saudis in 1981. J. Crawford Cook, a politically well-connected public relations man, in 1981 had a $470,000 contract with them.

Saudi Arabia, the Palestine Liberation Organization, the United Arab Emirates, Oman, Qatar, Libya, Kuwait, Egypt, and Jordan all have American agents. Israel and Israeli companies also have retained law firms and consultants, primarily for business and military advice, but occasionally to make political contacts.

Foreign agents advise their clients on political strategy, help prepare "propaganda," and informally rub shoulders with high-placed officials at dinners and social gatherings. Congressional aides said the effect is hard to measure, but most feel it was only marginally useful in a particular campaign, such as the AWACS battle.

"Although a good deal of attention and publicity are periodically attracted by the activities of foreign lobbyists or agents, a close examination of their activities shows that those lacking strong indigenous support acquire only limited or transient influence on American foreign policy," Mathias asserted in his *Foreign Affairs* article on ethnic lobbies.

The same assessment can be applied to foreign embassies as well. Most Arab embassies throw impressive parties but have little day-to-day contact with Congress, according to lawmakers and aides. Israel, by comparison, has a staff of congressional relations counselors who keep in touch with Capitol Hill. One congressional aide deeply involved in Mideast affairs said he could not remember meeting anyone from an Arab embassy except, in recent times, from Egypt's.

Christian Right

After making a strong early showing in the campaigning that led up to Michigan's August 5, 1986, Republican primary, television evangelist Marion G. "Pat" Robertson expressed jubilation about the early success of his exploratory 1988 presidential campaign. "The Christians have won!" he wrote to some 50,000 supporters in June. The comment seemed to sum up both the emerging political strength of Robertson and others on the "Christian Right," as well as, in the eyes of some people, the potentially dangerous impact of a powerful and growing religious movement on American political life.

As it turned out, Robertson did not do as well in the Michigan primary as some of his supporters had hoped. Most accounts had him finishing well behind Vice President George Bush in the first round of the state's lengthy and complex delegate-selection process for the Republican nominating convention. Robertson's modest showing was unlikely, however, to cause him to drop the idea of a presidential campaign. He announced September 17, 1986, via a nationwide, closed-circuit television broadcast that he would seek the GOP nomination if three million voters signed a petition within the next year agreeing to work for his election.

Whatever the outcome of Robertson's campaign, his fellow political conservatives among the nation's estimated 35 million "evangelical" Christians are becoming a major force in politics. These theologically conservative evangelical Protestants, who stress the authority of the Bible and the need for a personal relationship with Jesus Christ, are opposed to what they see as the moral decay of American society, as exemplified by legal abortions, the banning of prayer in public schools, and the toleration of pornography. In the past decade they have moved away from their traditional distrust of politics, and they are showing a growing allegiance to the Republican party. Along with other demographic groups who are moving to the Republicans, evangelicals may be contributing to a realignment process that could make the GOP the nation's majority party. Their new political activism, symbolized by such organizations as Robertson's Freedom Council and the Liberty Federation (formerly the Moral Majority) of Rev. Jerry Falwell, is reshaping the Republican party at the grass roots.

The Christian Right will be, in the words of University of Virginia sociologist Jeffery Hadden, "one of the most important social movements in this country for the remainder of the century."

But the movement is also stirring up a backlash among people who worry that zealots will use the power of government to force their religious views on others. If they are to achieve significant electoral successes, Robertson and others like him will have to overcome a long American tradition of hostility to organized political involvement by churches — a tradition that Robertson acknowledged. "There is an antipathy to the involvement of clergy in politics — especially if clergy tell people how to vote," he told a group of Washington reporters August 12, 1986. "I think it's wrong to stand up and say you're God's candidate."

The new political activism of the "evangelical" Christians, symbolized by organizations such as the Liberty Federation of Rev. Jerry Falwell, pictured above, is reshaping the Republican party at the grass roots.

A Republican Blessing

While evangelicals are found in all walks of life, they traditionally have shared some common characteristics. Evangelicals are found much more frequently in the South, especially in rural areas. They are predominantly white and mostly women. Their incomes have tended to be below those of members of mainline Protestant denominations, as has their degree of education. In recent years, however, the evangelical population has changed somewhat, particularly through the development of "super churches," with many thousands of members, in fast-growing cities of the Sun Belt. Those churches have drawn many upwardly mobile, better-educated people originally from other areas.

Those traditional characteristics had political consequences. Evangelicals' relatively low social standing made them less likely to be involved in politics. While they held conservative views on some social issues, such as school prayer and abortion, their economic condition often led to relatively liberal stands on issues such as government aid to the poor. Concentrated as they were in the South, they tended to be Democrats out of the historic loyalty of their region. But analysts generally argued that their religion did not constitute a major factor in determining their political viewpoints.

In recent decades, however, evangelical political attitudes have changed. Most importantly, evangelicals are leaving their traditional Democratic home and becoming Republicans in great numbers. The Republican trend in evangelical voting for president, evident since about 1960, had become a mass movement by 1984. The exceptions to this trend were in 1976 and 1980, when Jimmy Carter — who stressed his "born-again" experience and southern roots — captured the votes of many evangelicals in the South. According to television network exit polls and surveys by the University of Michigan's Center for Political Studies, at least 80 percent of white evangelicals backed President Reagan's reelection. Evangelicals also gave 75 percent of their votes to GOP congressional candidates in 1984.

A 1984 survey of Southern Baptist ministers, conducted by Furman University political scientist James L. Guth, found that 66 percent identified with the Republican party, while only 26 percent considered themselves Democrats. As recently as 1980, Democrats had outnumbered Republicans, 41 percent to 29 percent. According to Calvin College political scientist Corwin Smidt, the shift has been strongest among young evangelicals. "Young Southern whites in particular are showing a very strong movement to the Republican party," he said.

Evangelicals also are going to the polls in greater numbers, after many years of voting at lower rates than nonevangelicals. Indeed, in 1980 — when Reagan, Carter, and independent presidential candidate John B. Anderson all had ties to the evangelical movement — evangelicals voted at a higher rate (77 percent) than nonevangelicals (72 percent). Evangelical turnout fell back in 1984, to 70 percent, but remained at a level just below that of the rest of the population (76 percent). Christian Right groups have laid great emphasis on improving voter registration and turnout among evangelicals. The groups' efforts appear to have paid off in the election of at least seven Republican House candidates in 1984, according to election analyst Albert J. Menendez of Americans United for Separation of Church and State. In those seven districts, located in Texas, North Carolina, and Georgia, substantial evangelical populations and increased voter-turnout rates appear to have played a role in GOP victories. Stepped-up evangelical voting also apparently helped Sen. Jesse Helms, R-N.C., win a tough 1984 reelection contest.

The Republican party's stand on social issues has been the key reason for the shift. The party favors abortion curbs, school prayer, and other positions backed by most evangelicals. Moreover, Republicans have worked hard to woo them, appointing evangelical liaisons at the Republican National Committee and other party organizations. In contrast, many evangelicals see the Democratic party as abandoning them in pursuit of homosexual and feminist support. "One party has chosen to appeal to them [evangelicals], and one party has cultivated other constituencies," said Robert P. Dugan, Jr., director of public affairs for the National Association of Evangelicals (NAE).

Voter Drives

The mass movement of evangelicals to the GOP has been accompanied by the emergence of a smaller cadre of activist evangelicals who are highly involved in politics. The best-known representatives of this activist core are several national organizations, including Falwell's Liberty Federation and Robertson's Freedom Council. The Liberty Federation has a mailing list of about six million households, although many fewer people are active in the organization; the Freedom Council says it has about 500,000 members. Among other national groups is Christian Voice, a 350,000-member lobbying and political organization that distributes a "Biblical Scoreboard" on the voting records of members of Congress. The American Coalition for Traditional Values (ACTV) claims to represent the leaders of "110,000 Bible-believing churches" in a battle against "secular humanism," the philosophy that man, not God, is at the center of life.

In the 1986 election year, these organizations and other similar ones put their main efforts into increasing political participation among evangelicals. According to Gary Jarmin, consultant to Christian Voice, the aim of that group was to spread "campaign technology as applied to the church." The organizations tried to create networks of activists on the state and local level to mobilize evangelical voters and provide grass-roots support for lobbying campaigns in Congress. While avoiding specific endorsements of candidates, the groups hoped to aid candidates of the Right. "If you go fishing in a conservative pond, you're going to catch conservative fish," said Falwell administrative assistant Mark DeMoss.

The legislative agenda of these organizations focuses on social issues. ACTV's 10-point program, for example, listed constitutional amendments banning abortion and allowing voluntary prayer in the public schools as top priorities. The organization also called for opposition to gay rights legislation, pornography, and the Equal Rights Amendment. The Christian Right groups emphasized some foreign policy and economic issues as well. Christian Voice's 1986 scoreboard listed support for the Strategic Defense Initiative, aid to anticommunist guerrillas in Angola and Nicaragua, and a balanced-budget constitutional amendment as representing the "biblical" position.

Despite their high profile, however, these organizations represent only a relatively small sector of the evangelical community. A Robertson presidential campaign could not count on the support of evangelicals as a bloc; an April 1986 poll of church leaders by NAE found that Robertson ran well behind Rep. Jack F. Kemp of New York and Sen. William L. Armstrong of Colorado as the preferred Republican presidential candidate. "The organizations on the Christian Right are separate from the larger movement of evangelicals," said Guth. "I think that these groups really aren't tapping the political potential of the larger movement. They tend to be skeletal organizations, made up of mailing lists. There's no hard membership core."

The Christian Right organizations also face theological and personal differences among themselves. Although all stress their nonsectarian nature, observers have found that their memberships tend to follow splits within the larger evangelical movement. Many of the leaders of the old Moral Majority, for example, were members along with Falwell in the Baptist Bible Fellowship denomination, representing the theologically conservative fundamentalist wing of the faith that adheres strictly to a literal reading of the Bible. The Freedom Council has special appeal to people like Robertson, who are part of the "charismatic" wing of evangelicism, some of whose members are thought to have special powers of healing and communicating after being infused with the Holy Spirit. In addition, the groups are divided by the strong personalities of their leaders. "This religion has been built around very dramatic personal leaders; these people tend to compete with each other," said Brookings Institution scholar A. James Reichley. Falwell is backing Bush, not Robertson, for president in 1988.

In spite of the obstacles facing the national Christian Right organizations, grass-roots activism appears to be increasing among evangelicals. Activists are recruited through television ministries, such as Robertson's, and local churches. Kenneth D. Wald, a University of Florida political scientist who studied church political involvement in the Gainesville area, said: "Something appears to happen in the evangelical churches that is not overtly political, but enables them to mobilize politically," he said. "People in the evangelical churches don't see their involvement as political — they see it as acting out their religious beliefs."

Wald also noted that "people who are persuaded that they hear the voice of God are very active political workers. If I were running for office, those are the kind of people I'd want supporting me. There's nothing they won't do for you." In the Michigan primary campaign, 4,500 people ran as Freedom Council delegates for seats at GOP county conventions, which was the first stage in the delegate-selection process for the 1988 Republican presidential nominating convention. The fact that so many people — more than Bush or Kemp were able to enlist — were willing to seek those positions showed the enthusiasm and energy of Christian Right activists.

In several instances in 1986, conservative evangelical forces were able to take control of the party organs that run the GOP at the local and state level. In Iowa, Freedom Council members controlled the Polk County (Des Moines) party; in Nebraska, Christian Right forces dominated the party organization in Douglas (Omaha) and Lancaster (Lincoln) counties. Christian conservatives elected 40 percent of the delegates to the Minnesota Republican convention, and the Washington state GOP was seen by many observers as dominated by the Christian Right.

Religious activists also had some successes in winning GOP congressional nominations for their candidates in 1986. Guth said that he had identified two dozen House districts where the Christian Right was particularly active in supporting the GOP candidate. The most dramatic Christian Right primary victories as of September 1986 were in Indiana. State senator James Butcher, who had close ties to local conservative church groups, and Nazarene minister Rev. Donald J. Lynch won House nominations against candidates backed by the GOP establishment. In Oregon, Baptist minister Joe Lutz did not win the Republican Senate nomination but finished with a surprisingly strong 43 percent against incumbent Bob Packwood.

Narrow Constituency

The 1986 political contests also revealed the vulnerability of the organized Christian Right. The Michigan primary showed that religious activists could have trouble expanding beyond their limited base of support to win many elections. *Wall Street Journal*/NBC News exit polls showed Robertson favored by only 9 percent of Republican voters, compared with 40 percent for Bush. Robertson even lost out to Bush among "born-again" Christian voters: 23 percent of that group backed Robertson, while 37 percent favored the vice president. Among other Republicans, Robertson's strength was virtually nonexistent, with only 1 percent of non-born-again voters indicating support for him. To some extent, Bush's large advantage reflected his vastly superior name recognition among voters. But it was also true that Robertson was the only potential candidate in a field of five about whom a plurality of those surveyed expressed unfavorable opinions. A late August *Detroit Free Press* poll of GOP county delegates elected in the primary showed 45 percent backing Bush, 21 percent favoring Robertson, and 16 percent supporting Kemp.

The defeat of Rep. Mark D. Siljander in Michigan's GOP 1986 congressional primary was another setback for the Christian Right. An outspoken evangelical conservative, Siljander had feuded with the Republican establishment in his district ever since his election in 1981. He was locked in a close contest with challenger Fred Upton until a few days before the primary, when the incumbent released a taped statement to the local clergy asking for support "to break the back of Satan." The tape's implication that Upton was backed by the devil was sharply criticized in the district, and the challenger went on to win with 55 percent of the vote.

Comments like those of Siljander — or Robertson's controversial June 30, 1986, claim that Christians "maybe feel more strongly than others do" about patriotism and love of family — fuel the anxiety that many people feel about the mixture of politics and religion. Polls show that many people are disturbed by candidates who suggest, even indirectly, that God is on their side. A July 1986 *Wall Street Journal*/NBC News survey found that nearly 80 percent of the public opposed politicians who claimed to be acting on divine instructions. Robertson and other religiously affiliated candidates are likely to be vulnerable to the criticism that they are trying to impose their faith on the political system. Bush workers in Michigan distributed leaflets to primary voters urging them to "help keep religion out of politics."

Concern over the role of the Christian Right was evident within evangelical circles, too. "For Christians to step across the line and try to assume for the church a role of being power brokers or a power bloc is not only being untruthful to the faith, but it invites a backlash," Senator Armstrong was quoted as saying in the August 3, 1986, *Denver Post*. "They should never, never, never give the impression that . . . they are somehow speaking with authority of scripture or church or God." The NAE's Dugan expressed a similar view: "We are committed to urging Christian involvement in politics, but in the right way. I'm chagrined at seeing some of the things evangelicals are doing. Robertson has not had a lot of wisdom in some of the things he has said. When he tells the National Religious Broadcasters 'we're going to take over,' it scares people to death."

As several of the 1986 GOP primary contests demonstrated, Christian activists were coming into increasingly sharp conflict with other elements of the party. Many veteran GOP officials at the local level felt threatened by the influx of evangelical activists, whom they saw as trying to take over a party they only recently joined. The struggle for control of the local party machinery was exacerbated by social and cultural differences between traditional party leaders — frequently described as being dominated by an upper-class "country-club set" — and the religious activists, whose roots were often in the middle and lower-middle classes. "At the local level, these county chairmen want to protect their little fiefdoms," Jarmin of Christian Voice observed. "The establishment types just don't understand or mix well with our people. You have three-martini Episcopalians and teetotaling Baptists — socially, culturally and religiously they just don't mix."

Conflict Over Political Role

Throughout the history of the American evangelical movement there have been conflicting strands of opinion about how believers should relate to the rest of society. One tendency, still evident today, has been to avoid politics and other efforts to change society, in favor of concentrating on religious conversion and awaiting the impending return of Jesus Christ to the world. The Christian Right represents a modern manifestation of a different stance: that Christians should seek to use politics and government to improve the moral and religious condition of society.

The origins of evangelicalism as a separate tradition within American Protestantism go back to the second half of the nineteenth century. Around 1870, the leadership of some Protestant denominations began to develop relatively liberal theological doctrines on issues such as the literal truth of the Bible. That led to a split that created two separate wings of Protestantism — the liberal wing, which allowed for a looser reading of the Bible, and the orthodox wing, which held to a stricter reading. Another major cause of the fracture was liberal advocacy of the "Social Gospel" — the belief that Christians had a responsibility to improve society. In contrast, the orthodox group put its stress on personal salvation.

By 1920, the orthodox Protestant movement had come to be known as "fundamentalism." Combining a strict adherence to biblical doctrines with an insistence on separation from all those with different beliefs, the movement pulled further and further away from the liberalism that held

The legislative agenda of the Christian Right focuses on social issues, such as banning abortion and allowing voluntary prayer in the public schools.

sway in most denominations. At the same time, however, the fundamentalists also became increasingly willing to become involved in movements to change society. Their chief goal was to resist secular trends they disapproved of. They were a leading force in the antialcohol movement that culminated in 1919 with Prohibition. Outraged by the scientific attack on the biblical account of creation, they also pushed state laws barring the teaching of the theory of evolution in schools.

The fundamentalist attacks on alcohol and evolution theory, though, both ended in failure. The nation had overwhelmingly rejected Prohibition by the time it was repealed in 1933. The famous 1925 Scopes "monkey trial," in which a Tennessee teacher was tried for breaking a state law against teaching evolution theory, marked a decisive public defeat for anti-evolution forces. Fundamentalists, attacked in the press as anti-intellectual reactionaries, retreated into their shell, abandoning politics to concentrate on religious concerns.

Fundamentalism continued to be a religious force, however, and by the 1940s some theological conservatives had become dissatisfied with the movement's rigidity. The critics argued that fundamentalism had to become more open to working with other Christians and encourage intellectual development. The formation of the NAE in 1942 signaled the birth of moderate evangelicalism, which now represents the centrist element of the movement. To the theological right are the fundamentalists and charismatics, whose views conflict in many respects.

The most important representative of moderate evangelicalism is Rev. Billy Graham, whose touring revivals and televised sermons have made him the best-known religious figure in American life since World War II. In the decades following the war, Graham and others spearheaded the rapid growth of evangelicalism. While the mainline Protestant denominations, such as the Presbyterian, Episcopalian, and Methodist churches, have experienced steady declines in membership, many evangelical churches have grown rapidly. The evangelical Southern Baptist Convention, for example, grew by 17 percent, to 14.5 million, between 1973 and 1985.

It has only been since the mid-1970s that the evangelical movement has turned to politics. Before then, the conservative religious political movement was limited to a small group of zealots. By the late 1980s the Christian Right was capable of mounting a politically significant campaign for the presidency.

The growth of the Christian Right is all the more remarkable in light of the strong theological objections that the evangelical movement — particularly its fundamentalist wing — traditionally had to politics. A religion that believes in the individual nature of salvation and the impending end of history would not appear to provide fertile ground for growing political militants. The traditional attitude of many fundamentalists was typified by Falwell in a 1965 sermon: "We have few ties to this earth. We pay our taxes, cast votes as a responsibility of citizenship, obey the laws of the land and other things demanded of us by the society in which we live. But, at the same time, we are cognizant that our only purpose on this earth is to know Christ and to make Him known." Contrast that thought with this current-day statement by Tim LaHaye, ACTV president, of whose executive board Falwell is a member: "At this crucial time in history, every Christian should do one or the other — run for office or help someone else run."

Academic observers of the Christian Right and the activists themselves attributed the increasing political involvement by evangelicals to deep social changes in American society since 1960. Seeing a world where abortion was legalized, homosexuality and promiscuity were tolerated, and school prayer was banned, many evangelicals began to feel that their traditional, family-oriented lifestyle was profoundly threatened. According to Seymour Martin Lipset and other political sociologists, groups that experienced such social alienation were prime candidates for conservative political movements.

Evangelicals had come to feel that their values were being challenged. Reichley said, "The political side of it was something they could get their hands on. When some of the television preachers began urging them to get into politics, it provided them with a release. A lot of them realize that the world won't change that much, but at least it's something they can do."

Christian activists say they moved into politics to protect themselves from secularization imposed by the rest of society. "People try to portray us as the intolerant oppressors, who want to go out and ram our values down their throats," said Jarmin. "The opposite is true — we are the ones who feel oppressed. Christians look around at the culture and feel like aliens. The whole culture is against them. We feel that we are the majority tyrannized by the minority."

However, not all evangelicals have accepted the idea that political involvement is a Christian imperative, or that the Christian Right is the correct way to become involved. Rev. Bob Jones, head of fundamentalist Bob Jones University in South Carolina, repeatedly warned that politics would entangle Christians in worldly affairs, distracting them from spiritual life.

Rev. Graham, on the other hand, evolved in a different direction politically. In the early 1970s, he was a prominent ally of President Nixon. Disillusioned by the Watergate scandal, however, he moved away from close identification with politicians and kept his distance from the organized Christian Right. Most of his political pronouncements in recent years have stressed the need for world peace and an end to the nuclear competition between the United States and the Soviet Union.

Televangelism

Robertson and his fellow televangelists played a key role in the growth of the Christian Right. The conservative political message that they pushed encouraged many evangelical viewers to become committed political activists.

The impressive growth of televangelism in recent decades has been linked to changes in the broadcast industry, particularly the development of cable systems and the proliferation of small, independent stations. With little prospect of getting air time from the networks or major local stations — which favored religious programming provided by the established Protestant denominations — evangelical preachers began during the 1960s to purchase blocks of time from independent stations. With that air time, they were able to raise increasing amounts of money by asking viewers for contributions. Soon, they began buying some of the small stations. Robertson, for example, purchased the Virginia Beach station that became the foundation of his Christian Broadcasting Network (CBN) for $37,000 in 1961. The development of cable systems in the 1970s allowed the televangelists to reach even larger audiences.

By the mid-1980s religious broadcasters — most of them conservative evangelicals — were a major force in the television and radio industry. There were about 200 religious television stations, as well as more than 1,000 religious radio stations. Several networks offered broadcast and cable programming from an evangelical point of view, including CBN, the Trinity, and PTL (Praise the Lord) networks. CBN alone had an annual budget of $250 million. In addition, evangelical preachers such as Falwell, Jimmy Swaggart, and Oral Roberts regularly purchased air time on hundreds of independent television stations around the country.

Surveys indicated that the televangelists reach a sizable audience. A 1985 study by the A. C. Nielsen Co. found that 61 million people watched at least one of 10 major religious programs during the course of one month. The survey, commissioned by CBN, also found that one or more of the shows was watched on a weekly basis in 21 percent of the 86 million American households with a television set.

The most popular religious television show is CBN's flagship program, "The 700 Club," which reaches a monthly audience of nearly 29 million people. A combination of talk show, news program, and old-fashioned revival, "The 700 Club" features Robertson and cohosts Ben Kinchlow and Danuta Soderman. A typical show includes a documentary presenting the politically conservative viewpoint on some current event, an interview with a guest whose life was changed by accepting Jesus, appeals for contributions, and sessions in which Robertson sought to use prayer to heal viewers with physical ailments.

The televangelists are not without their problems, however. Dependent on viewer contributions, which could vary greatly over time, they frequently are faced with financial crises because of the high cost of air time. Even CBN, the giant of the industry, was forced in early 1986 to cancel its experiment with a nightly news program, while other religious broadcasters had to lay off employees to stay afloat. A basic difficulty for the networks is that most people, no matter how strong their beliefs, do not want to watch religious instruction exclusively. CBN greatly expanded its audience in 1981 when it began adding other types of shows — including old movies and reruns of family-oriented television series from the 1950s and 1960s — to its religious programming.

Some of the televangelists avoid discussion of political issues. Among those that do discuss politics, though, the viewpoint is almost exclusively conservative. The styles vary — from Swaggart, with his fiery denunciations of modern immorality, to Robertson, with a detailed analysis of Federal Reserve Board monetary policy, for example. But the common message is that America has gone far down the wrong road and only Christians can put it back in the right direction.

The audience the televangelists are reaching is receptive to their appeals. In a 1984 study of evangelical voters, Stuart Rothenberg and Frank Newport found that frequent viewers of religious programs were strongly inclined to base their political opinions on their religion, suggesting that "there is a potential for these religious programs to be a significant and potent political force in this country." Observers think that many of the Christian activists around the nation were first inspired and recruited by the televangelists. "Television is clearly the catalyst that is used to energize and mobilize people," said Hadden of the University of Virginia. "You don't have to watch 'The 700 Club' very long before the political aspect becomes clear."

Uncertain Future

Despite its advances, the Christian Right faces an uncertain future. Because of Robertson's problems with reaching beyond his evangelical base — and, indeed, with winning solid support from his fellow evangelists — he has little chance of winning the GOP presidential nomination. But strong showings in some primaries could give Robertson and other religious activists a significant voice in choosing a candidate and writing the 1988 GOP platform. If so, the convention could find itself debating and voting on platform planks similar to those adopted by the Texas GOP in early 1986, which denounced secular humanism and called for teaching the biblical theory of creation in the public schools and a quarantine of AIDS (Acquired Immune Deficiency Syndrome) victims.

Critics of the Christian Right say that a strong Robertson showing could lead to disaster for the GOP in the 1988 elections. If the party is seen as dominated by religious activists, these critics speculate, it could lose support from many younger voters who have been attracted to Reagan's economic policies but have little interest in social issues. According to Menendez of Americans United for Separation of Church and State, the strength of the Christian Right also could weaken the party's base in the Western states, where libertarian sentiments are strong. "You get a Robertson on the ticket, or the Republican party is seen as captured by the religious right, and the party could lose the whole West," he said.

John Buchanan, a former Republican House member from Alabama who lost a 1980 renomination bid to a Christian Right-backed candidate, also warned of the dangers to the party. "The Republican party has been pushed too far to the right already; sometime it's going to fall off the edge," he said. "The party stands to lose some of its best elements, replacing them with ultra-fundamentalists, who in many cases have no long-term loyalty to the party." Buchanan, a Baptist minister, serves as president of People for the American Way, an organization sharply critical of the activities of the Christian Right.

Other observers see the Robertson candidacy as adding to tensions between the Christian Right and established forces within the GOP. If he does well in the 1988 presidential campaign, and religious conservatives start winning substantial numbers of Republican nominations for other offices, the conflicts that are simmering just below the surface may boil over into open political warfare. "The Robertson candidacy will exacerbate the divisions in the party," said Jarmin. "The tensions will continue to build. You could have a bloody civil war in the party on your hands." Some Christian Right activists are even discussing the possibility of an open split, leading to formation of a new political party.

That apocalyptic scenario seems unlikely in the near future, however. Another possibility is that, as they gain more experience in politics, Christian Right activists will become more attuned to the need for conciliation and compromise. As time goes on, they may begin to be seen as one interest group among many, one that represents a substantial number of people but does not evoke the strong feelings, positive and negative, so evident in the mid-1980s. "If they insist on the purity of their agenda, they are likely to lose some of their political effectiveness," said Reichley of Brookings. "Once they're in politics, they begin to be willing to compromise. If the evangelicals are willing to do that, then the Republicans have a good chance of becoming the majority party." Said Dugan of the NAE: "The way a lot of my fellow evangelicals are going into politics is an embarrassment to me. But we're growing in our wisdom. People will learn from the mistakes Robertson is making."

'Contra' Aid

After two years of sustained battles, President Reagan in 1985 won congressional approval — if not full-hearted support — for U.S. involvement in the war against the leftist government of Nicaragua. Congress authorized and appropriated $27 million for nonmilitary aid to the "contras," who are seeking to overthrow the Nicaraguan government. It was a victory for Reagan, who had thrown the weight of his presidency behind the contras' battle against the Sandinistas.

The 1985 fight over aid to the contras was fought not only by the president, however. Congress found itself in the middle of a massive lobbying campaign involving a large cast ranging from the Nicaraguan government and American church groups to Hollywood celebrities, impoverished Central American peasants, and European politicians.

Background

Congress in 1984 cut off U.S. aid to the contras, who over three years had received some $70 million in pay and equipment from the Central Intelligence Agency (CIA).

In the fiscal 1985 continuing appropriations resolution (PL 98-473), Congress approved $14 million more for the contras but said it could not be spent until after February 28, 1985, and only if the president returned to Congress with a request and got both houses to approve it.

In the weeks before a vote on continued U.S. aid to Nicaraguan guerrillas was expected, Congress was lobbied on the issue both by the Reagan administration and the Nicaraguan government.

President Reagan, Vice President George Bush, Secretary of State George P. Shultz, and other officials made speeches attacking the Nicaraguan government and calling on Congress to vote aid for the contras.

In a weekly radio broadcast on February 16, 1985, and at a nationally televised news conference February 21, Reagan made some of his harshest attacks ever on the policies of the Sandinistas and acknowledged publicly for the first time that he was seeking to overthrow the Managua regime. Reagan and his aides for three years had given several purposes for aiding the antigovernment guerrillas, but the ousting of the Sandinistas had not been among Washington's official aims.

In the February 16 radio broadcast, Reagan called the Nicaraguan guerrillas "our brothers." Leaders of several guerrilla organizations had stated repeatedly that they wanted to overthrow the Sandinista regime. And, asked at the news conference if U.S. policy was to remove the Sandinista leaders in Nicaragua, Reagan responded: "Well, removed in the sense of its present structure in which it is a communist, totalitarian state." The United States, he added, had "an obligation to be of help where we can to freedom fighters" in such places as Nicaragua and Afghanistan.

In his radio broadcast, Reagan compared the contras with Americas who fought the British during the American Revolution. The United States should aid the contras now, he said, just as the French aided the Americans then.

The president insisted that the Sandinistas were bent on spreading communism throughout the Western Hemisphere. "We must remember that if the Sandinistas are not stopped now, they will, as they have sworn, attempt to spread communism to El Salvador, Costa Rica, Honduras and elsewhere." The Sandinistas denied that claim.

At his news conference, the president repeated his longstanding contention that the Sandinistas violated pledges they made to the Organization of American States in 1979, when they and other groups overthrew Nicaraguan dictator Anastasio Somoza. Among those pledges was the holding of free elections. Instead, he said, the Sandinistas established a totalitarian government that was "brutal, cruel."

Reagan said the United States would ease its pressure on the Sandinistas "if they'd say: 'Uncle. All right and come on back into the revolutionary government and let's straighten this out and institute the goals' " of the 1979 revolution.

Shultz told the House Foreign Affairs and Senate Budget committees February 19 that the Nicaraguan regime was "bad news" not only for its own people but also for "its neighbors in Central America and for our security interests here in the United States."

Nicaragua's deputy foreign minister, Victor Tinoco, visited Capitol Hill the week of February 25 to lobby against the contra aid. Nicaraguan president Daniel Ortega on February 27 invited members of Congress to travel to his country to inspect the military bases that Reagan said threaten other countries in the region. Ortega also offered to send home 100 Cuban military advisers and impose a moratorium on Nicaragua's acquisition of new weapons systems.

Proposed Peace

After three years of asking Congress for money to support a guerrilla war against Nicaragua, Reagan April 3 shifted tactics and proposed a peace of at least 60 days. Reagan officially asked Congress for renewed U.S. funding of the contras — coupled with a cease-fire and offer of church-mediated negotiations.

The request put Reagan's Capitol Hill critics on the defensive. Democrats who had opposed his Central America policies were forced to quibble with the vague details of his plan and to scramble to come up with their own alternative, while Reagan declared that he was promoting peace. House Speaker Thomas P. O'Neill, Jr., D-Mass., called Reagan's plan a "dirty trick" to win over wavering members of Congress.

Administration officials and congressional leaders agreed that Reagan had significantly improved the prospect that Congress would approve his request for $14 million in resumed aid to the Nicaraguan guerrillas. Robert C. McFarlane, Reagan's national security adviser, said "the climate is changing" in Congress. And Richard G. Lugar, R-Ind., Senate Foreign Relations Committee chairman, said the plan could be a "breakthrough" for Reagan on one of the most contentious disputes with Congress.

McFarlane conceded that the Reagan plan was put together to overcome Hill opposition to aiding the guerrillas. Asked by

reporters if Reagan would have advanced such a plan if he already had the votes in Congress, McFarlane said: "I don't have a good answer for you on that."

Reagan sent Congress his request for the $14 million in a secret report on April 3 and publicly announced his "Central American Peace Proposal" the next day. Senate leaders scheduled a vote for April 23 on a resolution (S J Res 106) approving release of the $14 million, and House leaders agreed to a vote in their chamber by April 30.

Reagan pegged his plan to a declaration in Costa Rica on March 1 by key Nicaraguan opposition leaders, all of whom had gone into exile and some of whom had taken up arms against the Sandinistas. The declaration demanded that the Sandinistas agree to negotiations, in return for a cease-fire. The cease-fire offer was to expire on April 20.

Under Reagan's plan, the contras would extend their offer of a cease-fire to June 1. In the meantime, Congress would be asked to free up the $14 million, with Reagan's pledge that the money would be spent for food, clothing, medicine, and "other support for survival" of the contras — but not for arms or munitions.

If the Sandinistas do not accept the cease-fire by June 1, Reagan would use what was left of the $14 million to resume contra arms aid.

If the Sandinistas agree to negotiations, Reagan would retain his pledge of nonmilitary use of the $14 million. But he said he would not allow the talks to "become a cover for deception or delay"; if there is no agreement between the Sandinistas and the contras within 60 days after talks start, he would resume the arms aid unless both sides asked him not to do so.

The major contra group, the Nicaraguan Democratic Force, immediately accepted Reagan's request for an extension of the cease-fire negotiations.

But Nicaragua's government rejected the plan. Carlos Tunnermann, ambassador to Washington, said the contras would have an incentive to drag out negotiations past 60 days so they could receive more U.S. military aid.

Compromise Agreement

Confronted by opposition in both houses of Congress, Reagan on April 18 backed down from his $14 million aid request. Reagan agreed tentatively to a compromise, advocated by Republicans and conservative Democratic senators, restricting contra aid to nonmilitary purposes — at least through the end of the 1985 fiscal year, September 30.

Reagan began the week of April 15 hoping for a narrow victory in both houses on his request for $14 million to aid the guerrillas, together with a plan for a cease-fire in Nicaragua and talks between the ruling Sandinistas and their U.S.-backed opponents. But the option to resume military aid if the government did not agree to negotiations, or if it tried to drag them out, generated deep opposition on Capitol Hill, and on April 16 Republican leaders told Reagan that his plan could not pass the House and was in danger of failing in the Senate. Two days later, after Sen. Sam Nunn, D-Ga., added his voice to that appeal and Secretary of State Shultz privately met with 54 restive senators, Reagan agreed reluctantly to a compromise.

A White House official said Reagan coupled his agreement with a demand that Congress generally endorse his call for Nicaraguan peace talks, and that Congress not take any action that could be interpreted as abandoning the contras.

Lobbying

As the debate over U.S. policy in Nicaragua heated up in mid-April, a massive lobbying effort also was underway. The White House found itself on the defensive, with Reagan's persuasive influence giving way to a well-organized drumbeat of opposition to his policies in Central America.

Reagan attempted at the outset of the week of April 15 to take the offensive on his plan to provide $14 million to the contras. In a speech April 15 at a dinner to raise money for Nicaraguan refugees, Reagan said a vote against his aid plan was "literally a vote against peace."

But the Democratic-controlled House blunted the administration's lobbying effort by pushing up its Nicaragua vote to April 23, the same day as the Senate vote. The House originally was not scheduled to vote until the following week. The accelerated vote was designed to prevent the administration and congressional allies from concentrating their attention first on the Senate and later on the House.

"Lobbying is one on one. It may not frustrate the White House but it would stop them from lobbying both at the same time," said Christopher J. Matthews, an aide to Speaker O'Neill. Before a group of newspaper editors from around the country April 18, Reagan denounced the House maneuver as "immoral."

Reagan's Pitch. Throughout the week, members of Congress were invited to the White House to hear Reagan's pitch for his original Central America proposal, a tactic that appeared to work well during the successful lobbying campaign in March 1985 for continued production of MX missiles.

Some, like Rep. Ed Zschau, R-Calif., attended the meetings but remained opposed to Reagan's plan for military aid. Others, like Rep. Tom Tauke, R-Iowa, declined to attend the sessions. "I simply couldn't make it when they wanted me to go," said Tauke. He also said he had already made up his mind to oppose military aid and felt little need for Reagan and other White House officials to appeal for his vote.

Reagan had attempted to sell his proposal as one that would benefit the security interests of the United States. But some legislators were at least equally interested in the political consequences in their home districts of a vote for or against contra aid.

Rep. Paul E. Kanjorski, D-Pa., said he heard mostly from constituents strongly opposed to Reagan's initiative. "I'm trying to discern whether there is a strong silent group that is for it," he said. The president is popular in Kanjorski's blue-collar district centered in Wilkes-Barre. And the freshman legislator worried that Reagan could cause political headaches for potentially vulnerable Democrats like himself by portraying them as soft on defense and foreign policy. "If that perception is in fact occurring out there, then I would want to destroy it by voting for this thing," said Kanjorski, referring to Reagan's contra proposal.

Coincidentally, former ambassador to the United Nations Jeane J. Kirkpatrick, who lobbied for the contras in Washington, was in Kanjorski's district April 15 to speak at a fund-raising dinner for a possible Republican opponent in 1986. Her topic: the need to assist the Nicaraguan rebels.

As the week — and congressional support for Reagan's original plan — wound down, the president eased his own efforts to push the plan. When a group of GOP senators spent an hour with Reagan the evening of April 18, he devoted his remarks to the federal budget without discussing Central America.

Patrick J. Buchanan, White House communications director, reportedly urged a stronger presidential push for the contras, including a televised speech. But other aides were said to resist Buchanan, believing that Congress would still defeat Reagan's plan. Their fear was that a loss would jeopardize the president's strength on other issues, notably the budget.

Religious Opposition. Organized against the president was a lobbying drive by an assortment of church groups and liberal peace organizations aimed at generating pressure on legislators in their home districts and in Washington.

The U.S. Catholic Conference, representing Roman Catholic bishops in the United States, played a leading role in marshaling opposition to Reagan's proposal for aid to the contras. "It's the non-combatants [in Nicaragua] who are suffering. The contras simply can't be seen as a means of bringing pressure [on the Sandinistas] when this means destroying the lives and property of many innocent people," said the Rev. William Lewers, director of the conference's Office of International Justice and Peace.

Some congressional offices reported receiving hundreds of phone calls from church members and others insisting that legislators vote against Reagan's contra-aid plan.

Sen. Arlen Specter, R-Pa., said that many from his state's large Quaker population traveled to Nicaragua and told him of brutal behavior by contra forces. Specter was one of four Republicans who voted against Reagan's original $14 million request April 18 when the Senate Appropriations Committee approved it on a 15-13 vote.

Organized against the Reagan administration was a lobbying drive by an assortment of church groups and liberal peace organizations.

In Minnesota, more than 100 members of a coalition of religious and peace groups staged a demonstration April 16 in the Minneapolis office of Republican senator Dave Durenberger. Durenberger had indicated his opposition to Reagan's Nicaraguan plan, but the demonstrators hoped to convince other members of the state's congressional delegation to vote against it. More than 4,000 peace activists around the state pledged to resort to a 1960s-style form of protest if Congress approved aid to the contras, according to Jack Wieczorek, director of Minnesota Clergy and Laity Concerned.

Central Americans Visit. In Washington, Capitol Hill corridors were crowded with visiting Central Americans brought by various lobbying groups to press on both sides of the contra issue.

The conservative Citizens for America budgeted $300,000 on a public relations campaign in support of Reagan's original contra proposal. As part of its effort, the organization flew 22 Central American business officials to the United States, fanning them out across the country for media appearances and speeches. Jack Abramoff, the group's executive director, said the purpose of the nationwide tour was "to take the president's case right to the people, to hop right over the national media and get them [the Central Americans] right to the local areas."

Some of the visiting Central Americans came to Rep. Peter H. Kostmayer's district in Pennsylvania, where they received local press attention. But Kostmayer, a liberal Democrat and ardent foe of Reagan's Nicaragua policy, was not persuaded by their efforts.

Following the tour, the Central Americans came to Washington for three days of lobbying appointments with individual members of Congress. "What we thought was a nationalist revolution [in Nicaragua] turned out to be a Marxist revolution," Maria Teresa Bendana, a Nicaraguan teacher, told Rep. Richard H. Stallings, D-Idaho, during a 25-minute meeting with the freshman April 16. Stallings, at the time uncommitted on the contra issue, listened politely as Bendana and two others, an attorney from Costa Rica and a newspaper editor from El Salvador, urged the lawmaker to support the contras. But Stallings said little to indicate his position and brought the meeting to an end when he was called to the floor for a vote.

Another organization, the Nicaraguan Refugee Fund, paid for five Nicaraguan refugees to come to Washington, where they issued a plea for U.S. support of the contras. The official purpose of their visit was to help raise funds for a refugee relief effort. "The contras and the United States are our hope for returning to Nicaragua. For me, communism is ashes and the contras are fighting for our freedom," said Juan Ortega. Speaking in Spanish, the 54-year-old farmer told reporters through an interpreter he left Nicaragua for Honduras in 1981 after a Sandinista patrol tortured him and killed his wife and eight children.

Still others from Central America journeyed to Washington with tales of brutality said to be committed by the contras. Gladys Bolt told reporters that her husband, Noel Rivera, was killed by contra guerrillas in July 1984. She described her husband as someone who only wanted to be left alone to make a living as a coffee producer. "He was never a Sandinista," she said. Bolt participated in a press conference called by the Committee for a Sane Nuclear Policy, known as SANE, which has been lobbying against Reagan's Central America plan.

The controversy over U.S. policy in Nicaragua brought others to Washington to lobby on both sides of the issue. Actors Mike Farrell of TV's "M*A*S*H" and Robert Foxworth of the "Falcon Crest" series urged a rejection of Reagan's plan at a Capitol news conference and in individual meetings with members.

On the other side, a group of Western European politicians and writers, called Resistance International, endorsed U.S. aid to the contras at an April 18 White House meeting. The group included Winston Churchill II, grandson of the late British prime minister.

Senate Action

The Senate April 23 narrowly approved, 53-46, $14 million in aid to the contras. That approval came only after Reagan had promised not to use the money for military purposes, had agreed to resume

During a news conference held on Capitol Hill, actors Mike Farrell, right, and Robert Foxworth, left, urged a rejection of President Reagan's policy in Nicaragua. Seated in the middle is Rep. Richard A. Gephardt, D-Mo.

U.S. negotiations with the Nicaraguan government, and had given a nod to building sentiment in Congress for economic rather than military pressure on Nicaragua.

Administration officials started with the proposition that they would be defeated on a straight up-or-down vote on Reagan's request, and that the only way of gaining a victory was to offer concessions responding to widely held concerns.

The administration at first tried to work with a broad spectrum of Democrats, in hopes of fashioning a compromise that would give the president an overwhelming Senate victory and put pressure on the House. But when the White House concluded that it could not swallow putting into law a plan offered by the Democrats, it returned to its traditional tactic of negotiating with individual Democrats.

The Democrats had a source of leverage: For parliamentary reasons, the Senate could not consider anything other than Reagan's original request unless the rules were suspended by a two-thirds vote, and Democrats had enough votes to block that move. The Democrats hammered out their compromise proposal the weekend of April 20-21 and presented it to the administration on April 22.

The negotiations between the White House and the senators were an extraordinary exercise in executive-legislative decision making.

Sitting around the massive oval table in the Cabinet Room on April 22, the two sides were attempting to draft the details of legislation that would allow Reagan to continue his Nicaraguan policies and allow the Democrats to claim they had forced the president to shift direction.

Although the day's negotiations went on for more than eight hours, Reagan himself participated for little more than a half hour at the beginning of the day. National security adviser McFarlane led the administration team. Fourteen senators, evenly divided along party lines, participated at one point or another.

About 100 yards away, police arrested more than 300 demonstrators who were protesting Reagan's policies, particularly the war in Nicaragua.

As the negotiations began, Republicans and Democrats each offered a proposal for providing $14 million in humanitarian aid to the contras and calling for a mutual cease-fire in Nicaragua. Neither side proposed giving the contras outright military aid for the foreseeable future.

The primary differences between the two proposals were over what conditions would be attached to the money. The Republicans proposed to put pressure on the Sandinistas by demanding that they negotiate with the contras and that they not engage in a further military buildup. The Democrats sought to use release of the $14 million as a lever to force Reagan to resume direct U.S. talks with the Sandinistas.

A secondary disagreement was over the method of disbursing the $14 million to the contras. Administration officials insisted the CIA was the best organization to channel the money — in part because the $14 million on which Congress was voting already was authorized to that agency. Senator Durenberger, Intelligence Committee chairman, admitted that "there is a trust problem" with the CIA but insisted that requiring public accountability would eliminate any chance that the money would be used for military rather than humanitarian purposes.

While not spelling out which agency should provide the money, the Democrats opposed using the CIA because it had been the conduit for military aid to the contras. Patrick J. Leahy, D-Vt., said the Democrats were concerned that any money handled by the CIA might become "a backdoor way of running an army."

At the conclusion of the White House talks April 22, a senior official told reporters that the administration was insisting on Congress's including in its resolution a call for direct talks between the Sandinistas and the contras.

On April 23, the scene shifted to a more familiar format in the Capitol: Democrats caucused in a cramped room tucked behind the bank of elevators outside the Senate chamber, and Republicans met with Secretary of State Shultz and Vice President Bush in a more spacious, ornate room named after former Democratic leader Mike Mansfield, D-Mont. (1953-77). Early in the day, the administration abandoned negotiations with the full Democratic Caucus and shifted strategy to building support for the president's position based on a letter accepting some, but not all, of what the Democrats had proposed. One administration lobbyist called that strategy "picking off Democrats one by one."

The administration made changes in the letter to win converts. For example, a threat to use economic sanctions against Nicaragua was toughened at the request of Lloyd Bentsen, D-Texas, and others.

As the administration expected, some of the conservative Democrats quickly grabbed the opportunity to support the president. And the president's firm promise not to use any of the $14 million for military purposes — and to limit all his spending on the contras to $14 million — brought support from several senators who had agonized over the issue.

Reagan Defeat

The House on April 23-24 handed Reagan one of the most serious defeats of his presidency by rejecting the resumption of

U.S. aid to the contras.

Democrats for weeks were confident that they had enough votes to defeat arms aid to the contras, even if the president mounted a high-pressure lobbying campaign. But Reagan's April 4 and 18 concessions on using the aid for humanitarian purposes gave new impetus to the effort to draft a Democratic alternative.

Michael D. Barnes, D-Md., and Lee H. Hamilton, D-Ind., intended their alternative to emphasize diplomatic, rather than military, pressure on Nicaragua. It split Reagan's $14 million request into two parts: $10 million for aid to Nicaraguan refugees, including contras outside Nicaragua, and $4 million to help implement any regional peace treaty. The proposal also threatened unspecified action against Nicaragua if the Sandinistas failed to make internal reforms, and it retained indefinitely the legal ban on military aid to the contras.

House Republicans also drafted an alternative to Reagan's original request, which, for procedural reasons, was worded as providing military or paramilitary aid to the contras. Offered by Minority Leader Robert H. Michel, R-Ill., the plan would have funneled $14 million in humanitarian aid to the contras through the Agency for International Development.

The House took four votes on the issue. First, by a 180-248 vote April 23, it rejected Reagan's request (H J Res 239) for $14 million in direct aid to the contras. That vote effectively killed the request because approval by both houses of Congress was needed.

On April 24, the House voted three times on a separate resolution (H J Res 247) on the Nicaragua issue.

By a 219-206 vote, the House tentatively adopted the Barnes-Hamilton proposal, with 15 Republicans joining 204 Democrats in support. Then came the key vote on the Michel alternative; if adopted, it would have overturned the earlier action on the Barnes-Hamilton plan and given Reagan a watered-down victory. As with most high-stakes votes in the House, the tally was close throughout the allotted 15 minutes. When the time expired, the vote was tied 205-205, and O'Neill, who rarely voted, plucked a "no" card from a table in the well of the House in case it was needed. But the vote was held open for nearly a minute longer while 16 more members cast their ballots, half on each side. Finally, two Democratic loyalists, Edward R. Roybal, D-Calif., and Henry B. Gonzalez, D-Texas, arrived to cast the deciding votes.

O'Neill took the chair and rushed the House into a final vote on the underlying bill. After a few minutes, it was clear the bill would go down to defeat, and a stampede against it ensued. The final vote was 123-303, with a majority in both parties voting no.

Renewed Effort

The Senate reaffirmed its support for contra aid June 6-7 by approving $38 million for food, clothing, and other nonmilitary aid in fiscal years 1985-86.

The action came a little more than a month after Congress rejected President Reagan's previous request for aid to the contras. That rejection, which appeared to leave the United States in the position of not having a policy toward the Nicaraguan regime, troubled many moderate and conservative Democrats. Congressional second thoughts were heightened by a late April trip to Moscow by Nicaraguan president Ortega.

The administration took advantage of the new political climate by renewing its quest for contra aid and by revving up its rhetorical engines against Nicaragua. Reagan on June 5 called Ortega "the little dictator" and demanded that Congress back his policy.

The Republican-controlled Senate was the first to respond. Acting on a routine

Rebel forces, known as "contras," are fighting the Sandinista-led government of Nicaragua.

authorizations bill (S 1003) for the State Department, it approved the $38 million in nonmilitary aid by a 55-42 vote on June 6.

It provided $14 million in fiscal 1985 and $24 million in 1986 for "food, clothing, medicine or other humanitarian assistance" for the contras. The aid was to be monitored by the National Security Council, and sponsors said they expected the CIA would administer the aid. The Senate plan also repealed a current bar on military or paramilitary aid and specifically authorized the CIA to provide intelligence information to the contras.

House Action. In a stunning turnaround, the House June 12 agreed to supply $27 million in nonmilitary aid to the Nicaraguan rebels. The House attached the aid to a fiscal 1985 supplemental appropriations bill (HR 2577).

The House voted directly on the contra issue four times on June 12 and supported the president by comfortable margins each time. The first, closest, and most important vote came on the issue of whether to extend indefinitely a legal ban on any U.S. aid for "military or paramilitary operations in Nicaragua." That prohibition, which the House had supported consistently since 1983 and which has been U.S. law since last October, is called the "Boland amendment," after Edward P. Boland, D-Mass., former chairman of the Intelligence Committee. Boland on June 12 offered his provision as an amendment to an underlying amendment by Michel that provided the aid for the contras. The House rejected Boland's amendment 196-232, with 58 Democrats joining all but seven Republicans in opposition to it.

About an hour after rejecting the Boland amendment, the House turned back the Democrats' second attempt to thwart aid to the contras. By a 172-259 vote, it rejected an amendment by Richard A. Gephardt, D-Mo., that would have postponed implementation of the aid for six months — with the money available then only if Reagan made a new request and both houses approved.

By a 248-184 vote, the House then approved the basic Michel amendment, offered by Joseph M. McDade, R-Pa., providing the $27 million in aid to the contras.

And after two more hours of debate, the House rejected a broad alternative offered by the Democratic leadership, 174-254. Sponsored by Hamilton, the Democrats' plan would have provided $14 million in aid, through international agencies such as the Red Cross, to Nicaraguan refugees outside of their country. It also would have authorized an unspecified amount of economic aid to help implement a regional peace treaty, and would have extended indefinitely the Boland ban on aid to Nicaragua military operations.

Finally, by a 271-156 vote, the House passed the supplemental. Leaders of both parties had a multitude of explanations for the turnabout on the issue. Among the most important appeared to be:

- Reaction to Ortega's trip to Moscow after the House April 24 rejected Reagan's previous request to aid the contras. Wright said Ortega's "maladroit behavior" embarrassed some Democrats because it seemed to confirm Reagan's contention that the Sandinistas are Soviet pawns.
- The House's April 24 action gave the impression that Congress, and Democrats in particular, were opposed to doing anything about the situation in Nicaragua. That impression was inaccurate, the Democrats said, because Republicans provided the bulk of the votes to defeat the bill (H J Res 247) containing the Nicaragua provisions.

247) containing the Nicaragua provisions.

- Many Democrats were cowed by sustained attacks in which Reagan and his supporters accused them of lacking the will to resist communism. Reagan portrayed the decision on contra aid as a stark choice between freedom and communism, putting members who opposed his policies in the position of appearing to choose communism. Boland said he had never seen "such frenetic rhetoric" from a president. Wright charged that Reagan's attacks amounted to "McCarthyism" based on "the most simplistic of terms." The attacks frightened some Democrats, he said, because "nobody wants to be vulnerable to being portrayed as as friendly toward communism."
- It was difficult for members to oppose something labeled "humanitarian" aid for the contras, even though everyone understood that the money would be used to keep a military force fighting in the field.
- The administration targeted those members most vulnerable to Reagan's persuasion on the issue: moderate Republicans who could be worried about opposing him too frequently, and conservative, southern Democrats whose constituents worried that a communist victory in Central America could lead to a tidal wave of refugees. The lobbying efforts, including telephone calls from the president and a mass meeting at the White House the day before the vote, paid off. Only seven Republicans deserted Reagan on the Boland amendment vote.
- The Michel amendment was designed to have the broadest possible appeal. In addition to providing nonmilitary aid, it excluded CIA or Defense Department involvement and appeared to rule out the resumption of military aid.

Final Action. Congress August 1 cleared HR 2577, which included $27 million for nonmilitary aid to the contras to be distributed by any U.S. agency except the Defense Department or the CIA. The funds were available through March 1986.

Iran Arms Connection

The controversy over Nicaragua took a startling turn in late 1986 when the Reagan administration disclosed that profits from secret U.S. arms shipments to Iran had been diverted to the contras.

At a hastily called November 25 news conference, a grim and obviously shaken Reagan said that he had not been "fully informed" about the Iran arms deals. "This action raises serious questions of propriety," he said. However, he continued to insist that his Iran policy was "well founded." He conceded only that "in one aspect, implementation of that policy was seriously flawed."

Attorney General Edwin Meese III said at the news conference there was evidence that the Iranians had been overcharged for the arms and that the $10 million-$30 million profit had been placed in Swiss bank accounts accessible to the contras. Contra leaders denied they had received the money but conceded someone could have used it to buy arms for them.

Reagan announced that he had fired the National Security Council (NSC) staffer who had helped manage the Iran operation, Marine Corps Lt. Col. Oliver L. North. The NSC director, Vice Adm. John Poindexter, who Meese said knew about the diversion of money to the contras, resigned and asked to be returned to the Navy.

Poindexter and North later invoked the Fifth Amendment protection against self-incrimination in refusing to answer questions of congressional committees. On December 16 President Reagan asked that they be given partial immunity so that their testimony could not be used against them.

The sales to Iran already had been controversial on other grounds since they first became known early in November. Such sales had been barred in the wake of the takeover of the U.S. Embassy and the seizure of American hostages in Tehran in 1979-81. Reagan said he had partially lifted the embargo as an overture to Iranian moderates. He denied that the weapons were a form of ransom for American hostages being held in Lebanon. Iran presumably wanted the arms to help in its long and bloody war with neighboring Iraq.

An independent special counsel was to be appointed to probe possible violations of law by White House and other officials. In mid-December, the House and Senate appointed special committees to supersede the investigations being conducted by several congressional committees.

Reagan appointed a three-member committee, headed by former senator John Tower, R-Texas, to conduct "a comprehensive review" of the operations of the president's 80-member National Security Council staff. Other committee members were former senator and secretary of state Edmund Muskie, and President Gerald R. Ford's national security adviser, Brent Scowcroft.

Members of Congress, top State Department officials and former NSC staffers said Reagan needed to reorganize White House operations to prevent similar policy mistakes. "There's something wrong if the president doesn't know what is going on in the basement of the White House," said Senate Democratic Leader Robert C. Byrd, W.Va.

Many Hill leaders said privately that, as part of his shake-up, Reagan should fire White House staff director Donald T. Regan. But in congressional testimony Regan denied any knowledge of the diversion of funds to the contras.

Within hours of Reagan's press conference, the most widely quoted statement on Capitol Hill was the famous question that Sen. Howard H. Baker, R-Tenn. (1967-85), repeated during the Watergate hearings of 1973: "What did the president know and when did he know it?"

Gun Control

When you think of guns, do you visualize them in the hands of the pioneer, the Western lawman, the sportsman, and the soldier whose markmanship helped preserve American liberty? Or do you view guns as the tools of outlaws, urban hoodlums, gangsters, and political assassins? The answer probably determines your position on gun control. But the questions also illustrate the American gun dilemma: how to balance the rights of legitimate gun owners against the demands of citizens to be protected from illegitimate uses.

There may be as many as 200 million guns — rifles, shotguns, pistols — in private hands in the United States, nearly enough for every man, woman, and child to have one. Most of these weapons are owned by law-abiding citizens who use them responsibly for legitimate purposes like hunting and target shooting. But many are held by criminals; firearms were used in more than half of all murders committed in 1984, not to mention those used in holdups, burglaries, rapes, and other crimes. About 1,800 people die each year in firearms accidents, and approximately 12,000 people use guns to kill themselves.

Gun control is one of the few issues on which the opposing camps are so far apart, with so little apparent willingness to compromise. Gun advocates, led by the well-financed and aggressive National Rifle Association (NRA), accuse the gun controllers of disarming law-abiding citizens, leaving them vulnerable to armed marauders. Antigun activists, represented by Handgun Control Inc., the National Coalition to Ban Handguns, and others, assail the gun lobby for sacrificing thousands of Americans to their Second Amendment principles. Each side has its list of statistics and examples, convincing when viewed in isolation but contradictory when compared with the other side's evidence.

It is thought that hunters own more than half of all firearms — primarily rifles and shotguns. Hunters have objected so loudly to attempts to restrict ownership of hunting weapons that antigun groups are now focusing their efforts almost exclusively on handguns.

"We don't deal with rifles and shotguns; we have nothing against hunting," said Josh Sugarmann, public affairs director for the National Coalition to Ban Handguns (NCBH).

NRA statistics indicate that most of the estimated 50 million-60 million handguns in the United States are owned for the purpose of self-protection. "It may well prove to be the most immediate means of thwarting criminal activity," an NRA pamphlet reads. "In that sense, it serves to provide security in a manner similar to health or life insurance."

Gun control advocates counter with statistics showing that it is far more likely for a "self-defense" handgun to be used to commit murder or suicide, be involved in a fatal accident, or be stolen by burglars than to prevent a criminal act. Antigun groups are also concerned about the proliferation of machine guns and semiautomatic military-type weapons in private ownership — and their use in several mass-shootings.

Applying their famous slogan "Guns Don't Kill People — People Do," the gun lobby is adamant that any restriction on gun ownership by law-abiding citizens is an abridgment of the Second Amendment, which guarantees the right to keep and bear arms.

Primary Users

The earliest American settlers depended on their guns to hunt game, which was a vital part of the colonial diet. Today most hunting is for sport. "Nationally very few people hunt for food," said Jack Berryman, the executive director of the International Association of Fish and Wildlife Agencies (IAFWA). Berryman added that most states prohibit wastage of game meat. Hunters have "got to eat it or give it to somebody to eat," he said.

Like most issues involving the use of firearms, it is hard to determine how many Americans actually use guns to hunt. More than 16 million people hold hunting licenses; the NRA says there are 28.8 million hunters. Whatever their numbers, hunters as a group are most protective of their right to own guns. Calling gun control advocates "gun-grabbers," many hunters subscribe to the "domino theory" of gun control — that the banning of any kind of firearm or ammunition is the first step on the road to confiscation of all weapons.

Periodically hunters have faced serious image problems. The massive and unsportsmanlike slaughters that wiped out or endangered such species as the passenger pigeon and buffalo in the late nineteenth and early twentieth centuries fueled an antihunting movement and spurred the conservation efforts of President Theodore Roosevelt, himself an avid hunter. More recently, the number of fatal hunting accidents and what Berryman called "hunting vandalism, bad manners and poor ethics . . . threatened the sport." In September 1981 the IAFWA recommended that the states adopt a mandatory certification process for hunters that would include education on wildlife and their habits, the safe handling of firearms, and other elements of hunter safety. In October 1985, Wisconsin became the 34th state to require some form of hunter training.

Yet many hunters complain that antigun forces and urban elitists continue to stereotype them as machismo-motivated primitives. Hunters say they hunt not because of bloodlust but because they appreciate the sport as a form of outdoor recreation. "Someone has to defend hunting as being worthwhile, as important to our growth and development," Berryman said. "There is something good and worthwhile in people going outdoors and pursuing game, as long as they do it with respect. It is part of what we are. . . . Something of the American personality is lost when people don't go out-of-doors."

The Friends of Animals, the Humane Society of America, the Fund for Animals, and other animal rights' organizations strongly disagree. They believe hunting is cruel to animals. Wild animals must be released "from the bondage of the arms manufacturers and the gun and ammo magazines," wrote Cleveland Amory, president of Fund for Animals. The fund joined in a successful effort to block a 1985 bear hunt in Wisconsin. Antihunting activists have gone so far as to walk through woods playing music to scare animals away from hunting areas.

Hunters counter that they are the real conservationists. In 1984 the $292 million paid for state hunting licenses, $89.2 million in excise taxes on sporting arms and ammunition, and $13.8 million for duck stamps went to state wildlife management agencies, wildlife restoration projects, and wetlands acquisition. The National Wildlife Federation, Izaak Walton League, and Wildlife Management Institute are among the conservation-oriented groups that support hunting. "The conservation movement and in fact the environmental movement really had its beginnings with hunters," Berryman said. "It was hunter and fisherman's dollars that supported the only conservation program a state had, the state fish and game department. . . . They were the only ones who showed an interest in pesticides and wetland drainage and other environmental issues."

Most hunters use long guns, but the National Shooting Sports Foundation (NSSF) says 1.5 million hunters use handguns; 49 states permit handgun hunting for small game and 37 states allow big-game handgun hunting. "Because of the limitations of the equipment used, handgun hunting demands a high level of marksmanship as well as excellent hunting and stalking skills to bring the shooter within effective range," an NSSF pamphlet entitled "Handgun Hunting" reads.

However, the antigun lobby has long insisted that any inconvenience to the relatively small numbers of handgun hunters caused by handgun controls is minor compared with the benefits that would be gained from restricting or banning handgun use. "Because the vast majority of hunters use a rifle or a shotgun, there is no reason why their pursuit of game (and sport) should be affected by handgun control," wrote Pete Shields, chairman of Handgun

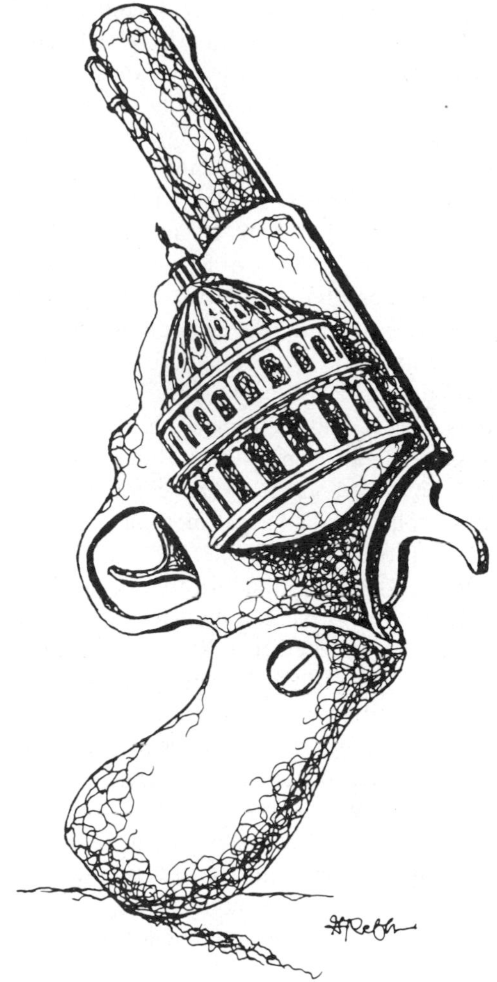

Control Inc. Sugarmann said the effort of NSSF and other groups to promote handgun hunting was really a political strategy "to make the handgun control issue a hunting issue, saying, 'Look at this, they're going to take away your handgun to hunt with.' And basically, yeah, we are. We look at hunting and you use long guns, there's a readily replaceable method for using a handgun."

Handguns and Crime

Guns are lethal whether they are fired at animals or humans. Hardly a day goes by without a report of some senseless gun slaying. On a single day in October 1985, two high school students in the Washington, D.C., area died of gunshot wounds, including one who was shot while resisting a robbery in a school building. In Baltimore the same day, a high school football star died after a friend playing with a handgun accidentally shot him. In suburban Philadelphia the next day, Sylvia Seegrist, a former mental patient with known violent tendencies walked into a shopping mall and allegedly shot 10 people, 3 fatally, with a semiautomatic rifle. In the 1980s alone, tens of thousands of Americans have shared a grim distinction with President Reagan and John Lennon: they have found themselves on the wrong end of a gun.

Of the 16,689 reported homicides in 1984, 9,819 were killed with guns. Of those, 7,277 murders were committed with handguns. The number of murders has declined steadily since 1980. However, the percentage committed with handguns has remained fairly constant, about 50 percent. Handgun murders are double the number of stabbing murders, the second most common method. In addition, handgun-wielding assailants rob, rape, or threaten countless thousands of people each year. Shotguns and rifles are used in about 10 percent of all homicides each year.

Gun control groups contend that murder and suicide rates would fall if it were harder for criminals to obtain handguns. Handgun Control Inc. notes that handguns account for 90 percent of firearms misuse, although they comprise only 30 percent of firearms in private possession. The organization refers to the current situation as The Great American Handgun War, pointing out that during the peak years of the Vietnam War, 40,000 American soldiers were killed in action, while 50,000 civilians were killed by handguns on the streets of America.

A recently issued National Institute of Justice (NIJ) study found that 50 percent of the state prisoners surveyed had used guns in crimes, and 22 percent said they had used them frequently. Criminals prefer handguns because they are concealable, easy to use, and relatively cheap. Guns with barrel lengths of three inches or under, known as snub-nosed guns, "snubbies," or "Saturday night specials," can often be purchased for less than $100. Although it is widely believed that criminals rely on these guns, the prisoners surveyed in the NIJ study said they preferred larger caliber, more powerful handguns and often stole them or bought them "off the street."

Gun control advocates also observe that hardened criminals do not commit all the murders. FBI statistics show that 57 percent of all murders in 1984 were committed by relatives or persons acquainted with the victim. "Millions of the handguns now in America were acquired for self-protection . . .," Jervis Anderson wrote. "Yet a terrible irony of this justifiable precaution is that guns bought for family and self-protection end up doing far more harm to the owners, their loved ones, and their personal acquaintances than they do to intruders."

Gun control advocates contend that a family argument is more likely to end in murder if a gun is available. "If you have a handgun around, it lends itself well to spontaneity, unfortunately," Sugarmann said. This spontaneity is also blamed for the large number of suicides by handgun. In an average year, between 11,000 and 12,000 Americans kill themselves with handguns. "While pills, gas, or razor blades allow time for a change of heart, there are no second chances with a bullet," an NCBH suicide fact sheet reads. In addition, handguns are blamed for approximately 800 accidental deaths each year. Overall, between 1,800 and 1,900 people die each year in firearms accidents.

The NRA and its supporters say the high crime rate is not caused by widespread handgun ownership but by failures in the justice system. "To the extent that government's sole effective mode of deterring crime is criminal law enforcement, the crime rate is itself a barometer of the success of the criminal justice system. . . .," sociologists Randall R. Rader and Patrick B. McGuigan wrote. "In that sense, the statistics and accounts of growing lawlessness are both a stern indictment of current criminal law enforcement standards and a verification that those standards have become more lax over the past decades."

According to sociologists James D. Wright, Peter H. Rossi, and Kathleen Daly, "there is little or no conclusive evidence to show that gun ownership among the larger population is, per se, an important cause of criminal violence. It is true by definition that gun crimes require guns, and it is true that guns, mainly handguns, are involved in a very large share of criminally violent incidents. . . . But it does not follow from any of this that reducing the private ownership of weapons would be accompanied by similar reductions in the rates of violent crime, or (what amounts to the same thing) that private weapons ownership is itself a cause of violent crime."

Gun advocates also deny that the presence of handguns contributes to the frequency of "crimes of passion." NRA director of public education John Aquilino believes gun control supporters "take the FBI statistics on the homicides by acquaintances and try to make people think those are just normal, wonderful, loving people who become unloving and murderous because of the presence of a gun." Aquilino said many of these murders occur in families with histories of domestic violence or are committed by criminals who choose their neighbors or partners in crime for victims.

Right to Self-Defense

The NRA and other like-minded organizations also contend that bans or restrictions on handguns would deprive law-abiding citizens of an effective means of self-defense. The NRA claims that 300,000 to 350,000 Americans use handguns each year to scare off would-be burglars, rapists, muggers, and murderers, a figure hotly disputed by gun control groups. "Literally tens of millions of Americans disagree with the prohibitionist position," an NRA self-defense pamphlet reads. "They see their handguns as critical tools that might spell the difference between becoming the victim of a crime or the victor in a confrontation with a criminal predator."

The NRA also maintains that "firearms in the hands of law-abiding citizens can and do produce a chilling effect on criminal behavior." In the NIJ survey, 56 percent of the prisoners interviewed agreed that "a criminal is not going to mess around with a victim he knows is armed with a gun," and 74 percent said "one reason burglars avoid houses when people are at home is that they fear being shot."

Some advocates of gun ownership say that law-abiding citizens should be trained as an auxiliary to local police and be permitted to carry guns. "Hoodlums are only brave when the odds are all in their favor, when they can predict what's going to happen," said Roy Innis, chairman of the Congress of Racial Equality. "If he hears of this plan, that there are growing numbers of citizens legally armed and trained, when he plans to victimize his next prey he has to think, 'Is this prey really a prey?' "

Many applauded Bernhard Goetz, New York's "subway vigilante," after he shot four youths he claimed were threatening him in December 1984. But gun control advocates reject the idea that even more guns in private hands will prevent crime. "We have 50 to 60 million handguns," Sugarmann said. "Why is all this crime going on? It's because there is no relationship between stopping crime and ownership of handguns."

The Constitutional Issue

The gun debate goes beyond the question of whether the easy availability of guns contributes to increased crime and accidental deaths. Gun owners regard ownership as a constitutional right guaranteed by the Second Amendment. Their opponents contend that the amendment does not apply to ownership restrictions on private citizens.

Both the tradition of gun ownership in the United States and the Second Amendment have their roots deep in English history. When the Anglo-Saxons ruled England 1,000 years ago, all able-bodied men were required to own weapons so that they were prepared for military service and to respond to the "hue and cry" sounded when a criminal was being pursued. By the time English settlers arrived in the New World, a militia composed of the entire male population was deemed preferable to a standing army in Britain. In 1765 Sir William Blackstone, the English jurist, wrote that the possession of arms was a "natural right of resistance and self-preservation, when the sanctions of society and laws are found insufficient to restrain the violence of oppression."

Universal arms ownership carried over to the American colonies out of necessity — hunting was not only a vital source of food, but weapons were needed to defend against attacks from hostile Indians and wild animals. But as the colonies moved toward independence, state militias comprised of all adult males assumed new importance. It was members of the local militias, calling themselves the Minutemen, who confronted British soldiers at Lexington and Concord in the opening battles of the American Revolution.

Several of the original 13 states also required all adult men to serve in the state militia and guaranteed the right of private citizens to keep and bear arms. When addition of the Bill of Rights to the Constitution was being considered in 1789, those guarantees were a priority of legislators who feared that a strong central government with a standing army could usurp the power of the states.

As ratified, the Second Amendment of the Constitution reads: "A well-regulated militia being necessary to the security of a free state, the right of the people to keep and bear arms shall not be infringed." Had it simply guaranteed the right to keep and bear arms, there likely would be little debate today. However, the link between the right to own arms and the need for a trained militia has created confusion for almost two centuries and remains at the core of the debate over gun control.

To those favoring private possession of firearms, the Second Amendment implies an *individual* right to keep and bear arms. This belief is based in part on the theory, widely held in the early days of the Republic, that a militia was to be composed of "the body of the people." Don B. Kates, Jr., wrote in the *Michigan Law Review* that the authors of the Second Amendment understood the individual right to own arms as a given. "They must necessarily have known that their undefined phrase 'right of the people to keep and bear arms' would be understood by their contemporaries in light of common law formulations like Blackstone's 'absolute rights of individuals,' " Kates wrote.

Gun control theorists emphasize the militia aspect of the amendment's wording. "Alone among the provisions of the Bill of Rights, the Second Amendment contains a statement of its rationale: 'a well-regulated militia being necessary to the security of a free state . . .,' " wrote Martin C. Ashman, attorney for Morton Grove, Ill., one of the few communities in the United States to ban handguns. "The circumstances surrounding the adoption and ratification of the United States Constitution and its Second Amendment, however, reflect debate

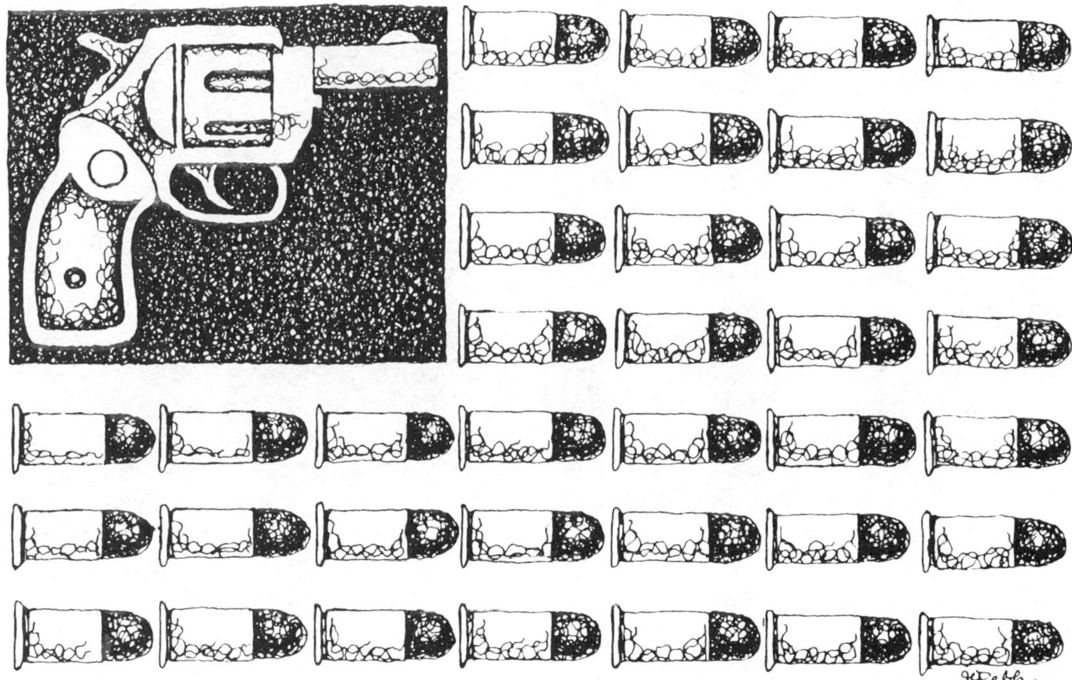

over the proper balance of power between state and federal governments with respect to armed forces — and not over a right to arms for any individual purpose."

Viewed this way, the right to keep and bear arms is a *collective* right, applying to the people as a militia in defense of the state and not the people as individuals. Many say even this collective right is now an anachronism. Once feared as a threat to civil liberty, a standing army is now accepted as a necessity of national security. Gun control advocates say the states' National Guards, funded and armed by the federal government since 1903, have become the militias to which the Constitution referred.

Court Interpretations

The Supreme Court has never ruled on the meaning of the militia clause. However, it has affirmed the authority of the state and federal governments to restrict the use or ownership of firearms in several cases. In *United States v. Cruikshank* (1876), the court ruled that private ownership of arms, even for a lawful purpose, was not "a right granted by the Constitution." In *Presser v. Illinois* (1886), the court upheld an Illinois law barring parades by armed paramilitary organizations, stating not only that the paraders had abused their right to keep and bear arms, but that the Second Amendment applied only to acts of Congress, and not to restrictions imposed by the states.

While not defining the term "militia," the court ruled on its scope in *United States v. Miller* (1939). The defendant had been convicted of interstate transportation of an unregistered sawed-off shotgun under the first federal gun control law, the National Firearms Act of 1934, which required registration of "gangster-style" weapons. The court ruled that the Second Amendment protected only those weapons necessary for the preservation or efficiency of a well-regulated militia and that the defendant had failed to prove that a shotgun with a barrel length of less than 18 inches fulfilled such a purpose.

On numerous occasions, state courts have upheld state and local gun control laws, some basing their decisions on the collective right theory of gun ownership. In October 1983, the Supreme Court declined to hear an appeal of a ruling by the Seventh Circuit Court of Appeals in Chicago that upheld the Morton Grove, Ill., handgun ban. The appeals court said that "the Second Amendment is not applicable to Morton Grove and . . . possession of handguns by individuals is not part of the right to keep and bear arms. . . ." And in October 1985 a Maryland court held the manufacturer of a Saturday night special liable for damages caused when a man was shot with such a gun during a holdup.

Gun Control Laws

Congress enacted three gun control laws in reaction to periods of extreme violence. The gangsterism of the Prohibition period and the rise of organized crime led to passage of the National Firearms Act of 1934, which required registration of machine guns and sawed-off shotguns, and the Federal Firearms Act of 1938, which prohibited unlicensed dealers from selling guns across state lines and made it illegal to sell firearms to convicted felons and fugitives.

Clamor over the political assassinations, crime wave, and urban riots of the 1960s resulted in passage of the Gun Control Act of 1968 (PL 90-618). The law barred the mail-order or interstate shipment of firearms and ammunition. It revised licensing procedures for those manufacturing, importing, selling, or collecting guns. It also banned importation of most firearms, but not of gun parts.

There are about 23,000 state and local gun ordinances, creating a legal patchwork that both gun control supporters and opponents condemn. In 13 states — Alaska, Arizona, Colorado, Delaware, Idaho, Kentucky, Maine, Montana, Nebraska, Nevada, New Hampshire, New Mexico, and Wyoming — the only prohibition is on carrying concealed handguns. At the other end of the scale three Chicago suburbs — Morton Grove, Oak Park, and Evanston — have banned handgun ownership.

Chicago and Washington, D.C., banned new handguns from their jurisdictions; people who owned pistols prior to the laws' enactment may legally keep them. A 1982 San Francisco law requiring owners to give up their handguns was overturned by a state court, not on Second Amendment grounds, but because the state gun law preempted such local actions. In reaction to the attempts to ban handguns, several communities have followed the lead of Kennesaw, Ga., and passed laws requiring each household to own a firearm.

Federal Gun Law Weakened

The 99th Congress acted to ease major provisions of the 1968 Gun Control Act.

The Senate, 79-15, passed S 49 on July 9, 1985. Sen. James A. McClure, R-Idaho, sponsor of the bill, said the large margin of victory was in part a reaction to "abusive enforcement" of the 1968 law. But one Senate aide said the vote was a tribute to the gun lobby. "This place is marching in lock step with the NRA," he said.

House action came after some initial reluctance. A House bill (HR 945) similar to S 49 faced strong opposition from key members of the Judiciary Committee. Sponsors of the measure, led by Harold J. Volkmer, D-Mo., attempted to force the legislation out of committee through a discharge petition. Once 218 members — a majority of the House — have signed a discharge petition, the full House must act. Besides speeding up floor action, discharge petitions generally provide for more limited debate than regular House procedures.

In a rare display of unity March 11, 1986, the House Judiciary Committee unanimously approved a compromise bill

(HR 4332). The committee's unusually quick action was in part an effort to beat Volkmer's petition. Volkmer secured the needed 218 signatures on March 13. His petition did not directly affect HR 4332, but it played an important political role. With the backing of half the members, Volkmer could virtually dictate the terms under which his bill and HR 4332 would be considered by the full House.

On March 19 the Rules Committee approved a rule that foreclosed a yes-or-no vote on HR 4332. Instead, Volkmer was given the chance to offer his bill as a replacement for the Judiciary bill. In addition, Rules limited the number of hours the bill could be debated, which in effect limited the number of amendments that could be offered.

The House passed HR 4332 April 10 on a 292-130 vote. As passed, the bill would make it easier to buy and sell rifles and shotguns and to transport them interstate. The House, however, refused to lift the restriction in the 1968 gun law that bars interstate sales of handguns.

Congress cleared S 49 on May 6. The major provisions of the bill were identical to HR 4332. The Firearms Owners' Protection Act (PL 99-308) included the following provisions:

• Made legal the interstate sale of rifles and shotguns as long as the sale was over-the-counter and legal in the state of the buyer and seller.

PL 90-618, the 1968 Gun Control Act, barred the interstate sale of rifles, shotguns, and handguns, although residents of one state could buy long guns in a contiguous state.

• Relieved ammunition dealers of record-keeping requirements.

• Narrowed the definition of who must get a license to sell guns to cover only those people who "regularly" import, manufacture, and deal in guns with the "principal objective of livelihood and profit."

• Allowed licensed dealers to conduct business at gun shows and provided that records of gun show transactions can be inspected.

• Maintained record-keeping requirements for firearm transactions, while prohibiting the Treasury Department's Bureau of Alcohol, Tobacco and Firearms (BATF) from issuing any regulation requiring centralized dealer records. The law also bars the establishment of any firearms registration plan.

A dealer would not be required to keep a record of any transaction involving his personal collection unless the gun is disposed of within one year of being transferred from the dealer's business inventory to his personal collection.

PL 90-618 required the dealer to record all firearm and handgun ammunition transactions, including those involving guns from a personal collection, and to maintain such records indefinitely.

• Allowed federal officials to make one unannounced inspection of a dealer's premises each year. PL 90-618 allowed federal officials to make unannounced inspections of dealers' premises at "reasonable" times.

• Allowed federal officials to inspect a dealer's premises without a warrant during a criminal investigation of someone other than the dealer or when tracing firearms.

• Barred federal officials from denying or revoking a dealer's license because he allegedly violated provisions in the law if the dealer is acquitted or the case is terminated prior to trial. If denied a license or if a license is revoked for another reason, the dealer would have the right to a full trial on the denial in federal court.

PL 90-618 allowed federal officials to deny a dealer a license for failing to meet certain statutory criteria or for a "willful" violation of any provision of the gun control law or BATF regulation. Judicial review of the denial was limited.

• Made clear that the Treasury secretary

may not deny import permits for firearms and ammunition meeting statutory requirements for importation, and barred the importation of barrels for firearms that do not meet the criteria for "sporting purposes."

PL 90-618 gave the Treasury secretary greater discretion.

• Kept the mandatory penalties for using a firearm during the commission of a federal crime of violence and added drug felonies and carrying a handgun loaded with armor-piercing bullets to the crimes covered by this provision.

The law set a mandatory 5-year prison term for a first offense and 10 years for a subsequent offense.

• Imposed new penalties of 10 years for a first offense and 20 years for a subsequent offense for carrying or using a machine gun or a gun equipped with a silencer during commission of a federal crime of violence.

• Incorporated into the Gun Control Act provisions of the 1968 Omnibus Crime Control and Safe Streets Act that bar categories of people, such as those convicted of certain crimes, from transporting or owning a firearm.

• Specified that state law governs in determining whether a person, by reason of a previous conviction, is barred from handling or possessing firearms. This is similar to PL 90-618.

• Allowed all persons barred from handling or possessing firearms because of a prior conviction to get their eligibility restored by BATF. This includes persons with previous convictions involving the use of a firearm.

A state pardon for a crime would automatically carry with it a restoration of eligibility. An individual denied a restoration of eligibility is entitled to a full trial on the issues in federal district court.

PL 90-618 automatically barred anyone from a restoration of eligibility if the offense involved use of a firearm. And a state pardon did not automatically mean that the person could once again own or deal in firearms.

• Restricted the circumstances under which federal officials could seize firearms or ammunition as a result of a violation of the Gun Control Act. S 49 barred such seizures unless the government could prove by "clear and convincing evidence" that the person intended to violate the law and that the violation involved specified crimes, such as crimes of violence, drug felonies, and illegal exportation of firearms.

PL 90-618 allowed federal officials to seize any firearm or ammunition involved in any violation of the gun control law.

• Required the government to return property to the alleged violator if he is acquitted of the criminal charges on which the seizure of property was based. PL 90-618 contained no similar provision.

• Required the government to prove that a person "willfully" violated certain provisions of the law, such as failing to obtain a dealer's license. For other violations, such as selling a gun to a person not eligible to own one, the government would have to prove only that the person knew he was violating the law. The bill also reduced to a misdemeanor violations involving record keeping.

PL 90-618 did not require the government to prove that a person "willfully" violated the law, and that all violations were felonies.

• Permitted a person to travel interstate with a firearm as long as the gun was not loaded and not readily accessible. This provision would override state and local laws that may bar possession or transportation of a firearm. However, the provision would not block a state from enforcing its own gun laws on its own citizens.

• Barred the future possession or transfer of machine guns. Persons lawfully owning machine guns prior to the date the president signed S 49 were not affected. They could sell or swap their machine guns after the date of enactment as long as the machine gun was lawfully owned at that time.

● Allowed a court to award "reasonable" attorneys' fees to a person who prevails against the government in getting his seized property returned. PL 90-618 had no such provision.

Lobbying Efforts

Weakening of the 1968 Gun Control Act was a victory for the NRA, which had been trying for more than a decade to soften the law's regulatory scheme. Gun owners and dealers were persistent critics of the 1968 law, claiming it put too many restrictions on their activities and subjected them to harassment by overeager federal authorities.

Taking an unusually strong advocacy position, nearly all major police organizations — including the International Association of Chiefs of Police, the Police Executive Research Forum, the National Organization of Black Law Enforcement Executives, the Fraternal Order of Police, and the National Troopers Coalition — joined with the gun control forces to oppose changes to the 1968 law. In the past the police groups had often supported and rarely vocally opposed the positions of gun lobby groups like the NRA. However, they came out strongly against S 49.

There were two new things about the law enforcement lobbying effort: First, that it happened at all, and second, that there was so much unity among groups that do not often agree with one another.

"I've been in police work for almost 24 years, and I have never seen anything like this," said Hubert Williams, president of the Police Foundation. "You have forged together in unity competing and divergent interests that exist within organizational structures such as police unions and police chiefs."

Marty Tapscott, an assistant chief of police in Washington, D.C., and president of the National Organization of Black Law Enforcement Executives, said the lobbying was "a new approach for us, trying to urge congressmen to listen to our point of view."

The fight over gun legislation was billed as a showdown between the police and the NRA. It turned out to be a rather mismatched affair. While the police groups were able to get more than 100 uniformed officers to Washington, they were, in the words of some members, too little too late.

"The police misunderstood the force of lobbying," Rep. Buddy Roemer, D-La., said. "Lobbying is not standing in long lines at the door. Lobbying is good information early; it is a presence when minds are being made up," he said.

Rep. William J. Hughes, D-N.J., and other members attributed the NRA's success to the millions of dollars it has poured into congressional campaigns. But an equally important factor is the organization's ability to generate broad grass-roots support.

"Sixty to seventy million people own a firearm — 40 percent of American households," Wayne LaPierre, NRA legislative director, said. "They see it every day. It becomes like a set of golf clubs, and they say, 'Why does everybody want to take it away from me?' "

Although the police groups were unable to block passage of S 49, they did win some concessions in clarifying legislation (S 2414) that was cleared by Congress June 24, 1986.

Ever since the House passed its version of S 49, McClure and Orrin G. Hatch, R-Utah, chief sponsors of S 49, had been talking with Sen. Howard M. Metzenbaum, D-Ohio, a chief opponent of the bill who was representing the concerns of police groups and gun control advocates unhappy with S 49. While these organizations were pleased that S 49 retained the ban on interstate sales of handguns, they opposed lifting the ban on interstate sales of long guns, and they contended that easing the

Taking an unusually strong advocacy position, nearly all major police organizations — including the International Association of Chiefs of Police, the Police Executive Research Forum, the National Organization of Black Law Enforcement Executives, the Fraternal Order of Police, and the National Troopers Coalition — joined with the gun control forces to oppose changes to the 1968 Gun Control Act.

licensing requirements would make it more difficult to trace firearms used in a crime.

A coalition of police groups drafted a package of amendments they wanted the Senate to consider. For nearly three weeks their efforts bore little fruit, but when police spokesmen were able to speak to Judiciary Committee chairman Strom Thurmond, R-S.C. — a longtime law enforcement supporter — Thurmond set about trying to bring McClure, Hatch, and Metzenbaum together. Finally, on the afternoon of May 6, 1986, Thurmond got the three into a room and they hammered out S 2414, with language similar to what the police groups wanted.

S 2414 applies licensing and record-keeping requirements to anyone who engages in the regular purchase and disposition of firearms for criminal purposes or terrorism; requires gun dealers to keep records of gun transactions involving their personal collections; and allows the interstate transportation of a gun only when it is legal of the person to own a gun in the states in which he begins and ends his journey.

Other Issues

The police groups and the gun lobby have been at odds on other gun issues as well. The police organizations favored bills that would ban the sale of armor-piercing bullets, also known as "cop-killers" because they can penetrate most bullet-proof vests. "Any legislation that would restrict the availability of this ammunition . . . will help to ensure the safety of those who have dedicated their lives to protecting the public against crime," said David Konstantin, research associate at the Police Executive Research Forum. The gun lobby denied that armor-piercing bullets were a danger to police officers and claimed that the proposed bills would bar the sale of large-caliber hunting ammunition that is also capable of penetrating armor.

On August 13, 1986, Congress cleared a bill (HR 3132) barring the manufacture and importation of armor-piercing bullets. The bill exempted bullets made for rifles and sporting purposes, and ammunition sometimes used in oil well and gas well perforating devices. Earlier versions of the bill were opposed by the NRA, which claimed that the legislation amounted to a foot in the door for gun control. NRA, however, did not actively opposed HR 3132. The Senate Judiciary Committee had approved a similar bill (S 104) in July 1985. Action on that bill was blocked by Sen. Steven D. Symms, R-Idaho, who believed the legislation was unnecessary and was an intrusion on citizens' rights under the Second Amendment.

Law enforcement officials also have expressed concern about the growing number of machine guns and semiautomatic military-type rifles, some of which are convertible to automatic use, in circulation. Most of these guns are used by target shooters, but they are also being used by criminals to devastating effect. Semiautomatics were used in a July 1984 shooting rampage in a California McDonald's and the 1985 shootings in a suburban Philadelphia shopping mall. Drug dealers and racketeers are said to favor these weapons. And in April 1985, federal agents raided the rural Arkansas compound of the Covenant, Sword and Arm of the Lord, a fanatical anti-Semitic and racist group associated with the "Christian Identity" and neo-Nazi movement. They confiscated dozens of automatic and semiautomatic weapons, and reported that the Covenant was the likely arsenal for several violent right-wing hate groups.

Many police officials support federal legislative measures like those Hughes and Peter W. Rodino, Jr., D-N.J., proposed in the Racketeer Weapons and Violent Crime Control Bill of 1985. That bill would have banned future sales of machine guns and silencers to private citizens and established a 15-day national waiting period prior to the purchase of a handgun.

Gun control advocates believed police support for such legislation indicated that the tide was turning against the well-financed gun lobby. "The police were really taken aback when the NRA came out and fought them [on the armor-piercing bullet]. . . . They were stunned again by the NRA defending the right of people to own machine guns. . . .," said Charles Orasin, executive director of Handgun Control Inc. "When 'law-and-order' starts saying they're wrong, we think it's going to turn this thing."

The NRA's Aquilino denied that there is a schism between police and the progun forces. "It's a perceived split," Aquilino said, fueled by "some rather selfish individuals [from] gun control groups." He added that while "too many of the national [police] leadership groups are buying it," the police rank-and-file does not go along with everything their national leadership says. "I really feel that the other side is losing badly, losing a tremendous amount of support," Aquilino said. "One reason is that academics over the past decade are starting to delve into givens, and they're finding that their givens hold no weight."

Hydropower Relicensing

Electric utilities owned by private investors won a congressional battle for control of cheap hydroelectric power in 1986, when the 99th Congress determined that public utilities would not get any "preference" over private utilities when it is time to renew hydroelectric licenses.

Some public utility opponents of the electric utilities accused the private utilities of buying cosponsors for their bill (HR 44) to ensure victory. But a Congressional Quarterly analysis of political action committees (PACs) run by private utilities found that campaign contributions were not the decisive factor.

Money was certainly part of the atmosphere in which Congress considered hydropower relicensing — private utility PACs gave House members more than half a million dollars in 1985 — but there were far more important influences shaping members' positions.

The private utilities' success seems to be the result of compromise, coalition building, and old-fashioned convincing. Shaping members' decisions was the geography and politics of their states and districts, their philosophies about the role of government in people's lives, and the ability of the private utilities to sell Congress on the importance of one fact: Private utilities serve three times as many electric customers as public utilities.

The struggle, which spanned the 98th and 99th Congresses, was between two kinds of grass-roots democracy, one historical and the other quite modern.

The movement for public ownership of utilities harks back to the Populist Party that sprang up on the plains and prairies before the turn of the century and embraced the notion of "power to the people" — in both senses of the phrase. Private utilities, on the other hand, have adopted a more modern form of grass-roots democracy — one run from Washington, D.C., with the help of political consultants and based on a raw calculation of the greatest good for the greatest number.

The last round in the fight over the hydropower relicensing issue was played out by House and Senate confirees who settled differences in versions of the relicensing bills passed by the Senate April 17, 1986, (S 426) and the House April 21, 1986, (HR 44).

They agreed that utilities holding hydroelectric power licenses would not be favored but that a utility seeking to take over a hydroelectric dam would have to show that the public would benefit from the change in license-holders.

Congress cleared S 426 for the president October 3, 1986.

The Relicensing Issue

Hydropower sites are scattered throughout the United States, supplying approximately 13 percent of the nation's electricity needs — almost as much as nuclear, but considerably less than coal. Hydropower is perhaps the most prized fraction of the nation's power budget, however, because it is cheap, clean, safe, renewable, reliable, and not imported.

Under the Federal Water Policy Act of 1920, utilities planning new hydroelectric projects must get a license from the Federal Energy Regulatory Commission (FERC). When more than one application is filed, the law directs FERC to give the license to the applicant whose proposal is most beneficial to the public. When they show equal merit, the law gives a preference to state and municipally owned utilities. The law is ambiguous, however, on whether public utilities get a preference when the original license expires. Courts have given different interpretations of whether there is a municipal preference in relicensing.

The concept of a preference for public power is deeply imbedded in U.S. water law and policy, and its origins can be traced back as far as the Reclamation Act of 1902. The history of feuds between public and private interests over development of nonfederal hydro sites goes back almost as far.

Public power advocates argued that investor-owned utilities cannot be relied upon to serve the public interest because their purpose is to make a profit and because they are natural monopolies. Private power advocates said they could serve the public better because they are more efficient and have the financial resources to provide better service — and that the public interest is protected by extensive government regulation of utilities' performance and profits.

Most of the licenses coming due for renewal in the next decade are owned by private utilities that had the capital to invest in hydropower when the licenses were first offered. The private utilities were afraid of losing those investments if a public power preference were applied.

In 1984 Congress wrestled with the issue of which utilities in the Southwest should get the bargain-priced electricity from the Hoover Dam — one of the first of the large federally financed water projects of the 1930s to come back before Congress for legislative review of its pricing policy. The public power preference, although not the main issue, survived that debate unscathed. Federally-financed hydroelectric facilities that are still federally owned and operated, like the Hoover Dam, make up 51.4 percent of all hydropower plants in the country.

The dispute before the 99th Congress dealt with an entirely different set of dams — those owned by municipal and private utility companies.

Utility PAC Gifts

The private utilities asked Congress to settle the issue of relicensing, and that led to HR 44, introduced by Richard C. Shelby, D-Ala. Helping to build support for Shelby's bill was a grass-roots lobbying campaign funded by private power interests. It included leaflets mailed with monthly electric bills to private utility customers warning them of potential rate increases and urging them to write to their representatives and senators in Congress. The districts of key House Energy Committee members were targets for similar appeals mailed directly by a Washington, D.C., public relations firm.

Shelby introduced his bill on January 3, 1985, the first day of 99th Congress, with 58 cosponsors. Throughout the year, he picked up additional cosponsors, until by December, he had 182 — short of a House

The Hoover Dam was one of the first of the large federally financed water projects of the 1930s to come back before Congress for legislative review of its pricing policy.

majority, but within striking distance.

At that point, several congressional staff sources on the public power side of the question, speaking to reporters on the condition that they not be identified, charged that the bill's success was due to campaign contributions from private utilities. They said word had been spread that private utility PAC contributions were available to anyone who signed onto HR 44 as a cosponsor. Spokesmen for the Edison Electric Institute, which represents the private utilities, dismissed the charge, saying it was untrue and merely a case of sour grapes.

Congressional Quarterly attempted to study the effect, if any, of private utility campaign contributions by analyzing data on file with the Federal Election Commission.

The analysis covered all 1985 campaign contributions to incumbent House members from 78 PACs affiliated with private electric utilities. Municipal utilities generally are prohibited from operating PACs and were not included in the CQ analysis. But public power interests did make campaign contributions through association PACs, rural cooperative PACs, and donations from individuals.

Cosponsors of HR 44 did, on average, get more in campaign contributions from private utility PACs than those who did not sponsor the bill — but the relationship of utility giving to cosponsorship was less dramatic than its relationship to other variables such as geographic region or committee membership.

Utility companies with a lot of FERC-licensed hydropower did not give more to bill cosponsors than did utilities with modest amounts or none at all, suggesting that the hydropower issue was only one of many factors motivating their giving.

Nor did bill cosponsors, on the average, seem to get utility contributions very soon before or after they signed onto the bill. In fact, members who signed onto the bill during 1985 got less than those who began the year as original cosponsors — not what would be expected if the PACs were using contributions to induce members to come over to their side.

The average member of the House received $1,223 in 1985 from the private utility PACs. That includes 136 members who received nothing. Contributions of that magnitude would not constitute a large portion of the several hundred thousand dollars it takes to run a typical House campaign — and are far short of the maximum of $5,000 per election that members can receive legally from a single PAC.

The 253 members who did *not* cosponsor the bill got, on the average, $960; the 59 original cosponsors of the bill averaged almost twice that, $1,826. The 123 members who signed on during the year got an average of $1,476. As a group, all cosponsors averaged $1,589 in gifts.

The analysis turned up little linkage between time of cosponsorship and time of PAC donations. Only 71 of the 1,391 contributions counted were given to cosponsors within 30 days before or after cosponsorship. Of those 71 gifts, where the possibility for influence is theoretically the highest, 14, or almost one-fifth, went to a single member — Tommy F. Robinson, D-Ark. Another 10 went to Beryl Anthony, Jr., D-Ark., a member of the Ways and Means Committee. His spokesman said the timing of the contributions and the cosponsorship was "purely coincidental."

While cosponsorship does seem to have a statistically significant relationship to PAC donations, what seemed to influence PACs more was committee membership — especially a berth on the Energy Subcommittee on Energy Conservation and Power, the one that marked up the relicensing bill. Members of that panel averaged $4,804 in utility PAC donations.

Members of the key Interior subcommittee, which had influence but not direct jurisdiction over HR 44, also fared well. Members of Interior's Water and Power Resources Subcommittee averaged $3,132.

What region a member came from also seemed to be more important than cosponsorship of HR 44. Members in the Southwest averaged the highest amount of donations ($3,135), while those in the Northeast were lowest ($689).

While there are many reasons for regional variations, one is heavy giving by particular PACs. Several especially active Texas utility PACs — including four from the Texas Utilities Co. group and one from the Houston Lighting and Power Co. — helped boost contributions received by the average Texas member to $4,224 and pulled up the score for the whole Southwest region.

For the sake of comparison, CQ also examined utility PAC donations to a 35-member elite defined as the House leadership. It includes members holding party leadership positions and the chairmen of relevant committees and subcommittees. In the CQ analysis, leaders averaged $1,853 in contributions.

Statistical inquiries like this one can neither prove nor disprove assertions that PAC giving causes members to support a particular bill, or that their support of a bill causes PACs to give. There remains the possibility that members supported the bill because they were already inclined to be sympathetic to the concerns of private utilities, and that utilities simply give more to their known friends.

In sum, while the analysis shows there was a considerable amount of private utility PAC money being distributed while the hydropower bill was being debated, it does not uphold the charge of some public utility supporters that cosponsors of HR 44 were being systematically bought with private utility PAC contributions.

Consensus Politics

As heavily lobbied as HR 44 was, it is remarkable that the House eventually passed it by voice vote, under suspension of the rules, with no amendments, little debate, and scarcely any expression of opposition. That was possible because of compromises made and coalitions built by private power supporters while the bill was before the Energy Committee.

The changes included several environmental safeguards not in the original Shelby bill — among them a requirement that FERC consider environmental impact when renewing licenses and the elimination of some existing exemptions for private development of small dams.

By agreeing to these provisions, the private utilities were able to pick up support from environmentalists, who historically have opposed the utilities on hydropower issues.

The committee bill also contained financial compensation provisions that helped win over some of public power's friends in the House. Originally, some of the strongest objections had come from members like Robert T. Matsui, D-Calif., who represented customers of the Sacramento Municipal Utility District (SMUD). SMUD had already filed a challenge to a hydropower license held by a private utility and SMUD would have been seriously hurt by a bill that simply disavowed a public power preference. Instead of insisting on that, private power advocates agreed to a process allowing SMUD and other utilities that had already challenged licenses up for renewal to seek compensation from incumbent license-holders in return for withdrawing their challenges.

These changes represented compromises that helped the private utilities pick up additional support.

Still, there were other obstacles to overcome and other factors at work beneath the surface of the hydropower debate — including the legacy of an 80-year battle between public and private power.

Historical Context

Public power is still a kind of religion in some parts of the country.

To understand why, one has to go back to when Franklin D. Roosevelt built federal dams to reverse the ruin of a free market economy, to when Theodore Roosevelt was preaching that government should guard the nation's rivers as a sacred trust for its people, and to when electricity was something new and magical that promised to transform America into a technological utopia.

Theodore Roosevelt advocated public ownership of utilities as a reaction to perceived abuses of monopoly power. But others feared government control would be abusive and saw it as a threat to free enterprise. In 1931, Herbert Hoover referred to public control of power as "the negation of the ideals upon which our civilization has been based."

While electricity promised the infinite gifts of modern technology — freedom from drudgery, gloom, isolation, and ignorance — that promise was unfulfilled for most U.S. farmers in the early 1930s when Franklin Roosevelt picked up the mantle of public power. When Roosevelt became president, only one farm out of nine had electricity; by the end of his presidency, eight out of nine had it. That change was wrought not by the workings of the free market but by government agencies — the Tennessee Valley Authority (TVA), the Rural Electrification Administration, and the works program to build federal dams.

When Roosevelt proposed the TVA in 1933, private utilities opposed it, fearing it would force them to lower their rates, but

One incentive for Congress to settle the hydropower relicensing issue was the different interpretations the courts gave of whether there was a municipal preference in relicensing. In 1983 a court battle developed between two public utility districts and a private utility company over the use of the Merwin Dam in Washington state, pictured above.

Roosevelt prevailed. Two years later, he launched a full-scale war on the concentration of economic power in electric utility holding companies, which controlled more than three-quarters of the private utilities. He sent Congress legislation giving the Securities and Exchange Commission power to abolish the holding companies.

The private utilities and their chief spokesman, Wendell L. Willkie, countered with a massive lobbying campaign, claiming that individual liberty and the American economic system were in jeopardy. Some 800,000 telegrams poured into congressional offices in a two-week period — many of them paid for by utilities and signed by persons who did not exist, according to a congressional investigation.

Roosevelt called the utilities "the most powerful, dangerous lobby . . . that has ever been created by any organization in this country." But in the end his own power proved greater, and he signed the bill in 1935.

These fights were over more than just practical economics — they were a confrontation between fundamentally different approaches: the unfettered free enterprise system, and the New Deal concept of central social planning that critics said bordered on socialism.

Roosevelt himself said that selling electricity was not the main purpose of the TVA, which also involved soil conservation, recreation, public health, resettlement of farmers, manufacturing, and the creation of jobs. "We are conducting a social experiment," Roosevelt said. "We are trying to make a different type of citizen."

The New Deal also saw the building of

federal dams on an unprecedented scale, such as the Grand Coulee on the Columbia River. The power from these federally built dams was to be sold through federally created power marketing administrations, such as the Bonneville Power Administration. These entities not only formed the beginnings of the regional power grids we know today, but also enforced the preference for sale of federal power to public rather than private utilities.

Geography and Ideology

The politics of hydropower is closely tied to place — as are the rivers and dams that generate it and the factories and homes that use it. To understand a member's stand on the relicensing bill, it is usually necessary to understand where he is from.

One of the states with the strongest interests in HR 44 is Alabama. Most of the state's electric customers are served by the privately held Alabama Power Co., which controls major amounts of FERC-licensed hydropower and which for decades competed with the TVA for customers and dam sites. It was no surprise, therefore, that Shelby was the chief sponsor of HR 44.

Leading the lobbying effort for HR 44 was California's Pacific Gas and Electric Co. (PG&E) — the biggest private electric utility in the United States and the one with the most FERC-licensed hydropower. Needless to say, many members from PG&E's Northern California service area backed HR 44 and S 426.

Also predictably, some of the strongest opponents came from the area served by the TVA. Sen. Albert Gore, Jr., D-Tenn., denounced S 426 as a "giveaway." Sen. Jim Sasser, D-Tenn., cited the concern of the Tennessee Valley Public Power Association, formed by 160 municipal and cooperative distributors of TVA power, that the bill could undermine the public power preference.

The Great Plains states, with their abundance of rural cooperatives and where both water and people are scarce, also are strong public power supporters. Sen. Edward Zorinsky, D-Neb., was among those opposing S 426. His state is the only one served entirely by public power, a legacy of Sen. George William Norris, R-Neb. (House 1903-13; Senate 1913-43), a towering figure who fought for public power during the early decades of the century. Other senators from Great Plains states were among the minority voting with Gary Hart, D-Colo., April 15, 1986, when he offered an amendment to "recapture" privately held hydropower for the federal government upon license expiration.

Hart, a probable 1988 presidential candidate and one of only five senators to win a perfect rating from the liberal Americans for Democratic Action in 1985, spoke of "keeping faith with our own progressive political heritage," and "keeping faith with the conservation dream of our forebears." His pitch was populist. The issue, Hart said, was whether "to reverse 6½ decades of philosophy which said that power generated from the public waterways of this country belongs to the people of the United States."

But a very different kind of populism was expressed in letters sent out to voters in key congressional districts in 1985 by the Committee for the Electric Consumers Protection Act — the name used in the direct-mail campaign funded by private utilities. "In the 1920s and 1930s, utility companies were granted licenses to plan, construct and operate hydroelectric plants. They took the risks, invested billions of dollars, weathered bad times and put the plants in operation," the letter read. "Now, 50 years later . . . some government bureaucrats are trying to take advantage of a loophole in the law that may let them take over the hydro plants."

The letter appealed to antigovernment feelings — as basic an ingredient of American populism as the notion that government should express the will of the people.

Another response to Hart's arguments came from Sen. James A. McClure, R-Idaho, who played a large part in shaping the Senate bill as chairman of the Energy Committee. He is as conservative as Hart is liberal.

It was a less divisive, and ultimately more successful populist appeal. McClure argued that the mass of people who would benefit from low private utility rates is ultimately the same populace that would benefit from public ownership of utilities.

Liability Insurance

In 1984, Vernon Hayes, president of a machinery manufacturing plant in Fort Worth, Texas, paid $7,800 for $5 million in liability insurance.

The next year, after "going bare" for 38 days because he could not find any insurance, he paid $132,000 for $500,000 in coverage.

"It's outrageous," said Hayes. "I'm just so confused and frustrated that I've got no place to go."

When Americans feel they have no place else to go, they often find their way to Washington. That is what is happening now as manufacturers, doctors, municipal governments, hazardous-waste disposers, truckers, tavern owners, day-care providers, pharmaceutical companies, and other businesses find themselves facing huge premium increases for liability insurance. Sometimes they cannot obtain coverage at any price from the property-casualty companies that provide it.

"In certain industries, insurance is almost impossible to find," said Robert Seltzer, a Philadelphia insurance agent. "When you put the numbers together [for an estimate], it sounds like a telephone number."

"Washington is becoming Insurance City," reported an industry newsletter in the fall of 1985, as protests from angry businessmen poured in.

"Complaints are coming in to the members of Congress at a level that is unprecedented," said Rep. James L. Oberstar, D-Minn., chairman of the House Public Works and Transportation Subcommittee on Investigations and Oversight. "There is wholesale confusion, bewilderment, and sometimes outrage" among insurance purchasers, he said.

It is not clear what Congress can do to alleviate the problems of either the insurance industry or its customers. Consumer advocate Ralph Nader wants the federal government to provide last-resort insurance and to supervise the industry. Insurance companies want Congress to force changes in state liability laws. But insurance is unfamiliar territory for Congress. At the behest of insurers, the industry long has been exempted from federal regulation. And the McCarran-Ferguson Act of 1945 (PL 79-15) exempted the industry from antitrust laws.

"It's reminiscent of the blind men and the elephant," said one industry observer after watching various committees feel their way around segments of the problem that fall within their jurisdiction.

While most of the legislative action so far has been at the state level, Congress is getting interested fast.

"It's clear that for the economic health of the nation and the business community, we're all going to have to become more conversant with the mechanics of the insurance industry," said Rep. James J. Florio, D-N.J., chairman of the Energy and Commerce Subcommittee on Commerce, Transportation, and Tourism.

For the property-casualty industry as a whole, premiums went up 21 percent in 1985, compared with 9 percent in 1984. Industry economists predicted another 20 percent jump in 1986. Insurance companies said these price increases were necessary because premiums and investment income have fallen far short of claims and other expenses. They blamed most of their woes on the legal system, charging that costs have gone through the roof because of excessive litigation and outrageous settlements.

Consumer groups replied that the insurance companies are distorting their financial picture to pressure legislators to limit victims' rights to recover damages. "It's a staggering ripoff — there isn't an example in American history to compare with it," said Nader.

Background

The squeeze on insurance availability and affordability is concentrated in property-casualty insurance, which comprises about a third of the insurance market. Within that area, it is focused on commercial lines of insurance, where companies say their losses have occurred.

Industry spokesmen said 1984 was the worst year on record for property-casualty insurance companies, and that preliminary figures showed 1985 was just as bad. Even record-setting income from the companies' huge investments did not offset losses from basic operations — selling insurance policies and paying out claims. The companies lost $3.5 billion in 1984 and an estimated $5.5 billion in 1985, according to A. M. Best Co. Inc., which compiles statistics on the industry.

These statistics do not go unchallenged. "That is a fraudulent figure," Robert Hunter, head of the Nader-affiliated National Insurance Consumers Organization (NICO), said of the $5.5 billion "operating loss" claimed by the industry. Hunter and Nader held a press conference January 6, 1986, to assert that the property-casualty insurers actually earned $6.6 billion in 1985, after items such as capital gains and federal tax credits were included; they later revised that figure to $5 billion.

"The industry is not in any trouble — it's in fine shape," said Hunter. He said that property-casualty insurance company stocks rose 50 percent in 1985, compared with 28 percent for the Dow Jones industrial average.

Insurers were quick to denounce the Nader-Hunter analysis. Sean Mooney, an economist with the Insurance Information Institute, called their critique "inaccurate and misleading." Mooney said that it was improper to count unrealized capital gains, and that industry data relied on standard accounting practices.

The industry admitted that tax credits and other gains would make its 1985 bottom line profitable, although the Insurance Information Institute said profits in 1984 were only 1.7 percent, compared with 15 percent for Fortune 500 companies.

Insurance is a cyclical business, and in 1965 and 1975 profits dipped sharply. Both times the industry recovered without major changes, mostly by raising rates. But the industry has never shown such sharp swings as it has since 1977.

Why the Pinch?

A major reason for the industry's roller-coaster ride in recent years has been fluctuating interest rates. Insurance compa-

Consumer advocate Ralph Nader is a leading critic of property-casualty insurance companies. He wants the federal government to provide last-resort insurance and to supervise the industry.

nies make a significant portion of their income from investments, and the high interest rates of the late 1970s sent property-casualty companies scrambling for funds to invest. Price wars often put rates far below the levels actuaries said were necessary to cover the risks.

"Discounts of 50 percent from our advisory rates were not uncommon; some premiums were only 5 percent," said Mavis Walters, vice president of the Insurance Services Office, a nonprofit industry agency that estimates what premiums should be charged, using statistics from the companies.

State regulations limit the amount of insurance a company can write to a percentage of its financial reserves. Reserves went down in 1984, which meant companies could offer less coverage in 1985.

Another factor behind the crunch has been a shortage of "reinsurance," the insurance companies' own insurance to cover their largest claims. Reinsurance is an international market, with many of the largest companies — such as the venerable Lloyd's of London — based in Europe. These companies have raised rates and cut coverage in the United States, saying they have paid too many claims. "The present legal system in the United States makes it impossible for the liability or casualty underwriter to operate," said Peter Miller, chairman of Lloyd's, in a June 1985 speech.

Restoring Profits

The industry's first response to the situation has been to raise prices. While 1985 premiums increased an average of 21 percent overall for property-casualty insurance, the price hikes in certain industries have been far greater. Bus owners, for example, paid 1985 premiums that averaged 700 percent higher than 1984's, according to Wayne Smith, executive director of the United Bus Owners of America, a trade association. Other groups, such as day-care centers, nurse-midwives, and hazardous-waste disposers have gone through periods where no insurance was available at all.

Pollution insurance became almost impossible to obtain, for instance, after federal laws and court interpretations held companies liable for slow environmental damage even if their policies covered only "sudden and accidental" spills.

Insurers have been particularly wary of businesses with a "long tail of liability" — where an injury or illness can be discovered many years after the event. Even though the policy has lapsed, the original insurer is still liable for paying damages. Insurers pulled out of day care, for instance, after publicity about a few child abuse cases. They feared that teenagers would win large awards for pain and suffering, compounded by interest charges, for abuse that occurred years before.

Critics say these businesses have been victimized by speculation. "Insurers are expressing hysteria over the threat of child sexual abuse . . . but we couldn't find a case where an insurance claim had been filed," said George Miller, D-Calif., chairman of the House Select Committee on Children, Youth, and Families, after a July 1985 hearing.

Industry critics say the crisis was brought on more by cutthroat competition than by rising expenses. Lyndon Olson, chairman of the State Board of Insurance of Texas, criticized the "immense irresponsibility of insurers in giving away the business for the last four to five years." The industry, he said, "has competed itself into the ever-living ground."

Insurance company spokesmen say that the low premiums of the early 1980s were a bonanza to businesses, and that recent howls of protest are often overstated. "In actual fact, if you go back to 1980 and compare the rates charged then [with new rates], in many cases there's not much difference," said Seltzer, the Philadelphia agent.

Hunter and Nader charge, however, that the insurance companies' premium increases are excessive. They say that profits could be restored to healthy levels with an across-the-board 5 percent rate increase.

Flaws in Legal System?

Insurers say that a more fundamental cause of their problems than falling interest rates is the tort-law system. They say that court judgments have dramatically increased their cost of doing business by making it too easy for injured parties to win large damage awards.

"With minor exceptions, the availability problem is not a problem created by our industry. It is first and foremost a problem with the civil justice system," said William Bailey, president of Aetna Life and Casualty Co., in an October 1985 speech to agents.

Industry leaders say that judges have made insurers responsible for incidents that should not be covered, that juries have awarded outrageous sums to victims, and that attorneys have fueled the situation by their greed for large fees.

An underlying problem, they say, is a growing tendency in society to insist that someone — particularly someone with "deep pockets," such as an insurance company or a city — must pay whenever a person suffers a loss. "When I was mayor of Carlsbad [Calif.], a drunk had a head-on [collision] that killed somebody, but he didn't have any insurance," recalled Rep. Ron Packard, R-Calif. "The court determined that the city was 1 percent responsible for the accident because of the design of the highway, which had been in existence 100 years. The city ended up paying 100 percent of the settlement, well over $1 million."

Legislative Action

Product liability laws have been the focus of fierce struggles between manufacturers, who seek a federal law, and trial lawyers, unions, consumer groups, state judges, and attorneys general, who oppose most changes. Product liability has been debated in Congress for the better part of a decade, but no major bill has been enacted.

In May 1985 a measure (S 100), sponsored by Bob Kasten, R-Wis., that would have established comprehensive federal standards determining liabilily was blocked by an 8-8 vote in the Senate Commerce, Science, and Transportation Committee. A key provision required plaintiffs to prove negligence by the manufacturer — a tougher standard of proof than required in many states. Opponents of S 100 claimed that the bill would confuse, rather than simplify, the legal situation; would violate states' rights; and would result in denying victims compensation for injuries. They believed that the fear of large damage claims is necessary to pressure manufacturers to be sure their products are safe. Proponents of the bill said attorneys oppose reform because they want to preserve large legal fees. In 1984, legislation (S 44) similar to S 100 was approved by the committee but did not reach the floor.

Focus Changes

By spring of 1986, key members of the 99th Congress and the business community shifted their approach to changing the nation's product liability laws in an effort to avoid difficulties that stymied action in the past. For years attempts to overhaul the laws centered on crafting uniform federal standards that would preempt state laws determining liability for allegedly unsafe products. Proponents of change came to focus on putting federal limits on the money that could be recovered by people claiming injuries caused by unsafe products and on providing incentives for parties to settle disputes out of court. The new approach involved a less drastic preemption of states' rights, and states could set their own definitions of liability.

Senate Commerce Committee chairman John C. Danforth, R-Mo., revised a bill (S 1999) he introduced in December 1985 to emphasize award limits and incentives on out-of-court settlements, instead of uniform standards of manufacturing liability. S 1999 was unveiled May 12, 1986.

Business support for the change in direction marked "a fundamental reappraisal by the business community of its approach to product liability reform," said Leslie Cheek, vice president-federal affairs for Crum and Forster Insurance Cos., the nation's second largest underwriter of general liability insurance.

While consumer groups, which were actively involved in Danforth's revisions, are interested in encouraging out-of-court settlements, they are wary of limits on compensation to plaintiffs. Trial lawyers, who represent plaintiffs, are adamantly opposed to any federal changes to state liability laws and procedures.

Both groups were extremely skeptical of a Reagan administration proposals introduced April 30, 1986, by Kasten as an amendment to S 100. The proposals would revise the nation's personal injury laws involving the liability of product manufacturers, government contractors, and the federal government itself. The administration proposed a $100,000 cap on the amount a person claiming injuries from allegedly unsafe products could recover in awards for pain and suffering and punitive damages — so-called "noneconomic" awards. Courts distinguish this type of compensation from payments for actual out-of-pocket expenses, such as medical bills. Also proposed were restrictions on contingency fees charged by lawyers representing plaintiffs. Unlike Danforth's bill, the administration's measure did not offer incentives for parties to settle their disputes out of court.

In a speech to the U.S. Chamber of Commerce, President Reagan urged speedy passage of the measure, saying "tort law has become a pretext for outrageous legal outcomes — outcomes that impede our economic life, not promote it."

On May 20, 1986, Sen. Slade Gorton, R-Wash., offered a comprehensive amendment to Danforth's revised bill. Like Danforth's proposal, Gorton's approach also emphasized incentives for out-of-court settlements, but it incorporated an expedited settlement mechanism into the traditional court process. The Gorton proposal would require claims for punitive damages to be tried separately and would make it much more difficult for the plaintiff to recover punitive damages if he previously rejected a fair settlement offer by the defendant.

At a May 20 hearing by the Commerce Committee, the administration's bill won strong praise from some members of the

Different product liability plans were backed in the 99th Congress, from left, by Sens. John C. Danforth, R-Mo., Slade Gorton, R-Wash., and Bob Kasten, R-Wis.

business community but was attacked by consumer groups. Critics said that the $100,000 limit on noneconomic damages was too low and objected to including punitive damages. Punitive damages, they said, represent one of the few effective deterrents against outrageous conduct by makers of products.

Danforth's measure attracted favorable comments from both business and consumer groups, although each side expressed reservations. The business community — as well as the administration — was concerned that the out-of-court settlement track could become as cumbersome and costly as the current court system. Consumer groups were not reconciled to the bill's $250,000 cap on pain and suffering.

Gorton's plan was introduced the day of the hearing and was not the target of comments. However, consumer groups said they generally were pleased with it, especially because it took the least restrictive approach to caps on noneconomic awards.

Hopes Fade

Hopes for Senate passage of product liability legislation in the 99th Congress faded June 26, 1986, as the Commerce, Science, and Transportation Committee narrowly approved a package that key members vowed to fight on the floor.

The committee ordered reported, 10-7, a clean bill (S 2760) that included a bitterly contested provision crafted by Danforth setting a $250,000 limit on court awards for pain and suffering claimed by victims of unsafe products. Contained in an expedited settlement system that Danforth labeled the heart of the Commerce package, the cap would apply if a plaintiff rejects a pretrial settlement offer from a defendant. The Danforth plan also called for penalties against defendants who turn down offers from plaintiffs.

The Product Liability Alliance, an association of more than 200 businesses, expressed support for the package, saying "this bill has a greater chance of enactment than past efforts." Consumer groups, however, blasted the bill. "After spending a full year with this committee trying to devise a way to help people settle product liability cases in an equitable way, we are bitterly disappointed," said Joseph Goffman, an attorney for Public Citizen, a group founded by Ralph Nader. "Supporters of this legislation have to know that we are going to fight their unjust and unworkable proposal every step of the way."

Consumer groups were opposed not just to the caps but to a provision sponsored by Larry Pressler, R-S.D., that restricted joint and several liability to economic losses. That legal doctrine requires a defendant to pay more than his share of damages in cases in which other defendants are not able to pay their shares of fault.

As ordered reported by the committee, S 2760 also included:

- A compromise amendment that would require state regulators to share with the secretary of commerce data reported to them by insurance companies. Companies would be required to indicate whether compensation to claimants represented economic or noneconomic losses. Reporting also would be required from risk-retention groups and self-insured manufacturers.
- A provision that would allow punitive damages only if the plaintiff establishes by clear and convincing evidence the defendant's "conscious, flagrant indifference" to the safety of those who might be harmed by a product. Mere negligence, or imprudence, would not be sufficient justification for punitive damages, as is now the case in some states.
- A "government standards" defense against punitive damages that bars award of punitive damages for injuries caused by a drug that received premarketing approval from the Food and Drug Administration or by an aircraft-related product certified by the Federal Aviation Administration.
- A rule enabling a defendant to escape liability if the plaintiff was under the influence of drugs or alcohol and was more than 50 percent responsible for the injury.
- A "statute of repose" that limits the length of time for which a manufacturer can be held liable.
- A *forum non conveniens* rule that makes it more difficult for foreign plaintiffs to bring cases in U.S. courts.
- Sanctions on attorneys who make frivolous claims or prolong a trial.

S 2760 got as far as adoption September 25, 1986, of a motion to proceed with floor consideration. After the vote, Majority Leader Robert Dole, R-Kan., yanked the measure from the floor because Ernest F. Hollings, D-S.C., was prepared to filibuster to prevent a vote on the legislation.

Meanwhile, the House did not move beyond hearings on general liability issues in the 99th Congress.

Risk-Retention Bill

Legislation (S 2129) to make it easier for businesses, cities, and professional groups to form cooperatives to purchase liability insurance was cleared by Congress October 9, 1986. The measure was an attempt to help cities, manufacturers, medical personnel, truckers, bus drivers, and other businesses that are having trouble obtaining liability insurance because of high costs.

The bill would permit states to require "risk retention groups" to show they are financially sound. A risk group chartered to operate in at least one state would not have to obtain a charter to operate in any other states. The bill would allow cooperatives to purchase most types of liability insurance, except for personal insurance such as homeowner's or auto.

The new legislation broadens a 1981 law (PL 97-45) that allowed the formation of risk groups to provide product liability only.

A number of groups that have had difficulty obtaining liability insurance campaigned for the bill. Although some insurance companies do not welcome competition from risk groups, few actively opposed S 2129.

South Africa Sanctions

Throughout his presidency, Ronald Reagan's successes in Congress came in large part because of his ability and willingness to strike a deal at the right moment, even on issues that involved his fundamental principles. But on South Africa, Reagan staked out a position early in his presidency and steadfastly refused to make anything other than minor changes in it. He ignored or missed several opportunities to shape the course of political sentiment in the United States toward South Africa.

"To put it in the mildest terms," said House minority leader Robert H. Michel, R-Ill., "the administration has been less than brilliant in handling this issue."

Administration Policy Toward South Africa

In the early years of his presidency, Reagan himself seemed to ignore South Africa, leaving policy making to the State Department's Africa bureau, headed by Assistant Secretary Chester Crocker. Reagan devoted no speeches to and made no comments about South Africa until late 1984, when the movement toward sanctions was beginning to build.

Crocker in 1981 drafted and got Reagan's approval for a policy described as "constructive engagement." As envisioned by Crocker, the policy was to apply to all of southern Africa and was to include friendly persuasion not only toward racial reform in South Africa but also toward settlement of longstanding disputes involving South Africa and the neighboring countries of Angola, Mozambique, and Namibia.

In spite of Crocker's diplomatic success in negotiating limited agreements, the phrase "constructive engagement" was widely interpreted both in the United States and in South Africa as a policy of sympathy for the government in Pretoria. That interpretation was reinforced by some of Reagan's earliest actions toward South Africa — the easing of embargoes that President Carter had imposed on sales of computers and other items to security forces in Pretoria. Liberals and blacks in the United States condemned constructive engagement from the start, but it took several years for South Africa and Reagan's policy to become a major issue in the United States.

The key event was a demonstration at the South African Embassy in Washington on Thanksgiving Day 1984. Del. Walter E. Fauntroy, D-D.C., TransAfrica director Randall Robinson, and other civil rights leaders demonstrated at the embassy, deliberately getting themselves arrested.

In the following weeks, more than 20 members of Congress — including one senator, Lowell P. Weicker, Jr., R-Conn. — joined the hundreds stepping from the embassy picket line into police patrol wagons. Charges were not pressed against any of those arrested, but the demonstrations helped make South Africa a public issue.

Americans also were impressed by the eloquence of Anglican bishop Desmond Tutu, a black South African awarded the Nobel Peace Prize in 1984.

Antiapartheid groups in South Africa stepped up demonstrations early in 1985, provoking a cycle of crackdowns by security forces and more protests. Unrest in South Africa became daily news in the United States, forcing politicians to focus on the substance and results of Reagan's policy toward that country.

Sensing growing concern, many Republicans in Congress — especially those who had been involved in the civil rights struggles of the 1960s — urged Reagan to step up his pressure on South Africa. In December 1984, 35 House conservatives wrote the South African ambassador, Bernardus G. Fourie, threatening to support some economic sanctions unless Pretoria moved to dismantle apartheid.

The House in June 1985 overwhelmingly passed a bill (HR 1460) imposing modest sanctions on South Africa, such as banning bank loans to the government and businesses, barring new business investment there, and prohibiting importation of South African gold coins called Krugerrands. The Senate followed suit in July with an even more limited version (S 995) banning bank loans to the Pretoria government and prohibiting most nuclear and computer sales to South Africa, among other things.

A House-Senate conference on July 31, 1985, focused on the Krugerrand issue. Foreign Relations Committee chairman

Anglican bishop Desmond Tutu, awarded the Nobel Peace Prize in 1984, was an outspoken critic of apartheid.

Richard G. Lugar, Ind., pressed by the House and facing defections by other Senate Republicans, reluctantly agreed to the import ban on those coins.

The August recess interrupted congressional action on the conference bill and gave Reagan time to act on his own. On September 9, 1985, Reagan issued an executive order imposing many of the sanctions in the bill, including the Krugerrand ban.

Giving Reagan credit for acting, Lugar and Majority Leader Robert Dole, R-Kan., supported a Senate filibuster of the conference bill. Several attempts to stop the filibuster failed; to ensure the bill's death Dole and Lugar took the official copy from the Senate chamber and locked it in the Foreign Relations Committee safe.

Lugar and other Republicans said they hoped Reagan would follow up his executive order with new diplomatic pressure on South Africa for real changes in apartheid. Those hopes were dashed, however, by Reagan's willingness to accept assertions by

South Africa's president, P. W. Botha, that his government was moving as quickly as possible.

99th Congress Overrides Reagan's Sanctions Veto

South Africa on May 19, 1986, conducted bombing raids and commando attacks on suspected guerrilla camps and offices in three neighboring countries — Botswana, Zambia, and Zimbabwe. The raids, however, perhaps caused greater political impact in Washington than damage to the intended targets. Two days later key House and Senate members introduced major legislation (HR 4868, S 2498) to impose new punitive sanctions on South Africa.

South African president Botha defended the attack on alleged African National Congress (ANC) facilities as an "antiterrorist" move and compared it with the April 1986 U.S. bombing of Libya. Rejecting the comparison, the White House condemned the raids and said the United States "stands with the governments and peoples of those countries in expressing our sense of outrage at these events. . . ."

The proposed legislation would toughen substantially the sanctions Reagan imposed in September 1985. It would bar new U.S. business investments in South Africa and bank loans to private companies there. It also would end U.S. landing rights for South African Airways, prohibit U.S. involvement in energy production in South Africa, and bar imports of uranium, coal, and steel from the country.

If, after a year, Pretoria had not released all political prisoners and begun "good faith" negotiations to end apartheid, the legislation would prohibit computer exports to South Africa and require U.S. computer firms to withdraw operations there.

The administration strongly opposed the proposed legislation. Secretary of State George P. Shultz said on June 2 that imposing sanctions on South Africa amounted to "cutting and running" from that nation's troubles. And the State Department, in a June 5 statement to the Foreign Affairs Committee, said sanctions "will hold back efforts to promote early and peaceful transition to a genuine, non-racial democracy."

With tensions escalating in anticipation of hostilities surrounding the 10th anniversary June 16 of riots in the black township of Soweto, the Pretoria government on June 12 declared a nationwide state of emergency. Hundreds of antiapartheid activists were detained in the wide-ranging action.

Adding to the international pressure on South Africa was a report issued June 11 by the "Eminent Persons Group" composed of seven representatives of British Commonwealth countries. While stopping short of recommending economic sanctions, the group said such a course might be the only way to avoid "what could be the worst blood bath since World War II."

Reagan officials, however, continued to resist increased economic sanctions while reacting to Pretoria's action. Reagan, in a June 13 statement, said he had "communicated" with President Botha "to ensure that he and his government are aware of my deep feelings" about allowing nonviolent dissent. The same day, Shultz criticized the state of emergency and urged Pretoria to negotiate an end to apartheid.

On Capitol Hill, opponents of HR 4868 dismissed the bill as a political attempt to embarrass the White House and a ploy that ultimately would hurt South African blacks by disrupting the economy there.

House Action

The House Foreign Affairs Committee endorsed HR 4868 June 10 on a 27-14 vote.

The committee brushed aside last-minute pleas against the bill by Shultz and Secretary of Commerce Malcolm Baldrige, both of whom sent letters to committee members. Shultz called apartheid a "doomed system" that had "simply become unacceptable to the majority of the South African people." But he also said the sanctions in the House measure would undermine administration efforts to seek changes in South Africa's racial policies. "We do not believe it should be our purpose to harm the South African economy; nor do we believe that such action will hasten the end of apartheid," said Shultz.

A day after the Foreign Affairs action, the Ways and Means Committee approved the bill on a voice vote.

Dellums' Substitute

The House June 18 unexpectedly approved far-reaching sanctions against South Africa during debate of HR 4868, a milder sanctions bill pushed by Democratic leaders. The chamber on a voice vote adopted the tougher substitute offered by Ronald V. Dellums, D-Calif.

Under Dellums' legislation, U.S. firms operating in South Africa would be required to leave within six months of the bill's enactment. Direct investments in South Africa by those companies totaled $1.8 billion in 1984, with another $6.4 billion worth of indirect investments.

The Dellums' bill also would cut off all trade between the United States and South Africa. An exception would be made for strategic minerals from South Africa, such as chromium, when the president certifies to Congress that quantities needed for U.S. military purposes exceed domestic supplies.

Other Dellums provisions would permanently ban the sale of South African Krugerrand gold coins in the United States and deny U.S. landing rights for South African Airways. And the Dellums' substitute would not exempt any companies from economic sanctions.

The unanticipated approval of Dellums' substitute came as a jolting message of congressional opposition to the South African white minority government's policy of apartheid. "This is a vote that will be heard around the world," said Stephen J. Solarz, D-N.Y., a leading advocate of sanctions. He described the House action as "political shock therapy" for the Pretoria government.

William H. Gray III, D-Pa., and other supporters of the milder sanctions bill said they were delighted with the tougher bill, predicting that it would pressure both the Senate and the Reagan administration to consider strong steps against South Africa. Gray was the author of the bill superseded by Dellums' substitute.

The White House responded to the House action by repeating its opposition to economic sanctions against Pretoria. "We believe that legislation of this type would erode our capacity to promote negotiations in South Africa and would likely further separate an already divided society," said White House spokesman Larry Speakes. He said the administration would continue "active diplomacy" to achieve changes.

The House-passed bill prompted a sharp denunciation from Pretoria. "It is clear that the American House of Representatives do not give a fig for the black communities of South Africa," said Foreign Minister Roelof F. (Pik) Botha.

Conservative House Republicans opposed to sanctions insisted that approval of the Dellums package could doom approval of any bill. They reasoned that the Senate would not go along with the House, reducing the chances that the two chambers would be able to agree on a bill. If Congress produced a bill, opponents were hoping for a presidential veto.

"Dellums' bill is a lemon. Frankly, it's the kiss of death," said Mark D. Siljander, R-Mich., a leading opponent of South African sanctions. A key Senate source agreed that House Republicans "laid a little bit of a political trap" in handling the Dellums' measure, saying that approval of the milder Gray bill would have put more pressure on the Senate to follow suit.

As part of their strategy, Republican House members did not request a recorded vote on the Dellums substitute, paving the way for its uncontested approval. That decision was made after opponents of sanctions realized that the Gray bill would likely have passed by an overwhelming margin.

None of the Republican leaders was on the floor, leaving the last-minute quarterbacking to Siljander and a few other sanctions opponents. The Democrats "didn't call for a vote, and we just let it go through," said Dan Burton, R-Ind.

Reagan Address

President Reagan on July 22 hastened, rather than blunted, the drive for sanctions by delivering a speech staunchly defending his use of friendly persuasion to coax reforms from the white-minority government in Pretoria. Reagan's address, delivered at the White House, was his first devoted exclusively to South Africa. Although Reagan, largely in response to congressional criticism, had made several comments about apartheid since late 1984, he had never publicly addressed the full range of issues concerning South Africa.

The speech contained some of the toughest language Reagan has used against apartheid, calling it "morally wrong and politically unacceptable." He did not, however, directly criticize the Pretoria government. Instead, he praised reforms instituted by the government as a sign of "dramatic change."

Reagan repeated past calls for more changes, including setting a timetable for eliminating apartheid laws, freeing imprisoned ANC leader Nelson Mandela, legalizing all black political movements, and beginning a dialogue between the government and black leaders.

But the major thrust of Reagan's comments was aimed at Congress, not South Africa. Much of the speech was devoted to denunciations of sanctions, descriptions of the strategic and economic importance of South Africa, and a defense of his past policy. In perhaps the key section of the speech, Reagan called on Congress "to resist this emotional clamor for punitive sanctions. If Congress imposes sanctions, it would destroy America's flexibility, discard our diplomatic leverage, and deepen the crisis."

As originally conceived by Senate GOP leaders and some Reagan aides, the speech was to cap an intensive policy "review" by announcing new initiatives to prod the Pretoria government and reassure blacks of U.S. concern. Shultz, according to administration and congressional sources, advocated making some concessions to Capitol Hill in hopes of delaying or heading off sanctions legislation. But White House chief of staff Donald T. Regan and communications director Patrick J. Buchanan argued, successfully, for an approach basically defending Reagan's past policy.

Reagan made one symbolic concession to Capitol Hill, dropping the term "constructive engagement" as the official description of his policy. Reagan avoided the term, which had come to symbolize the friendly aspect of U.S. policy toward Pretoria, and a senior administration official told reporters he had been told not to use it.

Lugar called Reagan's decision to drop that title "an advance."

Reaction to Speech

Reagan's speech satisfied few members of the intended audiences, either on Capitol Hill or in South Africa. Among the few were white leaders in Pretoria, who were reported to be jubilant about the president's strong stand against sanctions.

In Congress, most Republicans expressed disappointment in the speech, which they had hoped would make a stronger denunciation of the South African government and take a more conciliatory line on imposing sanctions. Nancy Landon Kassebaum, R-Kan., chairman of the Foreign Relations Subcommittee on African Affairs, said the speech "gave no new direction to our policies toward South Africa and, perhaps most importantly, offered no renewed vigor in our pursuit of peaceful change there."

In expressing their dismay, however, the Republicans generally divorced Reagan personally from his policies, complaining about the contents of the speech and not about the attitude of the man who delivered it. One exception was Lugar, who said that "I hold the president responsible" for the policies. Lugar said he had hoped Reagan would use the speech to deliver "an extraordinary message to the world. He did not do so."

Some Republicans endorsed the president's approach, among them Larry Pressler, R-S.D., a Foreign Relations Committee member who had supported sanctions in 1985. Pressler said he had since traveled to South Africa and had come to believe that sanctions would be "counterproductive."

Democrats, with few exceptions, condemned the speech as a reiteration of a "failed" policy.

In an official response televised two hours after Reagan talked, Representative Gray said Reagan "condemns apartheid, but he refuses to back it with meaningful action." The Reagan administration, he said, was more interested in South Africa's "mineral wealth" than in that country's people.

Gray stressed the importance of the United States taking a clear stand on the side of blacks and other nonwhites in South Africa. "In the eyes of that country's majority, our nation is firmly aligned with the most oppressive system on earth," he said. "That is not good for America."

In South Africa, reaction to Reagan's stance fell along predictable lines, with most black leaders venting anger and dismay and the white government expressing relief. Desmond Tutu, who gradually adopted a more combative stance, said he found Reagan's speech to be "nauseating." Tutu told one interviewer: "Your president is the pits as far as blacks are concerned."

Reagan was backed, however, by one moderate black leader whom U.S. officials attempted to court: Zulu Chief Gatsha Buthelezi. He said Reagan was pursuing "realistic strategies."

The government-run television network in South Africa ran Reagan's full speech, and government officials praised its tone and content.

Shultz Testimony

Attempting to calm the furor, Shultz went before Foreign Relations on July 23 and defended Reagan's policy while smoothing some of the rough edges in the speech. For example, he hinted that the administration was open to a "mix" of actions and he took a more conciliatory stance than Reagan toward the African National Congress.

Shultz also insisted that there was a "broad bipartisan agreement on the guts of the matter" — that the United States wanted majority rule in South Africa. But he acknowledged differences over how it was to be achieved.

Shultz offered a detailed explanation of the argument against punitive sanctions, concentrating on their political and economic ineffectiveness. Pretoria was "sanctioning itself" by its repression and other actions that were convincing foreign firms to leave, Shultz said. The flight of business was sending "a deeper message" than would government sanctions, he added. Instead of looking for sanctions, Shultz argued, the

United States should be using "positive measures," such as boosting ties with black leaders and improving transportation links in neighboring black countries.

Shultz' explanations failed to satisfy most members, including Kassebaum, who called his reasoning "convoluted."

The emotional and political climax of the hearing was a sharp exchange between Shultz and Joseph R. Biden, Jr., D-Del. The senator defended Bishop Tutu's bitter reaction to the Reagan speech, saying, "Mr. Secretary, I'm amazed Bishop Tutu was as restrained as he was." Shultz responded that Tutu's statement was "nuts," and then the two men shouted at each other for nearly 10 minutes. At one point, Shultz accused Biden of "calling for violence" — a charge that Biden rejected by saying he was "ashamed of the lack of moral backbone" in Reagan's policy.

The key actor in the Senate for passage of a South Africa sanctions bill was Foreign Relations Committee chairman Richard G. Lugar, R-Ind.

Senate Action

As debate heated up in the Senate, there was general agreement that some form of sanctions bill stronger than Reagan wanted would be passed. "A large majority of senators would like to take some action on South Africa," Lugar said. "They would like to cast a vote that indicates their unhappiness." That unhappiness, he added, was with both the situation in South Africa and Reagan's response to it.

Other sources said senators up for election in 1986 were especially anxious to demonstrate to black voters that they cared about South Africa.

The Foreign Relations Committee August 1 adopted its South Africa bill (S 2701) by a 15-2 vote. Based largely on a proposal by committee chairman Lugar, the bill would impose several sanctions targeted at the white government in South Africa and demand steps toward dismantling of apartheid. The bill also would suggest stronger sanctions in one year if South Africa did not take significant actions to eliminate apartheid.

The bipartisan committee vote was a sharp rebuke to Reagan. Because of Reagan's stand, Lugar and other committee leaders stressed the need for a bill that could pass the Senate with at least a two-thirds vote. That figure did not "come out of the air," Lugar said, because it is the margin necessary to override a presidential veto. "If we are serious about legislation, we will look for what will have the most support," Lugar told his colleagues as they started work.

In the eyes of some senators, the South African government threw away its last chance to avoid sanctions on July 29, when President Botha rejected a plea by the European Community for changes. After meeting with British foreign secretary Sir Geoffrey Howe, Botha assailed outside pressure on his country. Howe, representing the European Community, had asked Botha to release ANC leader Mandela and to begin negotiations with that group.

"I can never commit suicide by accepting threats and prescriptions from outside forces and hand South Africa over to communist forces in disguise," Botha said.

Howe's mission was widely seen as a last-ditch effort by leading European nations to coax positive action out of South Africa and thereby avoid having to impose sanctions.

Breaking with Reagan, the Senate August 15 overwhelmingly passed HR 4868 to impose strict sanctions against South Africa. The vote was 84-14; all "no" votes were by Republicans.

Following are the major provisions of the Senate-passed South Africa sanctions bill.

Policy Goals

The bill set two kinds of policy goals for South Africa: immediate objectives, such as the lifting of the current state of emergency, and long-term, broader objectives, including the creation of a "non-racial democratic form of government."

The immediate goals of the bill were to encourage the South African government to:

- Suspend the state of emergency imposed in June 1986 and respect the principle of equal justice under law for citizens of all races.
- Release from prison ANC leader Nelson Mandela and his colleagues, black trade union leaders, and all political prisoners. While outlawed, the ANC is one of the most prominent black opposition groups in South Africa.
- Allow all South African citizens to form political parties, freely express political opinions, and participate in the political process.
- Establish a timetable for eliminating apartheid.
- Negotiate with representatives of all races for a new political system.
- End military and paramilitary actions aimed at neighboring countries.

The bill also calls on the ANC, the Pan African Congress, and their affiliates to: suspend "terrorist activities" so that negotiations would be possible with the government and other black groups, commit to a "free and democratic post-apartheid South Africa," and agree to enter into negotiations for the "peaceful solution" of that country's problems.

The bill supported the right of the ANC and other groups to negotiate with the government, but said the United States would withdraw that support if the South African government took certain steps and the ANC did not. The United States would back negotiations excluding the ANC and related groups, the bill said, if Pretoria agreed to negotiations without preconditions, abandoned "unprovoked violence" against its opponents, and committed itself to a free and democratic postapartheid South Africa — and if the black groups refused to abandon unprovoked violence during negotiations and refused to commit themselves to a free and democratic postapartheid South Africa.

The bill also called on the ANC to "strongly condemn and take effective action" against "necklacing," in which black militants place burning, gasoline-filled tires around the necks and legs of blacks suspected of cooperating with the government.

For the long term, the bill called for the establishment of a full-fledged democracy and the dismantling of apartheid, but it did not establish specific criteria for judging implementation of those goals. For example, it did not call for any particular political system, such as one-man, one-vote representation.

Sanctions

The bill imposed several new sanctions and directed the president to take other steps. It:

• Required the president, within 10 days of enactment, to direct the Transportation Department to prohibit any South African-owned airline (South African Airways) from operating in the United States, and required the secretary of state to terminate a 1947 air travel agreement between the two countries. It also prohibited U.S. airliners from taking off and landing in South Africa.

• Prohibited importation into the United States of articles produced by South African government-owned or -controlled organizations, called "parastatals." Strategic minerals would be exempt from the import ban, however, if the president certified to Congress that the amounts of those minerals produced in the United States were inadequate for military needs.

• Banned the importation of these specific items from South Africa: textiles, uranium and uranium ore, iron and steel, coal and agricultural products.

• Barred new U.S. loans to South African businesses, the Pretoria government, or any entity it controls, and forbade U.S. firms from making any new investments in South Africa. The ban on new investments, however, did not apply to firms owned by black South Africans. The ban also did not apply to renewals of existing loans, to short-term financings such as letters of credit, or to reinvestments by U.S. firms of profits earned in South Africa on their current investments.

• Prohibited U.S. banks from accepting deposits by any South African government agency, except for one account maintained in the United States for diplomatic and consular purposes.

• Prohibited exports to South Africa of crude oil and petroleum products.

• Barred the export to South Africa of any items on the official U.S. list of munitions (primarily weapons and military items), except for items that the president certified would be used solely for commercial purposes and not for use by the South African armed forces, police, or other security forces. The president must notify Congress 30 days before allowing such sales, giving Congress time to pass a joint resolution rejecting them.

• Prohibited U.S. government agencies from engaging in any form of cooperation, directly or indirectly, with the South African armed forces. The only exception was for activities "reasonably designed to facilitate the necessary collection of intelligence" — and those activities must be reported in advance to Congress, which has no formal power to stop them.

• Prohibited importation of sugar and sugar-related products from South Africa, and transferred South Africa's portion of the U.S. sugar import quota to the Philippines.

• Terminated immediately a 1946 U.S.-South African treaty intended to prevent businesses from paying taxes on the same income to both countries. Other U.S. laws, however, would continue tax deductions or credits to American individuals or companies in South Africa.

• Prohibited U.S. government agencies from contracting with or buying items from South African government-owned firms, except for those necessary for diplomatic purposes. U.S. agencies were urged to buy from black-owned businesses in South Africa.

• Prohibited use of U.S. government funds to promote tourism in South Africa or to promote or subsidize trade with that country. However, another provision authorized the secretary of agriculture to use U.S. subsidy and loan programs to encourage agricultural exports to South Africa.

• Stated that U.S. policy would be to impose more sanctions if South Africa did not make "substantial progress" toward ending apartheid in a year.

If the president determined, after a year, that substantial progress had not been made, he must recommend additional sanctions, such as: barring all South Africans from holding U.S. bank accounts, banning importation of South African diamonds and strategic minerals, and halting military aid to any country that supplied arms to South Africa. The last provision could affect Israel, which reportedly sold weapons to Pretoria in the past. Israel denied selling arms to South Africa in recent years, but to determine the facts, the bill required the president to report to Congress within 180 days on which countries were violating a U.N. arms embargo against South Africa.

- Established the following penalties for violations of the sanctions: a fine of up to $1 million for businesses and a fine of up to $50,000 and/or imprisonment of up to five years for individuals. Anyone guilty of importing the South African gold coins called Krugerrands could be fined up to five times the value of the coins involved.

The bill also declared that any action by foreign companies to take advantage of the U.S. sanctions would be considered an "unfair trade practice," potentially triggering retaliation by the administration.

The bill included two provisions encouraging other nations to act against South Africa. The most important required the president to begin negotiations with other countries toward an international agreement on sanctions and to report to Congress within 180 days on the results of his efforts. If the president reached such an agreement, he could modify the sanctions imposed by the bill to reflect the agreement — but only if he reported the agreement to Congress and Congress within 30 days passed a joint resolution approving his action.

Many of the sanctions in the bill were similar to those adopted by the British Commonwealth on August 4. The bill stated the sense of Congress that the U.N. Security Council should impose the same sanctions as the United States.

The bill also could have the effect of overturning state and local antiapartheid laws, such as those barring contracts to companies doing business in South Africa.

Lifting Sanctions

All sanctions imposed by the bill would be ended if the president reported to Congress that the South African government had done five things: freed ANC chief Mandela and all persons persecuted for their political beliefs or detained without trial; repealed the state of emergency and released all persons detained under it; legalized democratic political parties and permitted all South Africans to join political parties, to express political opinions, and to participate in the political process; repealed the Group Areas Act and the Population Registration Act, which restrict where nonwhites live and work, and did not institute other measures with the same purposes; and agreed to enter into good-faith negotiations with "truly representative" black leaders without preconditions.

The president also could suspend or modify any of the sanctions in the bill 30 days after reporting to Congress that Pretoria had released Mandela and the political prisoners, had taken three of the other four actions, and had made "substantial progress" toward dismantling apartheid and establishing a nonracial democracy. Congress could overturn the president's decision by passing a joint resolution within the 30 days.

Another provision allowed the president, acting on his own, to lift any of the sanctions against South Africa after six months if he reported to Congress that the sanctions would increase U.S. dependence for coal and strategic minerals on communist countries belonging to the Council for Mutual Economic Assistance, which included the Soviet Union, its East European allies, and Cuba.

The president could act if he found that U.S. dependence on communist countries for any of those materials

Black militants in South Africa place burning, gasoline-filled tires around the necks and legs of blacks suspected of cooperating with the government. The practice is known as "necklacing."

would increase over the average annual imports during 1981-85.

Reagan's Executive Order

The bill put into permanent law all of the sanctions that President Reagan imposed on South Africa in his September 9, 1985, executive order. Those were bans on:

- The importation of Krugerrands.
- The importation into the United States of arms, ammunition, or military vehicles made in South Africa.
- The export of computers, computer software, and related items to South Africa for use by government agencies and the government's weapons industries.
- Loans by U.S. banks or companies to the government of South Africa or any organization it controlled. Exempted were loans for educational, housing, or health facilities that were accessible to persons of all races.
- The export to South Africa of nuclear power equipment and supplies, except those needed for "humanitarian" purposes or, if South Africa commits itself to international standards, to reduce the spread of nuclear arms.

Aid to Blacks

The bill reaffirmed the U.S. commitment to help "the victims of apartheid" through direct financial aid and other efforts.

The bill authorized $40 million annually, beginning in fiscal 1987, for economic aid to disadvantaged South Africans, regardless of race. Of that amount, up to $3 million each year would be provided for training of trade unionists in organizing and other union-related skills. None of the funds could be provided to organizations financed or controlled by the South African government.

Another section of the bill authorized $4 million annually for scholarships for victims of apartheid. The bill also authorized $10 million for the purchase of housing for black South African employees of the U.S. government.

An additional $1.5 million annually was allocated for the State Department's human rights fund, which supported activities by rights groups in South Africa. Individuals or groups involved in necklacing could not receive aid.

U.S. firms employing more than 25 persons in South Africa would be required to adhere to the labor code formulated by the Rev. Leon Sullivan of Philadelphia. Under the code, companies were obliged to practice nondiscrimination and to provide housing, education, and other benefits for disadvantaged workers.

Other Provisions

In other provisions, the bill:

- Banned the importation of Soviet gold coins.
- Required the attorney general to report to Congress, within 180 days, on actual and alleged violations of the Foreign Agents Registration Act by representatives of governments or opposition groups in southern Africa, including the African National Congress. The foreign agents act required those lobbying in Washington on behalf of foreign governments or groups to register with the Justice Department. The attorney general also was to report on the status of any investigations into such violations.

Final Action

When Congress returned to work after its August recess, Lugar played a high-stakes game of hardball to force the House to accept the Senate's sanctions bill.

First, he warned that there was not enough time in the short September session for a conference committee to meet and resolve the two measures, and then for Congress to thwart a presidential veto. If Congress had failed to act before the very end of its session, Reagan could kill the bill by a pocket veto. Congress had a target adjournment date of October 3.

When House leaders — especially leaders of the Black Caucus — continued to resist, Lugar played his ace, appointing only two senators other than himself to serve on a potential conference committee: Jesse Helms, R-N.C., and Claiborne Pell, D-R.I. Lugar and Helms said they would refuse to accept any changes in the Senate bill, thus making a conference useless.

House leaders, including the Black Caucus, gave in to Lugar's pressure on September 10.

Two days later the House overwhelmingly passed and sent to the White House the version of the South Africa sanctions bill approved by the Senate in August. The 308-77 vote was more than enough to override a threatened White House veto. Backing the measure were 218 Democrats and 90 Republicans, while four Democrats and 73 Republicans opposed it.

Lugar insisted he would urge Reagan to sign it. If Reagan vetoes it, Lugar said: "I plan to support the override" in Congress — even if the president imposed his own sanctions by executive order to head off legislation.

State and Local Conflicts

As House leaders debated whether to accept the Senate bill or to insist on a conference, the issue of preemption of state and local laws arose as the surprise stumbling block. Most members of Congress had paid little attention to the question until press reports suggested that the Senate bill would wipe out scores of antiapartheid laws, possibly including a California measure forcing the sale of all state-owned investments in businesses working in South Africa.

During Senate action on the bill, Lugar had insisted that the measure would preempt state and local laws. The bill did so, he said, by "occupying the field," of U.S. policy toward South Africa. That interpretation was reinforced by the Senate's rejection of an amendment allowing state and local governments to maintain their antiapartheid laws. The Senate included a provision barring the federal government, for 90 days after enactment of the bill, from withholding funds for contracts to which any state or local government had applied an antiapartheid law.

House Democrats strongly rejected that interpretation, saying they did not want passage of a federal antiapartheid law to bar state and local governments from taking their own actions. Members of the Black Caucus said they would refuse to go along with adoption of the Senate bill if Lugar's preemption interpretation held.

As a compromise, leaders of the House Foreign Affairs Committee drafted a procedure under which the House would accompany passage of the Senate bill with a statement rejecting Lugar's interpretation of the issue. In a highly unusual move, that statement was included in the rule (H Res 548) governing House consideration of the bill. The House adopted the rule, and thus the preemption statement, on a vote of 292-92.

The statement said that "it is not the intent of the House of Representatives that the bill limit, pre-empt or affect, in any fashion, the authority" of state and local governments "to restrict or otherwise regulate any financial or commercial activity respecting South Africa."

The net effect, according to House and Senate sources, was to create confusion about the intent of Congress on the preemption, leaving a resolution to the courts.

Loopholes

Another last-minute issue that needed to be resolved between the House and Senate was whether the bill's ban on new bank loans and investments in South Africa contained major loopholes.

One important provision of the Senate-passed bill was a ban on new bank loans to South Africa and on new investments by Americans in businesses there. Although that ban largely reaffirmed what already was happening in the marketplace because of instability in South Africa, the ban was seen as significant because it could help deprive Pretoria for years of much-needed foreign exchange.

The Senate bill contained three exemptions to the ban, however: It permitted continued short-term trade credits for South African purchases of American goods, it permitted U.S. firms to reinvest in South Africa profits earned there, and it allowed American firms to make new investments if needed to allow their South African branches to operate in an "economically sound manner."

House leaders insisted those exemptions undermined the thrust of the bans on new investments and loans, and they argued that a conference meeting was necessary to narrow those exceptions. But Lugar insisted that the three exceptions were narrowly drawn and would permit only limited amounts of new U.S. capital to enter South Africa.

As part of an agreement under which the House accepted the Senate bill, Lugar inserted an explanation in the September 11 *Congressional Record* aimed at limiting the impact of the exemptions.

Veto and Veto Override

President Reagan on September 26 vetoed HR 4868. He said sanctions would be counterproductive, hurting the black majority in South Africa rather than the white-minority government.

Reagan decided not to accompany his veto with an executive order imposing his own sanctions. Such a course had been under consideration to help swing votes in the Senate to sustain a veto. But the president's veto message instead contained veiled hints that Reagan could be willing to issue such an executive order if Congress sustained his veto.

Reagan's veto had been expected ever since the House approved the Senate's sanctions bill. White House officials had said the president would attempt to kill the bill because of his longstanding opposition to sanctions against friendly governments. Officials also said Reagan saw the legislation as an unwarranted congressional intrusion into his foreign policy-making powers.

What was unexpected was Reagan's decision not to accompany his veto with an executive order incorporating many of the sanctions originally reported by the Senate Foreign Relations Committee. White House lobbyists carried a draft executive order to Capitol Hill on September 25 and told Senate leaders Reagan likely would sign it. Later that day, White House communiations director Buchanan said Reagan would not issue an order — indicating a split among the president's top aides.

Elbowing aside a president uncharacteristically resistant to compromise, the Senate on October 2, 1986, overrode Reagan's veto. The 78-21 vote enacted the bill into law (PL 99-440).

The House had acted on September 29, voting to override Reagan's veto 313-83. Reagan's aides did not lobby House members on the issue and made only limited efforts to block action in the Republican-controlled Senate.

Although fundamentally altering a major U.S. policy, the veto override was not expected to have a long-term effect on Reagan's ability to handle foreign affairs. There was widespread agreement on Capitol Hill that South Africa represented a special case in which Reagan was so out of step with the American public that Congress had no choice but to intervene.

"We believe the president was not being heard loud and clear" in his opposition to South Africa's apartheid system of racial discrimination, said Lugar. With passage of the bill, he said, "We're going to make sure we are all heard with one voice."

Reagan readily accepted the congressional action and promised to implement the law. In a statement issued by the White House after the vote, Reagan said the debate between himself and Congress "was not whether to oppose apartheid but, instead, how best to oppose it and how best to bring freedom to that troubled country." Nevertheless, Reagan insisted he had been correct in opposing sanctions because "they hurt the very people they are intended to help."

Not surprisingly, the white minority government of South Africa was not so receptive to the message from Capitol Hill. Foreign Minister Pik Botha said the United States and other countries should "leave us alone." Congress acted "regardless of our reform program, and no reason or argument could stop this emotional wave," he said.

Administration Efforts

In spite of the seriousness of the issue, the administration never pulled out all the stops to support the veto in the Senate. Reagan telephoned and met with several senators, and the State Department dispatched its senior black official — Alan L. Keyes, assistant secretary of state for international organizations — to the Capitol.

Reagan also took two steps to demonstrate his concern about South Africa: On September 29 he sent congressional leaders a letter promising to sign an executive order with limited sanctions if the veto was sustained, and the next day he named Edward Perkins, a senior black Foreign Service officer, as the new U.S. ambassador to Pretoria. Perkins replaces Herman W. Nickel, who served in South Africa since 1982.

In spite of those symbolic steps, one lobbyist said the vote was "never winnable" for the president, and so the administration decided not to use up valuable political capital on it.

The administration also made only feeble efforts to link the vote to Reagan's upcoming "presummit" meeting in Iceland with Soviet leader Mikhail S. Gorbachev. Talking to undecided Republicans on September 30, Secretary of State Shultz noted that Reagan would need congressional support for his sessions in Iceland. But most senators said the surprise announcement of the Iceland meeting had little effect on the vote because South Africa would not be on the superpower agenda.

Perhaps the most telling indication of the administration's willingness to accept the veto override was the proffered executive order. Its suggested sanctions were substantially weaker than draft proposals that White House lobbyists had floated on Capitol Hill in advance of the veto.

Reagan also got little productive help from his allies on Capitol Hill. While supporting the veto, Dole made only a faint stab at winning the vote. And Lugar, the man to whom most senators would turn for advice on foreign affairs, actively opposed Reagan.

The two senators who spent the most time supporting the veto carried little political clout with their colleagues: Helms and Pressler. In repeated speeches, they warned that sanctions would not force change in South Africa's racial policies and would instead strengthen the hand of radical black groups. "The thrust of this legislation is to bring about violence and revolutionary change and, after that, everlasting tyranny," Helms said.

Botha's Lobbying

The night before the Senate vote to override, Lugar and Helms exchanged charges about Helms' involvement in the lobbying of two farm-state senators by South African foreign minister Botha.

Lugar learned the afternoon of October 1 that Botha had told Sens. Edward Zorinsky, D-Neb., and Charles E. Grassley, R-Iowa, that South Africa would retaliate against sanctions by refusing to buy U.S. farm goods and by barring shipment of those products to neighboring black states whose transportation links were controlled by Pretoria. Lugar also said Botha had promised increased South African grain purchases from the United States if Reagan's veto was sustained.

Botha had telephoned Helms at the Senate Republican cloakroom; Helms then invited Zorinsky and Grassley to the telephone.

One provision of the sanctions bill barred U.S. imports of agricultural products from South Africa. Lugar and other senators long had warned that the provision likely would provoke retaliation by South Africa.

Lugar angrily charged that Botha's calls were "despicable" and amounted to "foreign bribery and intimidation to change the votes of members of the United States Senate. It is an affront to the decency of the American people." Further, Lugar said, Helms' involvement in the Botha lobbying effort was "inappropriate."

Helms immediately defended his actions and those of Botha, who he said had been a friend for 10 years. "Methinks Mr. Lugar doth protest too much," Helms said. "I think Ed Zorinsky was entitled to know that the farmers of America will be shot in the foot by Dick Lugar and Ted Kennedy and the others."

Foreign Minister Botha defended his lobbying and called "absolutely laughable" Lugar's complaints. He told reporters in Johannesburg: "If you rob us of our markets, we have to look out after the interests of our farmers."

After the Senate voted, Dole and others discounted the effect of Botha's lobbying, noting that Zorinsky and Grassley supported the veto override. "I don't think it made much of a difference," Dole said. "It's no big deal."

Tax Reform

On October 22, 1986, President Reagan signed into law the most significant rewrite of the federal tax code since 1942. The Tax Reform Act of 1986 (HR 3838 — PL 99-514), which was the product of more than two years' work by Congress, the Treasury Department, and the White House, dramatically reduced income tax rates for corporations and individuals and curtailed or eliminated dozens of tax breaks.

The House version, modeled after a sweeping tax-overhaul plan proposed by Reagan in May 1985, passed by voice vote in December 1985 after overcoming a Republican rebellion that threatened to kill the bill at the last minute. Only Reagan's personal appeal salvaged enough GOP support to keep the process alive.

The Senate Finance Committee started writing a bill that would have expanded the list of special tax breaks. In early May 1986, however, Chairman Bob Packwood, R-Ore., junked that version and pushed through his committee a bill that so radically cut both rates and tax breaks that it passed the Senate on a vote of 97-3 on June 24.

The conference bill reduced rates almost as much as the Senate version and considerably more than the House version. It also curtailed or eliminated more business breaks than the Senate bill and more individual breaks than the House bill. The House adopted the conference report September 25, and the Senate followed suit two days later. *(Changes in Major Provisions of the Tax Code Made by the Tax Reform Act of 1986, box, p. 162)*

From life insurance agencies, oil companies, and real estate firms to labor unions, churches, and charities, interest groups of every stripe fought to protect favorite deductions, exemptions, and credits under attack in the various tax plans proposed. Following are some of the major items that provided the liveliest encounters between tax reformers and the special interest lobbyists.

Capital Gains

"Money that is made by money should be taxed the same as money that is made by work," said George McGovern, the liberal Democratic candidate for president, in 1972. A proposal to tax capital gains at the same rates as ordinary income, ending a differential treatment that had been in the law, in one form or another, since 1921, received much attention during consideration of the tax-overhaul plan.

Treasury officials said that the difference in rates was one of the main sources of the complexity in the tax code they wanted to eliminate.

Backers of the preferential tax claimed that investment soared as a result of capital gains tax cuts enacted in 1978 and 1981. Rep. Ed Zschau, R, who represented California's "Silicon Valley," the center of high-tech industry in the West, said that since capital gains tax rates were cut, venture capital available to start up new firms rose from about $50 million a year to more than $4 billion a year. Some economists, however, questioned whether there was a relation between the two.

Opponents of the proposal said it would stifle investment, especially in risky new ventures, and mean the loss of hundreds of thousands of jobs. A coalition of industry groups, led by the American Council for Capital Formation, released a statement on capital gains revision warning that "it would be counterproductive to shut down this vital engine of economic growth."

The capital gains tax break also was generally popular on Capitol Hill. It is used not only by individual taxpayers but also by a broad cross-section of businesses, especially new high-technology firms that require large quantities of start-up capital. Favorable capital gains treatment makes it easier for such firms to attract investors. Of all the business tax breaks threatened in the tax bill, capital gains would be among the easist to defend, lobbyists believed, because it was not just a "big business issue."

The Senate Finance Committee in May 1986 reported a tax overhaul bill that would tax capital gains at the same rates as ordinary income. Committee chairman Packwood convinced his committee there was no need to keep the lower capital gains tax because the committee's bill cut the top individual tax rate to 27 percent.

All except one member of the coalition of industry groups vowed to continue the fight to get and preserve favored tax treatment of capital gains — the American Electronics Association (AEA). AEA decided to support the Finance Committee bill, rather than try to amend it on the Senate floor.

Part of the reason was the inclusion in the bill of some other things that AEA members wanted, according to Kenneth Hagerty, AEA's vice president for government operations. Among them were some proexport provisions and retention of the tax credit for research and development.

The problem of giving potentially too much of the tax relief to upper-income persons also caused the electronics group to stop working for a capital gains amendment in the Senate. Hagerty saw no way the Senate could restore the existing tax treatment of capital gains and keep the distribution of the measure's overall tax cut for individuals to any politically acceptable pattern.

"The architecture of the Senate committee bill makes the capital gains increase a load-bearing wall" for the distribution of the tax cut among income groups, he said. This was not the case in the House-passed bill, which kept the wealthy from getting a politically unacceptable share by imposing a tax rate of 38 percent on incomes above $144,000 (for a married couple.)

State and Local Taxes

The proposal to abolish the federal deduction for state and local taxes, which permits taxpayers to subtract the amount they paid in state and local taxes from their income that is subject to federal taxes, became one of the hottest issues to emerge in the debate over reforming the tax code.

The tax changes took on such importance because of the increasing reliance by state and local governments on federal tax breaks. Such indirect assistance made up about one-third of all federal aid to state and local governments in fiscal 1982, compared with one-fifth of federal aid in 1978, according to Helen F. Ladd, a specialist in state and local finance at Harvard University's John F. Kennedy School of Government.

A November 16, 1984, study by the Congressional Research Service (CRS) estimated that elimination of the state and local tax deduction could eventually result in a 15.5 percent decrease in revenues for state and local governments.

Supporting the Deduction

Most of the opposition to eliminating the deduction was generated in high-tax states such as New York, California, and Minnesota, where taxpayers would be hurt most. A host of state and local government organizations — including the National Association of Counties, the National Governors' Association, the National League of Cities, the National Conference of State Legislatures, the U.S. Conference of Mayors, the Council of State Governments, and the International City Management Association — opposed repeal of the deduction, as did labor unions that represented public sector employees. The unions were afraid that if state and local governments had to reduce their budgets, their members would lose jobs. Teachers' unions also were interested in keeping the deduction. Greg Humphrey, legislative director for the American Federation of Teachers, AFL-CIO, asserted that education would be especially hard hit because it was financed predominantly through state and local taxes. Elimination of the tax deduction could make it harder to obtain necessary tax increases, he said, because citizens would vote them down.

State and local officials argued that the deduction was necessary to allow them to keep taxes high enough to finance crucial government services. They said taxpayers who itemize are more willing to pay high state and local taxes if they know they get a federal tax break. For example, a $1,000 local tax bill would cost a taxpayer in the 40 percent tax bracket only $600. The rest would be subsidized indirectly by the federal government, which allows the taxpayer to deduct the $1,000 local payment from his taxable income.

The deduction also lessened the difference between tax burdens in high-tax and low-tax states, according to John Shannon, a senior fellow with the Advisory Commission on Intergovernmental Relations (ACIR), a bipartisan commission appointed by Congress and the president to monitor relations between federal, state, and local governments. "The most immediate effect [of its elimination] would be that upper-income people, who are the most footloose and fancy-free, would find it more advantageous to move to a state that is not quite as hard on the upper incomes," said Shannon.

That was one of the biggest fears of New York officials. They worried they would be forced to trim taxes to prevent taxpayer flight at a time when the federal government was cutting direct aid and turning over to state and local governments more responsibility for social programs. In a 1984 memo to other members of the New York delegation, Sen. Daniel Patrick Moynihan, D-N.Y., wrote that, without the deduction, the pressure to cut state spending for education, law enforcement, and prisons would be "enormous."

Nine of the 13 states that benefit the most from the deductibility of state and local sales, property, and income taxes — and would have the most to lose from its elimination — are in the Frost Belt, according to 1982 tax figures compiled by ACIR. The nine are: New York, Michigan, Maryland, Wisconsin, Minnesota, Massachusetts, New Jersey, Delaware, and Rhode Island.

The administration argued that the deduction forces taxpayers in low-tax states and those who do not itemize to subsidize wealthy taxpayers in high-tax states. Repre-

Changes in Major Provisions of Tax Code . . .

	Existing Law	HR 3838 (PL 99-514)
Individual tax rates	11-50 percent (14 brackets)	15 and 28 percent (lower rate phased out for high-income taxpayers)
Corporate tax rates	15-40 percent on first $100,000 of income; 46 percent thereafter	15-30 percent up to $75,000; 34 percent above $75,000
Capital gains	60 percent exclusion; top effective rate of 20 percent	Special exclusion repealed; taxed at same rates as regular income
Minimum tax	20 percent "alternative" minimum tax imposed on individuals who greatly limit their tax liability through tax breaks; 15 percent "add-on" minimum tax for corporations that use tax breaks to reduce their liability greatly	Increase the rate on the individual minimum tax to 21 percent and revise it to tax more so-called preferences; retain the 20 percent corporate minimum tax and redesign it to include more preferences, basing the tax on "book income" to include many firms that escape taxation
Personal exemption	$1,080 (1986)	$2,000 by 1989 for most taxpayers (exemption phased out for high-income taxpayers)
State and local taxes	Deductible	Income, real estate, and personal property taxes deductible; sales taxes not deductible
Charitable donations	Deductible	Full deductions for itemizers; none for nonitemizers; appreciated value of charitable gifts subject to minimum tax
Interest deductions	Deductions for home mortgage and nonbusiness interest	Unlimited deduction for mortgages on first and second residences; limits on mortgage borrowing for unrelated purposes;

sentatives of the Frost Belt region denied this is so. They noted that according to CRS, taxpayers in many high-tax states send more money to Washington than they get back in the form of federal outlays for grants and other aid. New Yorkers, for example, received only 92 cents in federal outlays in 1984 for every dollar they paid in taxes; New Jersey, another high-tax state, received only 70 cents.

"We know our region's balance of payments will deteriorate even further if the deduction for non-business state and local taxes is repealed," Frank Horton, R-N.Y., cochairman of the House's Northeast-Midwest Congressional Caucus, told the House Ways and Means Committee. "Of the new revenues generated by repeal," he said, "57

. . . Made by the Tax Reform Act of 1986

	Existing Law	HR 3838 (PL 99-514)
		no consumer interest deduction; interest paid on borrowing to produce investment income deductible equal to the value of the earnings
Retirement benefits	Tax-deductible Individual Retirement Account (IRA) contributions of $2,000 for each worker and $200 for each nonworking spouse; employer-sponsored 401(k) tax-exempt savings plans with maximum contributions of $30,000 annually	Limit tax-exempt IRA contributions to persons not covered by pension plans or those below specified income levels; restrict 401(k) contributions to $7,000 annually; make sweeping changes in private pensions to improve coverage and restrict benefits for high-income persons
Investment tax credit	6-10 percent	Repealed retroactively to January 1, 1986
Depreciation	Recovery periods of 3-19 years with accelerated write-off	Retain system of rapid write-offs similar to existing law; permit larger write-offs for most property, but over longer periods
Business expenses	Deductible	Deduction of 80 percent of business meals and entertainment costs; miscellaneous employee business expenses limited
Tax-exempt bonds	Bonds earning tax-free interest allowed for governmental and many nongovernmental purposes, such as sports arenas and mortgages	Cap use of nongovernmental bonds, exclude charitable organizations from the cap; some interest subject to minimum tax

SOURCES: Treasury Department, House Ways and Means Committee, Senate Finance Committee, Joint Committee on Taxation

percent will come from taxpayers in the Northeast and Midwest, which [have] 44 percent of the nation's population."

Argument for Elimination

The federal deduction for state and local taxes costs the federal government more than $30 billion a year. The Treasury Department argued that the deduction provided an unfair subsidy to high-income taxpayers who itemize their deductions, especially those in high-tax states. For example, in New York, the average taxpayer who itemizes would get a $1,133 federal tax break from the deduction in 1984, compared with $205 for the average itemizing taxpayer in Wyoming, where taxes are lowest.

In addition, the administration pointed out, 70 percent of taxpayers do not itemize and get no advantage from the deduction. The cost of the deduction "is borne by all taxpayers in the form of significantly higher" tax rates, the administration said. Democratic governor Bruce Babbitt of Arizona, where the average taxpayer who itemizes would get a $410 tax break from the deduction, said the federal government should not subsidize other levels of government through the tax code, but that states should pay their own way.

The administration also held that for individuals, the deductibility of state and local taxes provided a relatively small tax break. On the other hand, it costs the federal government a great deal of revenue. By repealing the state and local tax deduction, the Treasury would gain $34 billion in annual revenue by 1988.

Charitable Contributions

Perhaps no other provision in the tax code affects as many different taxpayers and organizations as one that permits deductions of contributions to charities and educational and religious institutions. Not surprisingly, it was relatively easy for charitable groups to mobilize a lobbying assault on a proposal to limit charitable deductions.

"To view charitable deductions as a loophole, we feel, is just not right," said Steve Delfin, public relations director at the United Way's national headquarters in Alexandria, Va. In 1984, the United Way's 2,200 local fund-raising operations around the country raised an estimated $2.1 billion that in turn was distributed to 37,000 separate charities.

Charity groups feared that taxpayers would cut back on donations without the charitable deduction, crippling their budgets. The United Way joined with Independent Sector, an association of 600 nonprofit groups, philanthropies, and corporations, in a letter-writing campaign aimed both at the White House and Capitol Hill.

Lou Garcia, who heads the United Way in California, used a slide show to lay out the case for retaining charitable deductions. The Board of Supervisors in Orange County — home to some of Ronald Reagan's most loyal supporters — responded by sending a resolution to the White House that urged rejection of the charity restriction.

Aides in several congressional offices reported large amounts of mail from constituents opposed to limits on charitable deductions. Many of them came from clergymen, worried that gifts to their churches would dwindle without tax incentives. Among the affected was the Rev. Jerry Falwell, a close political ally of Reagan, who stood to lose under tax plans that clamped down on charitable contributions. That was because Falwell's Moral Majority (now the Liberty Federation) lobbying group, though not tax-exempt itself, was bolstered by a separate foundation qualified for tax-deductible contributions.

The foundation's $10 million annual budget would be sharply reduced if the tax laws restricted charitable deductions. "We support the basic concept of tax reform but we want to ensure that it doesn't cut us off at the jugular vein," said Roy Jones, Moral Majority's lobbyist in Washington.

Charity advocates also worried that lowering individual tax rates would decrease the tax benefits of charitable deductions. But most charity groups realized the political futility of arguing against lower tax rates, so instead they concentrated on other proposals they considered harmful.

Of great concern was the suggestion that only those taxpayers who itemize on their returns be permitted to deduct charitable contributions. The 1981 Economic Recovery Tax Act (PL 97-34) allowed nonitemizeres to deduct charitable gifts, a provision that expired in 1987. Independent

Sector estimated that repealing the nonitemizer provision would cut $5.5 billion out of the $65.7 billion that Americans were expected to give to charity in 1986.

Numbers such as those, along with the argument that charitable deductions should not be available only to wealthier taxpayers who itemize, helped to generate sympathy among congressional tax writers.

"If you are going to encourage [charitable] giving at the top, you should also encourage giving at the bottom," Packwood said at a Senate Finance Committee hearing that focused on the effect of tax reform on charitable gifts.

Some groups that benefit from gifts of stock, artwork, and other items whose value appreciates over time, opposed a provision that could make such donations less attractive.

Under a part of the president's plan calling for a minimum tax to be paid by corporations and wealthy individuals, taxpayers would no longer be able to deduct the full current market value of items donated to charity when figuring out their minimum tax. For example, the founder of a successful company who contributes personally held stock in the firm would have his deduction limited to the original value of the stock, although it might be worth much more.

Museums and universities were particularly concerned because they benefited the most from large gifts designed to boost their endowment funds, finance new construction, or add to their collections. "You can't walk on the Stanford [University] campus without walking into something built by Hewlett-Packard stock," said Jack Moskowitz, a United Way official in Washington. David Packard, who began the California electronics firm, has been one of Stanford's major benefactors.

When Independent Sector's government relations committee met to discuss strategy on the tax bill, three or four members questioned the political wisdom of making the appreciated property issue a high priority. The committee members argued that fighting the issue would give the appearance of favoring only the wealthiest of taxpayers.

Rep. Bill Frenzel, R-Minn., agreed that the property issue could be a hard sale to make politically. But he also noted that studies showed a hefty amount of charitable giving coming from relatively few wealthy contributors.

Real Estate Industry

The real estate industry, which relied on tax breaks to lure customers and investors, had few positive things to say about President Reagan's tax plan, which threatened to eliminate many of those advantages. Industry officials said that without tax incentives, the cost of housing would increase and construction would decline, damaging the economy and especially harming the poor.

Although Reagan's proposals would preserve the homeowner's deduction for mortgage interest on a principal residence, it would eliminate the deduction for property taxes, end tax-exempt financing of below-market mortgages, and limit deductions for mortgage interest on second homes. Also, it would curb incentives for investing in real estate, such as stretching from 18 to 28 years the period over which a developer could deduct depreciation allowances and ending the favorable capital gains treatment for the sale of investment or business properties. Reagan also would eliminate several tax breaks used by developers of multifamily dwellings, such as the tax credit for rehabilitation of historic structures.

Without the tax incentives, industry groups said, investors would steer their money away from housing, which would slow housing construction, lower property values, and raise rents. That, they added, would harm the economy because real estate, directly and indirectly, generates about a third of the gross national product.

Hardest hit, industry spokesmen said, would be low-income families. Investors put funds into housing for the poor not for the limited rental income but for the tax advantages.

The Fairness Issue

Real estate officials complained that ending tax incentives for housing was unfair because the tax plan retained incentives for other types of investment, such as stocks and bonds, oil and gas drilling, and high-technology industries.

Rep. Dan Rostenkowski, D-Ill., chairman of the House Ways and Means Committee, said the elimination of various deductions and credits was intended to ensure that everyone paid his fair share of taxes. "Many people believe the real estate industry uses tax shelters to avoid paying taxes," he said. One goal in designing a tax bill, he said, would be to ensure that "tax avoidance is curtailed."

Although Reagan's proposal to eliminate the deduction for state and local taxes drew several members to their defense, real estate breaks had few vocal champions on Capitol Hill. "What you are seeing is an amateurish, unsophisticated pleading for tax subsidies," said Rep. Fortney H. "Pete" Stark, D-Calif., after a Ways and Means hearing. "They are not making economic or business sense. It's simply a request for a handout."

Industry spokesmen said they hoped to convince Congress that the public wanted to preserve the tax advantages that help housing.

Effect of the Plan

In a July 8, 1985, report, the National Association of Home Builders concluded that the loss of tax benefits targeted by Reagan would reduce single-family construction by 95,000 units in the first year after enactment.

Multifamily housing would be restricted even more, it said, with construction dropping by 230,000 units, chiefly because of the loss of tax-exempt financing for multifamily housing and deductions encouraging investment in apartments. The report predicted that rents would increase by between 21 and 28 percent for most apartment projects to make up for the loss of tax advantages. Property values for existing apartments would decline by as much as 25 percent because they would be less attractive to investors.

Supporters of low-income housing predicted even more dire consequences for the poor. They pointed out that direct federal spending on subsidized housing had declined from $30 billion a year to $11 billion since 1980 and private affordable housing for the poor was in short supply.

The effect, advocacy groups said, would be to wipe out gains poor families would make from other provisions of the tax plan, such as an increase in the personal exemption.

Critics of the tax breaks questioned the industry's doom-saying. Others said the tax advantages accorded real estate distorted the market.

Single-Family Breaks

The two-thirds of Americans who own their own homes could deduct from taxable income the amount of interest they paid on their mortgage, as well as what they paid in property taxes. In addition, many benefited from other tax advantages, such as tax-free bonds that resulted in below-market rate mortgages for first-time home buyers.

The Reagan plan threatened those breaks. It would retain the mortgage interest deduction for principal residences, the most widely used tax break for housing, but would reduce its value. Under the old tax code, the deduction for a family in the top bracket paying $1,000 a month in interest was worth $6,000 a year; if the top rate were lowered from 50 percent to 35 percent, as Reagan proposed, the deduction for the same family would be worth $4,200.

In addition, Reagan would limit mortgage interest deductions on second homes to $10,000 above net investment income from all sources, including income from interest, dividends, royalties, and limited partnerships. The cap would fall to $5,000 by 1996. That change could depress the market for new vacation homes. The home builders predicted that the current level of new starts of second homes of between 75,000 and 100,000 a year would drop by 20,000.

Eliminating the deduction for property taxes would add $400 a year to the after-tax cost of owning a typical home, discouraging purchasers and lowering property values, according to David D. Roberts, president of the National Association of Realtors.

The loss of tax-exempt mortgage bonds would close an avenue used by many moderate-income families to buy their first homes. In 1984, Congress reauthorized the use of such bonds, which are sold by state and local governments to investors, who accept a lower interest rate because income is exempt from taxation. Proceeds from the sale are funneled into home mortgage funds, which because of the low interest rate can result in mortgages at about 2 percentage points below the market rate.

In 1984, the home builders said, 246,000 families used mortgage revenue bond financing, about one-sixth of all first-time home buyers.

Rental Housing

Industry analysts predicted a more serious impact on multifamily housing, particularly for the poor. However, the revenue impact of the changes was relatively small. According to the Joint Committee on Taxation, historic rehabilitation, accelerated depreciation, tax-exempt financing, and low-income rehabilitation credits would cost the Treasury $4.8 billion in fiscal 1986, compared with the $37.3 billion cost of the mortgage interest and property tax deductions.

In recent years, much multifamily housing had been built with capital from participants in real estate syndicates, many of whom had invested not to earn income but to use tax losses generated from real estate investment to defer or reduce taxes on income that they have gained from other sources. Investors gain tax benefits by deducting losses from initial expenses, such as construction, before income from rents or the sale of property was generated. Also, profit from the sale of real estate and other property was taxed at the favorable capital gains rate, which in the top tax bracket amounted to an effective rate of 20 percent.

In addition, unlike other investors, real estate investors could claim losses from debt exceeding the amount for which they were personally liable, or placed "at risk." And they could claim a special tax credit for expenses incurred in the rehabilitation of structures certified as historic by the National Park Service.

Housing for low-income families received greater advantages. Developers of low-income projects could write off the cost of buildings or rehabilitation at a faster rate — 15 years, compared with 18 years for other rental housing. Also, low-income developers could deduct immediately the cost of interest and taxes on construction equipment and materials.

Proposed Changes

The proposal would change all of that, dramatically altering the way developers raise money. "Collectively," according to the home builders group, "these proposed changes would transform rental housing from a relatively favored status to a situation of relative disfavor, compared with other types of capital investment. The proposal would not only eliminate all distinctions between rental housing and other types of structures, but would also eliminate distinctions between low-income rental housing and rental housing in general."

The proposal would stretch to 28 years the period over which all investors could write off the cost of buildings, thereby reducing the amount of depreciation they could deduct each year. However, Reagan would index the value of the property to inflation, meaning that over 28 years, the total value of depreciation could be worth more than under existing law.

In addition, Reagan would eliminate the favorable capital gains rate of taxation for income-producing property, meaning that the profit from the sale of depreciable property held for business or investment purposes would be taxed as regular income. The administration argued that the inflation adjustment for depreciation could make up for the additional taxation on property sales.

And Reagan would eliminate the "at risk" exception for real estate.

His tax plan also would kill a provision that allowed developers to write off, over five years, expenses for rehabilitation of low-income apartments and eliminated the 25 percent credit available for rehabilitation of historic structures, which mayors and developers claimed had contributed to the revitalization of older cities.

Low-Income Housing

Developers of low-income projects testified that they could not attract investors without the lure of tax breaks. Without that capital, either they would have to charge more in rent or the project would not go forward.

Michael A. Liberty, a 24-year-old developer of low-income rural projects in Maine, told the Senate Finance Committee that his fledgling company had developed 1,000 housing units. "And what has made this possible?" he asked. "The sale of limited partnerships to private investors — something we'd be hard-pressed to accomplish under the tax proposal Congress is considering."

A developer of low-income projects in Chicago, Andrew Ditton of the Local Initiatives Support Coalition, outlined how the tax changes would affect one of his projects. The building, with 114 residential units and eight commercial units, cost $3.3 million, and he estimated he could charge $305 a month in rent for one-bedroom apartments and $400 a month for a two-bedroom unit.

To finance the project, the coalition raised $923,294 from limited partners, who Ditton said would not put up capital if Reagan's tax plan were enacted. Without that money, he said he would have to charge $378 a month for a one-bedroom apartment and $478 a month for two-bedroom units, rents higher than the market rate in the area and affordable only to families with incomes close to $20,000.

Reaction to House Bill

Officials from the real estate industry won some victories when the House Ways and Means Committee restored several tax benefits for real estate customers and investors that Reagan had sought to eliminate. Nevertheless, industry officials opposed the overall Ways and Means tax plan, because they say it would make their industry worse off than under existing law.

A spokesman for the National Association of Realtors called the Ways and Means plan "anti-savings and anti-investment," arguing that by lowering individual tax rates and raising taxes on business, the plan would shift capital away from investment and toward consumption.

The Ways and Means proposal would stretch out from 19 to 30 years the length of time an investor could write off the cost of buildings. Industry groups said that lengthening the depreciation period would reduce incentives for investing in real estate.

A further disincentive, the industry argued, was the committee's proposed minimum tax of 25 percent. This would cut into the ability of some investors to shelter their income from taxation by putting their money into projects that earn little or no income.

Advocates of low-income housing, while acknowledging that the committee directed several tax breaks to developers of projects for the poor, also said that they would oppose the bill.

Even while expressing opposition to the Ways and Means plan, industry groups acknowledged that the committee was more generous to real estate investment than Reagan. Ways and Means restored the current deduction on mortgage interest for second homes, which Reagan would have

Lobbyists lined up outside the House Ways and Means Committee meeting room, waiting for hearings on the tax overhaul plan to begin.

limited. Also, the panel preserved the current deduction for state and local taxes, including property taxes, which Reagan would have eliminated.

In addition, the panel restored several tax breaks for investors in multifamily housing. Reagan would have allowed investors to deduct from taxable income losses from an investment only to the extent that their investment was "at risk"; the committee, however, largely preserved existing law and exempted most real estate transactions from that limit.

The committee bill would also continue existing law and allow proceeds from the sale of real estate to be taxed at the more favorable capital gains rate, and would continue to allow states and cities to issue tax-exempt bonds to finance real estate development. Reagan would have eliminated those advantages.

Senate Consideration

Upon Senate Finance Committee approval of the tax bill May 7, 1986, industry groups largely came together in opposition to certain of its features that were aimed at scaling back tax benefits long enjoyed by those engaged in real estate sales and development. Scores of real estate agents and home builders visited congressional offices to complain, and leaders of trade groups sharpened the focus on what in the legislation required mending, and how the repair work could be accomplished.

But the industry did not joined hands on the crucial question of how to balance proposals to restore tax preferences while finding alternative ways to raise lost revenue. It was expected that amendments that would lose money would not be allowed on the Senate floor. Only those "revenue-neutral" amendments that balanced money-losing changes with additional revenue would be in order.

Most industry leaders acknowledged that offsetting revenues would have to come from within the industry — that the real estate sector could not credibly call for new taxes on outside sources.

'Passive Loss' Provision

The provision of the Senate Finance package that created the most concern in industry circles was the so-called "passive loss" limitation, which was intended to make it much more difficult for wealthy individuals to avoid paying taxes by sheltering their income with the aid of "paper" losses.

The Finance bill would effectively eliminate the tax advantages of the limited partnership, in which an investor makes contributions — or promises to make contributions over time — to a project in which he plays no active management role. Real estate projects tend to create tax-deductible losses in their early years and the losses are doled out to the limited partners in proportion to their stakes. Under existing law, the investor is permitted to count this "passive" or "paper" loss as a deduction against income sources not related to real estate, such as wages. Since losses often greatly exceed the limited partner's investment, the shelter becomes very attractive.

The Finance bill set up a five-year schedule for eliminating this deduction. Deduction of 65 percent of passive losses would be allowed in 1987; 40 percent would be allowed in 1988; 20 percent in 1989; 10 percent in 1990; and none in 1991 and thereafter. In less sweeping fashion, the passive loss limitation also applied to taxpayers actively involved in the management of rental property. These individuals, if their overall income was less than $100,000, would be able to deduct no more than $25,000 in real estate losses against their other income. The deduction would be progressively less generous for those earning more than $100,000 and would be totally eliminated for those earning $150,000 or more.

It would be unfair, many in the industry said, to apply new rules "retroactively" to investors who put up their money when the rules were dramatically different, and expected to reap benefits sometime into the future. They also said it was unfair to lump active participants in the same category as limited partners. It would be one thing to deny a deduction to the doctor who invested in a limited partnership; it would be quite another to say the operator of some other business could not take a loss on the rental housing project that he recently purchased.

Financial Institutions

Some officials said the passive loss limitation would threaten the stability of projects that had secured financing from banks on the basis of pledges of future capital contributions from limited partners. If the sum of the pledge was greater than the amount an investor could expect to save in taxes under the new rules, this reasoning went, there would be an incentive for the investor not to honor the promise. Furthermore, some in the industry said the stability of financial institutions could be threatened if their portfolios were heavily weighted with loans to real estate partnerships that were dependent on future contributions from limited partners.

Concern about defaults was particularly acute among developers of projects containing low-income housing units, whose trade group representatives in Washington said tax shelters offer virtually the only reason for investment in a project. Also alarmed, however, were the syndicators of deals involving shopping centers, luxury and moderate-income apartment complexes, and commercial office space.

Other objections to the Finance Committee bill included the lengthening by nearly 10 years of the depreciation recovery periods for rental residential structures and more than 10 years for commercial property; a shift to a less generous method of calculating depreciation; and the repeal of the capital gains exclusion.

No one accused the real estate industry of not trying to amplify its concerns. The National Association of Realtors, which was holding its annual meeting in Washington, D.C., sent 32 Greyhound busloads of real estate brokers to Capitol Hill May 13, 1986, just six days after the Finance Committee action. Some 40 members of the Kentucky Board of Realtors filed into the office of Sen. Wendell H. Ford, D-Ky., for example, and told the senator that the bill was the worst the industry had seen in 50 years. Ford said he was sympathetic with their concerns but noted the problem of finding new revenue to pay for money-losing changes to the Finance package.

The National Realty Committee used the occasion of a long-scheduled appointment May 13 with Paul A. Volcker, chairman of the Federal Reserve Board, to press home its point that the passive loss limitation could jeopardize the stability of financial institutions. Volcker had no comment, but reports of the complaints appeared in the *Wall Street Journal*.

A United Front

Industry leaders said they thought they could get more done when the bill came up for consideration on the Senate floor if they presented a united front. "We'd like to go in as a group," says Floyd L. Williams, tax counsel for the National Association of Home Builders.

The focal point for the effort to coordinate strategy was the Joint Real Estate Tax Committee, an informal alliance of the principal trade groups based in Washington. The committee met May 16 in the offices of Edward C. Maeder, who represented the International Council of Shopping Centers and was a partner in the law firm of Winston & Strawn.

The group resolved to write lawmakers citing common concerns and possible solutions, but not alternatives for making up lost revenues.

One revenue-raising idea discussed in industry circles was a "transfer tax" that would be paid to the federal government upon the sale of a development. Another was a "vintage" rule that would increase the permissible passive loss deductions for investors who have already pledged future capital contributions and cut them for those who have paid all their pledges and those who enter into such deals during the phase-in period.

But industry officials said it was doubtful that much money could be squeezed from the vintage approach, and it was a certainty that Realtors would vigorously oppose a transfer tax, since increasing the sales costs would likely cut down on the volume of sales and thereby reduce brokers' fees.

Efforts to develop a united front also were handicapped by support from some segments of the industry for the Finance bill and problems enlisting the aid of other industries that could have been expected to share real estate's concerns. For example, the American Bankers Association, which represents some 15,000 banks, favored the committee bill.

Anthony Downs, a senior fellow at the Brookings Institution, said he talked to a number of developers who felt the legislation was "a good thing for the country and a good thing for themselves." According to Downs, some developers calculated that the bill would serve to ease the glut of commercial office space and stabilize prices by decreasing the attraction of tax shelters and other real estate investments. An official of the National Association of Industrial and Office Parks said developers who are not personally dependent on income from nonreal estate sources, or on capital contributions from investors outside the real estate business, did not feel threatened by the bill.

House-Senate Conference

The real estate industry viewed the House-Senate conference on the tax bill with a mixture of hope and fear. The principal lobbying groups met with little success in trying to modify the crackdown on tax shelters imposed by the Senate and were not confident that things would go better in conference.

"We're facing a steamroller," said Edward C. Maeder, Washington representative of the International Council of Shopping Centers and coordinator of the Joint Real Estate Tax Committee, an alliance of major trade groups. Lawmakers "have a lot of momentum, and [tax reform] is apparently an idea whose time has come."

Notwithstanding the opposition of many trade groups, some in the industry vocally supported the blend of lower tax rates and sweeping restrictions on shelters. "A lot of people are saying that, in the end, our industry is dependent on the national economy . . . and what's good for the national economy is good for real estate," said J. Thomas Black, staff vice president for the Urban Land Institute, a nonprofit research and educational organization.

Trade groups appealed to conferees with much the same arguments they advanced against the Senate package. The reason those arguments made little headway, industry leaders said, was not that they lacked merit but that members had pledged not to make major floor amendments.

Individual Retirement Accounts

"We're hearing a lot from constituents," said Senate Finance Committee member John H. Chafee, R-R.I., during consideration of the tax overhaul bill. "What are they saying? They've got IRAs [Individual Retirement Accounts] and they like them."

A surprising wave of voter complaints turned the Senate Finance Committee's proposal to limit the tax deduction for IRAs into a target for change on the Senate floor.

As much as senators heard from voters back home, however, they did not hear from all of the traditional lobbying sources in Washington. The banking and thrift industries, which hold more than $90 billion of the estimated total $200 billion in IRA investments, generally backed off from trying to change the IRA provision on the Senate floor.

The American Bankers Association, representing 15,000 banks, endorsed the Senate bill. Some member banks voiced concerns that the bill would cause a sharp drop in lucrative IRA accounts, but the industry as a whole gave it a low priority. "We're going to lobby *for* this bill," said David Miller of Chase Manhattan Bank. "We're going to leave the IRA alone because we think other things are more important. We may close our eyes and cross our fingers, but we're not going to do anything."

Along with the reduced corporate tax rate, banks and thrifts strongly support another provision in the Finance bill that essentially maintains a deduction for additions to bad-debt reserves in excess of actual losses. The House voted to curtail bad-debt deductions sharply, so financial lobbyists worked hard to keep the Senate bill intact. They wanted some bargaining room when the bill went to a House-Senate conference.

"In a perfect world, we'd like to keep IRAs," said Beth Neese, a lobbyist for the National Council of Savings Institutions. "But we don't want to be in a position of appearing to oppose the bill."

The only visible lobbying effort to restore the IRA deduction was mounted by the mutual fund industry, which controls about $32 billion in IRA assets. The same day the Finance Committee approved its bill, May 7, 1986, the Investment Company Institute, the lobby for mutual funds, placed ads in 79 newspapers threatening, "Someone in Washington wants to kill your IRA." Institute officials said the one-day blitz succeeded greatly in inspiring newspaper stories about the loss of IRAs and in generating thousands of constituent complaints to Congress.

IRA Participation

The Finance panel delivered a broad attack on the so-called tax shelters that many middle- and upper-income taxpayers used to reduce their effective tax rates. Individual Retirement Accounts, among the most widely used shelters, under existing law allowed a worker to deposit up to $2,000 a year ($4,000 on a joint return) into an account of his own choosing and then deduct that amount from his gross income at tax time. Interest on such accounts was earned taxfree, but an IRA owner on retiring and withdrawing from the account would pay tax, though presumably at a low rate.

Congress first authorized IRAs in 1974 for workers not covered by company pension plans. In 1981, as part of a campaign to increase the saving habits of Americans, the tax advantages of IRAs were extended to all workers.

In 1981, the last tax year in which IRAs were limited to individuals not covered by company plans, IRA deductions were claimed on only 3.4 million tax returns. By 1983, IRA contributions were claimed on 13.6 million tax returns, at an average rate of $2,400. By 1985, surveys by various interest groups put the estimated number of IRA participants between 17.3 million and 28 million households — or nearly one-third of all households.

The Employee Benefit Research Institute, a nonprofit organization that worked for pension interests, estimated that only 6.5 million of the 50 million persons not covered by pension plans have opened IRAs. On the other hand, of the 56 million persons covered by pensions, 17.9 million have supplemental IRAs.

Why Deduction Limited

The Senate Finance Committee, for both philosophical and practical reasons, voted to eliminate the deduction for IRA contributions by workers already covered under company pension plans. Panel members cited arguments that IRAs were being used largely by those with incomes above $50,000 a year, and that IRAs have done little to increase the overall savings rate of Americans.

But more compelling for Senate tax writers, staffers said, was the fact of huge revenue losses to the Treasury under current laws governing IRAs. The cost of allowed IRA deductions was about $12 billion a year, which would fall to about $8 billion under the committee bill. By 1990, according to some estimates, the Treasury could recoup about $25 billion if the Finance panel's proposal became law.

Despite the obvious appeal of a big, new revenue source, many senators questioned the political price that could come with removing the IRA deduction. "I've heard from my constituents on this issue more than any other part of the tax bill," Pressler said. "It has struck a raw nerve across the country." An aide to Dodd suggested that an IRA is not so much a tax break for the rich as a treasured privilege of young, upwardly mobile voters. "It's like a barometric reading of having arrived in the middle class," he said.

Full Senate Action

The full Senate decided to limit deductions on IRA contributions, though not on interest earned. Only individuals who had no other pension plan, vested or not, would be able to deduct IRA contributions.

Financial industry lobbyists laid low on IRAs during Senate consideration because they believed they could successfully fight the battle in conference, particularly since the House bill retained most current rules on IRA deductions.

In addition, these observers believed House Democrats, who seemed to have lost their proprietary claim to "tax reform" (after successfully co-opting the issue from the Republican administration), would be looking for a way to regain the political initiative in conference. House Democrats could win that edge by championing IRA deductions, said lobbyists and Senate staff members.

However, the fire surrounding the Senate's debate over IRAs practically disappeared as the tax reform bill neared House-Senate conference. "It's just not as pressing a matter anymore," said a spokesman for Sen. Steven D. Symms, R-Idaho, who previously reported receiving 900 pieces of mail a week from constituents who wanted IRA deductions preserved. "There's still some [constituent] interest, but nothing like before," the spokesman said.

Banks, savings and loan associations, and other financial interests, for which IRAs have been big profit-makers, indicated they could live with a scaled-down version of the IRA tax shelter.

Business Investment

One of the most complicated tax battles was fought over the proposal to eliminate a generous tax break for business investment enacted in the 1981 tax law.

The accelerated cost recovery system (ACRS), which allowed businesses rapid write-offs of their investments in plant and equipment, would be replaced with a less generous depreciation system. In addition, the Treasury plan would eliminate the 10 percent tax credit allowed for new investment, a move expected to raise $147 billion by 1990.

Critics, including a wide range of industries that invested heavily in plant and equipment, charged that the proposals amount to a complete reversal of the tax policies the Reagan administration inaugurated in 1981. Prime movers behind the 1981 tax law, including top Washington tax lobbyist Charls E. Walker, argued that elimination of the tax breaks would cramp the investment they credit for the economic recovery.

Business lobbyists, however, were beset by divisions because the benefits of ACRS and the investment credit had been unevenly distributed among industries. This allowed some heavy industry firms to pay little or no taxes, while providing few benefits to businesses that relied more on people than equipment.

It was these discrepancies that led Treasury to call for elimination of the generous tax breaks. The department noted that some businesses must pay higher taxes to subsidize the tax breaks enjoyed by others. As a result, the proposal pitted capital-intensive firms against those, such as high-tech businesses, that did not benefit much from the 1981 tax law.

Investment Incentives

Many in the Frost Belt feared that proposed changes in tax breaks for business investment would adversely affect capital-intensive industries, predominantly located in the Northeast and Midwest.

On the plus side, the top tax rate on corporate income would be lowered, and the value of depreciable property could be indexed to offset the effects of inflation, allowing larger write-offs over the long run. In addition, companies could deduct from taxable income 10 percent of total dividends paid to shareholders.

But the plan would eliminate a 10 percent tax credit that firms received for investments in certain plant and equipment. It would replace the current "accelerated depreciation" system with one that would stretch out the period over which investments could be written off. And it would impose a controversial "recapture tax" to offset the tax "windfall" the administration said some firms would receive from the combination of lower tax rates in the future and accelerated depreciation of investments made under existing law.

Robert E. Mercer, chairman of The Goodyear Tire and Rubber Co., told the Senate Finance Committee that accelerated depreciation and the investment tax credit were vital to industries such as his that seek

PAC Gifts to Tax Writers

According to a Common Cause study, the debate over tax revision proved a boon for the campaign coffers of members on the congressional tax-writing committees. The citizens' lobbying group reported February 11, 1986, that 1985 political contributions to the 56 members of the House Ways and Means and Senate Finance committees were twice what they had been two years before.

The members received $6.7 million from political action committees (PACs) and $19.8 million in total receipts in 1985, compared with $2.7 million and $9.9 million, respectively, in 1983.

While most committee members denied that contributions influenced their votes on tax law, many recognized the financial benefits they reaped from the tax debate. When the tax bill was on the verge of being blocked from consideration on the House floor in December 1985, one Democrat was overheard suggesting to another that the party prevent a final vote so the bill would remain in limbo for a few more months. "Why kill the goose that laid the golden egg?" he asked.

to modernize to meet foreign competition. "Our concern is that the tax reform proposal under consideration achieves reduced tax rates at the expense of capital investment in the United States," he said. "Any tax reform package which does that will have a negative impact on jobs, economic growth and the ability of the U.S. manufacturing base to compete internationally."

Industry Opposition

While business support for a tax-overhaul measure had always been weak, many business groups refrained from outright opposition as long as they could.

"A lot of companies and a lot of trade associations have been reluctant to dump all over this until they absolutely had to," said Paul Huard, vice president of the National Association of Manufacturers (NAM). "Nobody's wild about the public relations appearances of business groups opposing a bill proposed by a popular president that has the main purpose of lowering tax rates."

But in an effort to influence the House Ways and Means Committee's final decisions on business tax changes, NAM took out a two-page ad in the *Washington Post* November 14, 1985, complaining that the package was "on the wrong track." The ad, endorsed by more than 1,350 firms, charged that proposed tax changes would retard business investments and impair the ability of U.S. companies to compete abroad.

A day earlier, the U.S. Chamber of Commerce held a press conference to announce that its board of directors had voted to oppose the direction the Ways and Means Committee package was taking. The Business Roundtable also released a statement November 14 calling for the committee to drop its tax-rewrite effort.

The Ways and Means draft approved November 23 would repeal the investment credit and provide less generous depreciation and foreign credit provisions. For many, the bill's proposal to reduce the maximum corporate tax rate from 46 percent to 36 percent was sufficient reason for support. For the opponents, in contrast, the lowered tax rate ceiling was less important because existing deductions allowed many manufacturers to slash their tax bills or eliminate them altogether.

Opponents included capital-intensive, heavy manufacturing businesses that were favored under the existing code, with its investment tax credit, accelerated depreciation, and foreign tax credit provisions. Supporters included small businesses and labor-intensive firms in the service, retail, consumer goods, food processing, and high-technology sectors, which tended not to benefit from existing investment incentives and generally paid higher effective tax rates under the existing tax code.

On November 26, the formidable U.S. Chamber of Commerce announced its mobilization to defeat the committee-approved bill after the Chamber's board voted 42-7 against it. Chamber president Richard L. Lesher conceded that small businesses would gain under the bill, but the overall effect of the package, he said, could be to "deindustrialize America." Though the existing tax code was "outmoded and archaic," Lesher said, it was still preferable to the proposed changes.

Noting that the bill would increase business taxes about $141.3 billion over five years, Lesher said the result would be slowed economic growth and "the stagnation we faced prior to 1980."

Allied with the chamber were the NAM and the Business Roundtable. NAM president Alexander B. Trowbridge said in a statement, "While overall rate reduction is welcome, the enormous added costs resulting from changes in the investment tax credit, the depreciation schedules, the international taxation rules and other items pose extremely high risks for the economy."

"You want the suicide rate, huh?" said Jeanne Campbell of the Invest to Compete

Alliance when asked for her group's reaction. Clients included U.S. Steel Corp., General Electric Corp., Boeing Corp., and machine tool and printing equipment companies.

The House bill, she said, had "so whacked the capital-intensive sector, I think they're reeling at this point." For example, Campbell said businesses generally expected the investment tax credit would be changed or phased out gradually, rather than ended abruptly in 1986, and that the minimum corporate tax would be less severe.

Some Support Remained

Meanwhile, other smaller business groups that consistently had backed House Ways and Means Committee chairman Dan Rostenkowski largely based on his commitment to a maximum 35 percent corporate tax rate, remained supportive despite a last-hour increase to 36 percent. Rostenkowski agreed to the change November 23 when his committee voted to continue the tax-free treatment of fringe benefits. The higher corporate rate would provide revenues to offset losses from the fringe benefit decision, in keeping with Rostenkowski's goal that a tax overhaul bill not add to the deficit.

The percentage point increase initially shook supporters. One alliance, the Tax Reform Action Coalition (TRAC), had an endorsement ready for release the night of Ways and Means' final drafting, but pulled it when the top corporate rate went to 36 percent. But after a November 26 meeting, the group, whose members included 250 businesses and associations ranging from small retailers and wholesalers to IBM Corp. and General Motors Corp., reiterated its support in a letter to Reagan.

Nick Calio, vice president for government relations of the National Association of Wholesaler-Distributors and another TRAC ally, said, "While elements of the package hurt our industry, the committee, by significantly reducing marginal tax rates, has provided across-the-board benefits for small and large businesses which cannot be duplicated by the parochial preferences which flaw the current code.

"For our industry, the corporate rate structure and the numerous provisions designed specifically to help small business will mean greater retained earnings and greater growth. This will benefit the economy."

However, two of TRAC's founding groups, the National Federation of Independent Business (NFIB) and the American Business Conference, had such problems with the bill that they decided to work apart from TRAC to seek improvements. Neither group, however, was so opposed that members wanted to join the Chamber forces against the entire bill.

The NFIB's unhappiness was somewhat surprising given the bill's generally favorable impact on the small businesses that NFIB represents. And spokesman Jim Weidman acknowledged that the bill was a major improvement over the president's package.

But various provisions, including the toughened minimum tax on individuals, could affect small-business owners adversely, Weidman said. Many of NFIB's members were individual entrepreneurs who were not in high business tax brackets, so the bill's reduction in the maximum corporate tax rate was less important to them than it was to most TRAC members, he said.

Weidman said NFIB had some concern that if investment declines, as big businesses claim it would under the bill, then small businesses that supply the major firms would be hurt, too. Also, he said, the group was disappointed in the bill's complexity.

Jack Albertine, president of the American Business Conference, said his group was "profoundly lukewarm" about the tax bill and, as a result, "we're not part of TRAC at the moment." The group had hoped Ways and Means would retain investment incentives and soften the impact of minimum taxes.

Albertine, referring to the Chamber, said he "disagreed with the notion the bill is a disaster for the economy." But, he added, the bill would shift the tax burden to businesses to an extent that, by 1991, they would be paying a share of taxes comparable to the 1981 rate, before Reagan's economic program of tax cuts was enacted.

The CEO Tax Group, a coalition whose 19 members included executives of J. C. Penney Co. Inc., TRW Inc., and General Foods Corp., released a statement applauding Ways and Means for reducing tax rates "without sacrificing revenues and increasing the deficit."

"Investment decisions appropriately will be based on economic rather than tax consequences and will build a solid foundation for sustained economic growth," the group said. Beneficial's Perkinson, a spokesman for the CEO Tax Group, said its membership was not eroded at all by Ways and Means' final actions.

Entertainment

Baseball, hockey, basketball, and football executives visited Capitol Hill to lobby against a part of Reagan's proposed tax overhaul plan that would end business deductions of tickets to sporting events as entertainment expenses. Others affected by the president's plan, including theaters, symphony orchestras, restaurants, and hotels, were afraid that the proposal to end entertainment deductions and limit deductions for business meals would threaten their financial health.

The Treasury Department estimated that proposals to limit meal and entertainment deductions would yield $6.9 billion in added tax revenues from individuals and corporations over a five-year period.

Some legislators expressed general agreement with the argument advanced by sports teams and others that business support was needed to keep ticket costs to entertainment events down for individuals. At the same time, other lawmakers questioned the fairness of permitting tax deductions for business dining and entertaining while ordinary citizens enjoyed no such advantage.

After a panel of sports executives testified June 26, 1985, before the House Ways and Means Committee, Rep. Beryl Anthony, Jr., D-Ark., said there was a "lot of sympathy" for their concerns among committee members. "Sports are such a strong part of the American fabric . . . that a well-reasoned argument that this [tax deduction] will help the average person afford this kind of entertainment, I think, will be looked upon favorably," Anthony said in a later interview. Still, Anthony said he was not sure that the tax code ought to subsidize "lavish" entertainment expenses, such as leasing or purchasing luxurious skyboxes that are found in many stadiums and arenas.

Some congressional tax writers were more skeptical. Sen. Dave Durenberger, R-Minn., noted that sports team owners already reap sizable tax benefits by depreciating the value of their players.

Businesses that take advantage of entertainment and meal deductions were not very vocal on the proposal to eliminate those deductions. That was largely due to their greater concerns with overall business tax rates, depreciation schedules, and other big-ticket items in the tax overhaul debate.
tax overhaul debate.

But sports officials were adamant about preserving the deduction. "Major-league baseball registers the strongest possible objection to the president's proposal to deny income tax deductions for the purchase by businesses of sports tickets," William Y. Giles, president of the Philadelphia Phillies, told the House Ways and Means Committee.

"The proposal is advanced by the president on grounds of economic efficiency and tax equity. The facts and reasonable analysis demonstrate, however, that the purchase of tickets to baseball games by businesses serves legitimate business purposes and is not subject to tax law abuse," said Giles. He and other sports executives tried to convince Congress that doing away with the business tax deduction would have a "catastrophic" effect on American sports by severely weakening the economic foundations of their teams.

The administration claimed that businesses each year purchase about one-third of all baseball tickets. But baseball commissioner Peter V. Ueberroth said a more accurate figure is 46 percent. The figure is above 50 percent for basketball and about 60 percent for hockey, according to officials at those leagues. These officials argued that ticket prices for ordinary fans would rise if businesses cut back on their ticket purchases.

In the case of the Phillies, Giles told Ways and Means members that he estimated a drop from 17,000 to 10,000 business-held tickets per game under Reagan's plan. That would mean a revenue loss to the team of somewhere between $3 million and $4 million each year.

Still, some lawmakers questioned the economic arguments advanced by baseball and other sports officials. A few complained that the real problem stemmed from the stratospheric salaries now commanded by many professional athletes.

Nonsports Entertainment

Nonsports segments of the entertainment industry also would be touched. About 15 to 20 percent of ticket sales at Broadway theaters are for business-related entertainment, according to theater officials.

"Attending theater with clients and customers is an ordinary and necessary business expense," said Gerald Schoenfeld, chairman of the Shubert Organization Inc., the nation's largest owner of stage theaters.

Opera companies and symphony orchestras worried that they would be hurt, too. In St. Louis, 13 percent of that city's symphony tickets are purchased by companies able to deduct the cost from their taxes.

Representatives from the arts community also were worried about proposed changes in the tax treatment of charitable contributions that could put a squeeze on fund raising by cultural organizations.

The administration's effort to cap deductions for business meals drew howls of protest from the restaurant industry. The National Restaurant Association told legislators that Reagan's proposal to limit the deductibility of business meals could cost 144,000 jobs in the food service industry. That figure came from a study by Chase Econometrics, an economic consulting firm commissioned by the restaurant association. The same study showed that restaurant sales would fall by $3.5 billion in the first year of Reagan's tax plan.

Members Lobby, Too

The lobbying against Reagan's meal and entertainment proposals was not restricted to outside interest groups. Members of Congress from states with sizable tourist industries worried that restaurants, hotels, and convention centers in their states could feel a pinch from the White House tax package.

"We believe this is both bad tax policy as well as being counterproductive to stimulating our economy. We believe it is fair to say that [Reagan] is trading what should be a business decision for a perceived political advantage," Rep. Bill Nelson, D-Fla., told the Ways and Means Committee. Nelson, a member of the Congressional Travel and Tourism Caucus, joined two other caucus members in testifying against the meal and entertainment provisions.

After the House acted to permit 80 percent deductions of business-related entertainment expenses, sports officials, restaurant owners, and others continued to press their case. "Obviously, the NBA [National Basketball Association] would prefer current law, but 80 percent is better than zero," said Kevin O. Faley, a lobbyist representing the NBA. The National Restaurant Association said it would accept nothing less than full deductibility for business meals.

Tax-exempt Bonds

Perhaps of greater concern to many local governments than the federal deduction of state and local taxes was a proposal to eliminate the tax exemption on interest from bonds issued by state and local governments that are used for "nongovernmental" purposes.

While many tax-exempt bonds are used to finance public activities, such as the construction of schools and roads, about half are sold to finance private projects ranging from factories to ski lifts. The Government Finance Officers Association reported that about $240 billion worth of tax-exempt bonds and notes were sold by state and local governments in 1985, up 68 percent from 1984. Of that amount, about $168 billion — or 70 percent — was for industrial development bonds used to promote economic development by private businesses, and the balance went to traditional general obligation or revenue bonds.

Many state and local officials argued that tax-exempt bonds were necessary to promote economic development. Because the interest was exempt from federal taxes, state and local governments could pay lower interest rates on the bonds but still be competitive with higher-paying taxable investments.

The tax exemption does cost the federal government, however. The Treasury was expected to lose about $19.6 billion in revenue in 1985 from tax-exempt bonds. Treasury officials said it was unfair for the average taxpayer to subsidize such bonds when the benefits were passed on to private business.

Some local officials, in fact, backed the plan to eliminate the tax break for private purpose bonds. They argued that the market had been flooded with tax-exempt bonds, driving up the interest that must be paid by state and local governments to finance traditional public projects. But they feared the Treasury, or Congress, would define the bonds still eligible for tax-exemption too narrowly. They said many activities of state and local governments, such as wastewater treatment, were conducted through contracts with private firms that might not be eligible for tax-exempt financing.

Others complained that lowering tax rates for all taxpayers would reduce taxpayer incentive to seek tax-exempt investments. But the administration proposed limiting other tax shelters, making investment in tax-exempt bonds more attractive.

The Public Securities Association, the main trade association for banks and brokerage houses dealing in tax-exempt bonds, waged a major "education" campaign to convince members of Congress that eliminating the tax exemption on interest from bonds issued by state and local governments would mean higher costs for local taxpayers. In addition, the group argued that fewer facilities, such as hospitals and mass transit facilities, would be built.

Banking Industry

The banking industry, like many others, professed strong support for Reagan's plan to overhaul the tax code — but for the concept, not the specifics aimed at it.

Several proposals would significantly change the way banks and savings and loan institutions (S&Ls) operate and compute tax liabilities. Credit unions would pay federal income tax for the first time, a prospect that could mean higher loan rates, lower dividends, and fewer services for more than 40 million customer-members.

Interest groups mobilized to change or kill the objectionable provisions. One, the American Bankers Association (ABA), whose member banks hold 95 percent of all bank assets, followed the example of many other businesses and reached outside for influential help.

The ABA retained lobbyists from the law firm of Manatt, Phelps, Rothenberg & Tunney, whose partners included Charles T. Manatt, former chairman of the Democratic National Committee and president of the California Bankers Association.

Banks and S&Ls opposed Reagan's proposals to limit their special deduction for reserves covering bad loans, to change the period during which they could claim losses for tax benefits, and to repeal the deduction for interest expenses related to tax-exempt obligations. And mortgage lenders and others complained that two provisions would harm the housing industry. One would limit the deduction for interest paid on second-home mortgages and other consumer loans. The second provision would disallow deductions for state and local taxes, including property taxes.

Countering 'Low-Tax Image'

But their greatest challenge was perhaps, in the ABA's words, to rebut "the continuing belief here in Washington that banks do not pay enough taxes." Banks, particularly large ones, generally pay taxes far below the maximum 46 percent corporate rate. In November 1984, the Joint Committee on Taxation reported that big banks it sampled paid an average annual tax of 3.8 percent from 1980 to 1983.

The ABA, however, distributed an industry survey contending that banks pay an effective tax rate of 43 percent if two "indirect taxes" are considered. Those "taxes" represent potential earnings that banks forfeit because of public policy. One such tax is the below-market interest that banks accept for investing in state and city bonds, which ABA called a subsidy to those governments. The other is the interest forgone on funds that banks must post with the Federal Reserve System.

Bad Debt Reserves

For both banks and S&Ls, Reagan would limit the current deduction for adding to a reserve covering bad loans. Over five years, from 1986 to 1990, the change would raise $5.1 billion, the administration said.

Under existing law, banks took tax deductions based on one of two accounting formulas, regardless of actual losses from loans. The administration wanted depository institutions to follow the same rule as other taxpayers: A deduction could be taken only for real losses as they occurred.

The industry said the idea was ill-timed. Federal regulators had been pressuring banks and S&Ls to build larger bad-debt cushions as protection against loan losses, which continued since the inflationary years of the late 1970s and the recession of 1981-82.

"The Treasury's proposals exhibit no consideration whatsoever of the current regulatory or economic environment in which savings institutions exist," W. Dean Cannon, Jr., president of the California League of Savings Institutions, told the House Ways and Means Committee July 26, 1985.

Under existing law, a depository institution was permitted to base deductions either on its past six years' record of loan losses, or on a percentage of outstanding loans.

The administration, in documents accompanying its tax plan, objected, "Because a bad debt reserve for tax purposes involves only bookkeeping entries with no set-aside of assets, the only practical effect of present law is either to increase the after-tax income of depository institutions or to enable depository institutions to offer loans at artificially low rates."

Banks and S&Ls also opposed a related proposal requiring them to count all existing loan-loss reserves as taxable income within 10 years. The administration said the "recapture" of taxes from current reserves would avoid double deductions; without it, amounts already deducted as reserves theoretically could be deducted again when loans actually became worthless.

Tax-exempt Bonds

Both banks and S&Ls would lose a deduction for interest expenses related to buying and carrying tax-exempt bonds. Changing existing law, which allowed a deduction of 80 percent of such expenses, would raise $2.2 billion over five years, the Treasury projected.

Banks' expenses are the cost of borrowing money to make the investments. For instance, if a bank pays 8 percent interest to depositors for use of their money, and earns 7 percent on municipal bonds, it appears to lose money. But, with the deduction for interest expenses, banks generally earn an after-tax profit on tax-exempt bonds, even though such investments offer lower interest rates than corporate obligations.

The administration said the tax break gave banks a competitive advantage over insurance companies, securities dealers, and other businesses that made similar investments without benefit of the deduction.

But Charles W. Wheeler, an ABA tax counsel, said repeal would hurt not only banks but also state and local governments that sell tax-exempt bonds to finance public projects. Banks are second only to individuals as investors in the bonds, holding one-third of those outstanding. If banks lose the deduction, Wheeler said, they would pass on the costs to governments through demands for higher interest on tax-exempt bonds.

Tax on Credit Unions

For the first time in their history, credit unions with assets of $5 million or more would have to pay corporate income taxes, under the president's tax plan. The tax would raise $1.7 billion over five years, the administration estimated.

Though only one out of five of the nation's 18,300 credit unions would be affected, that group holds about 85 percent of the industry's $100 billion in assets and represents more than 40 million of the industry's 52 million member-customers. The Treasury did not propose to revoke the tax exemption for smaller credit unions because, officials said, the administrative burden would be too great.

Credit unions are based on a European notion introduced in the United States early in the nineteenth century, whereby members pool their money to make loans to each other at reasonable rates. In 1937, Congress exempted such nonprofit, volunteer-run, and member-supported entities from federal taxes — a status it reaffirmed several times since.

The administration, however, argued, "Because of their tax exemption, credit unions enjoy a competitive advantage over other financial institutions."

Credit unions said that because they had no profits, any taxes they had to pay from retained earnings would reduce their cushion against losses, restrain expansion, and cost their members through lower dividends, higher interest rates on loans, or new service fees. Traditionally, credit unions have paid slightly higher dividends on savings and charged less for loans than banks and S&Ls.

The Consumer Federation of America

(CFA), which claimed to be the nation's largest consumer group, joined the fight. "As banks and savings and loans withdraw from low- and moderate-income markets, the services provided by credit unions have become even more essential to the consumers other institutions don't want. The proposal to tax credit unions poses a serious threat . . .," Alan Fox, CFA's legislative representative, testified.

In separate hearings of the Senate Banking, Housing, and Urban Affairs Committee and the House Ways and Means Committee in July 1985, members generally expressed Congress's traditional support for the consumer-oriented credit unions. Still, several echoed Senate Banking member Jim Sasser, D-Tenn., who said, "It gets a little bit harder to defend these special dispensations as the credit unions keep getting larger and larger."

Despite the widespread populist support for their institutions, credit union representatives worried. They ran direct-mail campaigns, urging their millions of members to contact Congress. Lobbyists supplied key members with information about the unusual services credit unions in their districts offer.

Energy's Concerns

Energy interests worked hard to preserve several tax breaks relied on heavily, including generous write-offs for "intangible" drilling expenses — such as labor costs — and an allowance for the depletion of natural resources.

The Treasury Department maintained that the breaks distorted investment and unfairly subsidized the energy industry at the expense of other businesses. Department officials also advocated repeal of the windfall profits tax, an excise tax on domestic oil proceeds enacted in 1980.

Industry representatives insisted the special industry tax incentives were needed to attract investors for risky drilling and exploration ventures upon which the industry depended. They claimed that without the tax breaks, investors would put their money elsewhere and the country would become more dependent on foreign energy sources.

"A current misperception is that the petroleum industry does not pay its share of federal taxes and that it is specially favored by tax preferences, tax breaks and loopholes. This notion is dead wrong," Charles J. DiBona, president of the American Petroleum Institute, told the House Ways and Means Committee June 18, 1985. He pointed to a 1984 study by the Joint Committee on Taxation that showed the petroleum industry paying a higher effective tax rate than the national average for large U.S. firms.

DiBona warned that further reductions in tax incentives for oil production and exploration could be devastating in a few years because of growing energy consumption and the nation's reliance on oil imports. The resulting shortages, he said "will make 1973 and 1979 look like a cakewalk."

James L. Stafford, executive director of the Oklahoma-based National Association of Royalty Owners Inc., also told the committee that provisions to phase out the so-called percentage depletion allowance for oil and gas royalty owners would deal a blow to the thousands of farmers and ranchers who invest in wells.

"In our state alone," Stafford said, "royalty owners would pay $210 million in increased taxes by 1990. This would be money siphoned largely from rural areas, and mark another direct hit on the extremely fragile farm economies of our state, Kansas, Texas, Louisiana and Arkansas."

Industry spokesmen admitted the oil business had an image problem. "The general perception of the press and the public has been that the petroleum industry has been awash in money and enjoys great tax breaks," said H. B. "Bud" Scoggins, Jr., general counsel and vice president for governmental relations of the Independent Petroleum Association of America, an independent producers' group.

To counteract this impression, said Scoggins, his group and others flooded the administration, Congress, and the public with materials arguing that elimination of the tax breaks would mean the loss of investment capital and cause serious setbacks for the industry. In the February 1985 *Petroleum Independent*, the group's magazine, oil and gas producers were encouraged to write to Congress and the administration and "when you are sending out those royalty checks [to investors] or paying a supplier's bill, why don't you enclose a note telling them about this tax idea and urging them to write Washington, too."

The industry won key allies at the Energy Department and among members of Congress from such oil states as Texas and Oklahoma. To broaden that support, independent oil producers formed a coalition with many of the more than 100 industries that extract minerals from the land. The coalition included the Independent Petroleum Association of America, the American Petroleum Institute, the American Mining Congress, the National Coal Association, and the Iron and Steel Institute.

Fringe Benefits

A proposal to treat employer-paid benefits — health and life insurance premiums, for example — as taxable income united such disparate forces as business groups and labor unions into a lobbying coalition.

The country's major health and life insurance companies — including Equitable Life and the Blue Cross and Blue Shield Association — pooled their resources in a massive public relations campaign to stir opposition to the taxation of employer-paid benefits.

Insurers worried that they would sell fewer policies if the tax laws were changed, because employers could drop coverage from benefits packages and employees in turn could decide they no longer could afford them.

Shortly after the administration announced the proposal, the American Council of Life Insurance convened a meeting of Washington lobbyists concerned about the tax treatment of fringe benefits. More than 300 showed up.

Joining the campaign against taxing employer-paid benefits were the U.S. Chamber of Commerce, National Association of Manufacturers, the Business Roundtable, and AFL-CIO.

Textile Imports

Arriving in Bangkok, Thailand, in August 1985, members of the House Ways and Means Subcommittee on Trade were greeted by something not usually seen by politicians junketing overseas — a demonstration against legislation that was at the hearing stage in Washington.

The protest by Thai factory workers was directed against a bill to limit clothing imports from countries such as Thailand. While the 99th Congress, increasingly concerned over trade issues, was set to debate comprehensive proposals to attack overall trade problems, it also looked at measures to protect specific industries — of which the textile legislation was the most prominent.

Debate on the issue of textile import restrictions brought about a heavy lobbing campaign waged by textile producers, retailers, and Reagan administration officials.

Background on Textile Industry

Despite the concentration of garment workers in the Northeast, the South dominates the U.S. textile and apparel industry. That supremacy came at the expense of New England, which was a world leader in textiles during most of the nineteenth century. There are important parallels between the demise of the New England textile industry and the current threat foreign competitors pose to the Southern states.

The spinning and weaving of natural fibers into cloth is an ancient craft rooted in utilitarian necessity. Until the industrial revolution began in the eighteenth century, textile making remained largely a cottage industry dependent on hand labor. The industry took hold in New England primarily because of the region's abundance of water power to drive the early textile machinery. Early in the century, workers poured in from the countryside to tend the mill machines. Later, waves of immigrants took their place.

When automation eliminated the need for artisans, many of the jobs went to women and children. Textile manufacturing became an entrepreneurial free-for-all. The first census of manufacturing, conducted in the year 1810, recorded 238 textile mills, including 26 in Rhode Island, 14 in Connecticut, and 54 in Massachusetts. By 1850, 896 mills were in operation in New England.

New England's hold on textiles was broken by the steam engine — a technological advance that made it possible to build a mill almost anywhere. Stationary engines freed textile manufacturers from river geography, and the steam locomotive made it possible to move raw materials and finished products great distances with new efficiency. Once they were no longer dependent on water power, textile manufacturers were free to migrate. And the South offered many powerful incentives. It was the region, as Steve Dunwell described it in *The Run of the Mill,* where "the cotton grows up to the doorsteps of the mills, and supply and demand clasp hands." It also was closer to the Appalachian coal needed to operate steam engines. And, perhaps most importantly, the Civil War had left the South with a surplus of poor whites ready to trade the uncertainties of farming for low-paying factory jobs.

At the same time, labor became an increasingly vexing problem for Northern industrialists. By the end of the nineteenth century, several New England states had passed laws forbidding children under certain ages to work. Other states limited the work day to 10 hours for women and children and prohibited them from working at night. Southern workers had no such protection. Child labor was common. Although New England mill wages were regarded as low, wages in the South were barely half those paid in the North. The wage gap in the two regions continued until the first federal minimum wage law was enacted in 1938. "In the meantime, poor white Southerners gave industrialists in their homeland the advantage that immigrants had given earlier to New England, an abundance of cheap, unskilled and tractable labor," wrote Dunwell.

Northern mill owners responded to the Southern competition by speeding up machines and assigning each worker to more machines. When too many goods were produced, owners placed workers on "short time," reduced workweeks. Labor unrest grew, setting the stage for the beginnings of unionization. The Fall River, Mass., strike of 1904 was a harbinger of things to come. Workers refused to accept a wage cut and were locked out of 85 of the city's mills for six months, throwing 30,000 out of work. Eight years later, organized labor won an important victory in a bitter two-month strike that idled over 23,000 workers in Lawrence, Mass. Management finally gave in to wage increase demands, causing a ripple effect of higher wages throughout New England. Organized labor won other battles in the coming years, but eventually lost the textile industry to the South, where management was unhindered by unions. In the 1880s, four-fifths of the American textile industry was concentrated in New England. Forty years later, the South had surpassed Northern textile production. By the mid-1980s, little was left of the New England textile industry that paced the world for nearly a century. And the South seemed caught in a similar downward spiral in its competition with low-wage foreign textile industries.

Origins of Quotas and Tariffs

The urge to protect the U.S. textile industry from foreign imports dates from 1816 when Congress passed a tariff of 6¼ cents a square yard on English cloth. Manufacturers had asked for a higher duty, arguing that they did not yet have power looms to compete on an equal basis with their English counterparts. Despite the tariff, the English flooded the U.S. market that year, causing a financial crisis for domestic mills.

Restraints on imports from Asian countries date from 1935, when the United States negotiated voluntary import quotas on Japanese cotton products. With the outbreak of World War II, U.S. manufacturers went into high gear to clothe the nation's troops and emerged from the war as the only major undamaged textile industry in the world.

By the end of the eighteenth century, several New England states had passed laws forbidding children under certain ages to work. Other states limited the work day for women and children. Southern workers, however, had no such protection, and child labor was common.

With U.S. aid, however, the Japanese rebuilt their industry and by the mid-1950s had again become a major exporter. As a result of Japanese imports, Congress, in the Agricultural Act of 1956, authorized President Eisenhower to negotiate agriculture and textile import limits with foreign governments. A five-year voluntary quota agreement on Japanese cotton textile products took effect January 1, 1957.

The United States, however, had no similar agreements with Hong Kong, Taiwan, and South Korea, which viewed establishment of a labor-intensive textile industry as essential to their economic development. Between 1958 and 1960, cotton textile imports doubled to just over one billion square yards. In May of 1961, President Kennedy called for a conference of the principal textile importing and exporting nations to develop an international agreement on textile trade. The conference produced the "Short-Term Cotton Textile Arrangement," which restricted cotton trade for one year and created a committee to study long-term solutions. The arrangement was accepted by 16 nations accounting for over 90 percent of the free world's trade in textiles. The Long-Term Arrangement Regarding International Trade in Cotton Textiles, concluded in February 1962, established a framework for participating nations to regulate trade in cotton products. The arrangement was extended in 1967 and 1970, and by 1973 had 82 signatories.

None of these agreements affected the

ever-expanding trade in man-made textiles such as polyester, rayon, and nylon. Imports from developing nations continued to disrupt textile industries in developed nations, prompting the assembly of an international trade council in 1973. The council devised the basis for the Multifiber Arrangement (MFA), formally known as the Arrangement Regarding International Trade in Textiles, which took effect January 1, 1974. Parties to the MFA may limit imports of cotton, wool, and man-made fiber by negotiating bilateral agreements with their trading partners. A major element of the original MFA stipulated that imports must be allowed to grow by a minimum of 6 percent a year, even if growth in domestic consumption is smaller.

The MFA was extended in 1978, 1981, and 1986. Each time more restrictions were added to protect textile industries in developed nations. The first renewal allowed importing countries to negotiate tougher annual growth quotas. Thus two countries, for example, could agree to reduce growth in sweater imports to 2 percent a year.

The MFA renewal in 1981 became entangled in U.S. presidential politics and remains a sore point for manufacturers. At the time, the U.S. textile industry was experiencing the adverse effects of the 1981-82 recession and a simultaneous surge in imports. Growth in the U.S. textile market remained almost flat while imports in MFA-controlled products climbed 18 percent between 1980 and 1981. U.S. manufacturers mounted a campaign for tighter import restrictions and pressed the issue during the 1980 presidential campaign. Candidate Ronald Reagan sent Sen. Strom Thurmond, R-S.C., a letter in September 1980 in which he promised, as president, to "make sure that these [textile] jobs stay in this country. . . . The MFA . . . needs to be strengthened by relating import growth from all sources to domestic market growth. I shall work to achieve that goal." Although the renewed MFA allowed participating countries to negotiate lower imports, U.S. imports grew by 25 percent in 1983 and 32 percent in 1984, putting pressure on Congress to erect protectionist trade barriers.

Free Trade Debate

The debate over protectionism is defined by economic theories first propounded by Scotsman Adam Smith (1723-90) more than two hundred years ago. In theory, free trade works to everyone's advantage because goods are produced and sold at the lowest price. Each nation specializes in products it makes at the lowest cost, those in which it has a "comparative advantage" in international markets. In reality, free trade can cause an array of economic and political problems, especially for developed nations whose basic industries are threatened by low-cost imports. Factories cut back hours or close down, throwing thousands out of work. In the United States foreign competition is hurting not only textiles, but steel, autos, shoes, radios, cameras, farm equipment, shipbuilding, and mining.

While closing the door to imports appears to provide a quick fix for saving American jobs, such protectionism has had disastrous results in the past. It is generally believed that international trade policies of the 1920s contributed to the Great Depression of the following decade. Economists warned against erecting a wall of trade barriers to stem the flood of imports that began after World War I. But Congress enacted several tariff laws anyway, including the Smoot-Hawley Tariff Act of 1930, which raised tariffs on imported durable goods to a record high level of 59 percent by 1932. Other nations reciprocated, throwing the international economy into a downward spiral.

Congress began to ease trade restrictions two years later with passage of the Reciprocal Trade Agreements Act of 1934, which gave the president authority to negotiate trade agreements with individual countries and lower tariffs in return for similar concessions. By 1947 the United States had trade agreements with 29 nations and had reduced duties on 70 percent of all imports. After World War II the United States took the lead in advocating tariff reductions and trade liberalization. In October 1947, the United States and 22 other nations signed the General Agreement on Tariffs and Trade (GATT), which established rules for regulating international trade. Under GATT, numerous trade barriers have fallen and others have been modified.

While the U.S. has been a leader in pushing free trade among nations, it frequently has departed from theory to practice various types of restraints. Protectionism remains politically popular because it tends to protect American jobs with little evident cost to the consumer. But those costs can be considerable. One study estimated that U.S. tariffs and other trade restrictions cost consumers $59 billion in 1980; about $15 billion of that was attributable to tariffs on imported textiles. Adjusted for inflation, the current cost to consumers of trade restraints on textiles is $23 billion a year, Michael C. Munger, author of the study, said.

The Reagan administration consistently defended free trade policies, a position that grew more difficult to maintain politically. Advocates of protectionist legislation contend they simply want "fair trade" to counter the unfair practices of the exporting nations. Many foreign governments subsidize their textile industries either directly or indirectly while erecting barriers to U.S. products. For example, the Indian government in 1980 agreed to subsidize 10 to 15 percent of the cost of producing blended and mixed textile items. The following year, Spain granted $1.42 billion in aid to its textile industry. Japan subsidizes textile research and development, offers large investment tax credits and various tax and depreciation advantages. South Korea, Taiwan, and China are among the nations that impose various types of nontariff barriers on U.S textile products.

Some economists contend that Adam Smith's theories no longer provide an adequate framework for fashioning international trade policies. In the past the colonial system kept nations like India and Indonesia from taking jobs from the West, economist John M. Culbertson wrote in *The Dangers of "Free Trade."* Political ideology prevented nations like China from competing significantly in international markets. But the end of colonialism and the relaxation of ideological restraints changed the world economic situation. Nations now have access to the same technology and factory management techniques. As a result, "areas and workers that in the past would have been quite incapable of posing a competitive threat to high-wage Western workers are now able to engage in wage-competition with Western workers on equal terms," Culbertson wrote. "That is a revolutionary change in the shape of the world."

Congressional Action on Textile Import Bill

Anti-import textile legislation (HR 1562) was the focus of a bruising lobbying battle between producers and retailers during the 99th Congress. The legislation would impose deep reductions on clothing and other textile imports from Thailand, China, Korea, and Taiwan. It would reduce total imports of textiles and apparel by nearly one-third.

Support and Opposition

The cornerstone of the argument for new import limits was a simple equation: increases in textile imports lead to decreases in U.S. jobs. The countries that would be hurt by the bill were the ones responsible for the surge of foreign-made clothes that threatened to push the "Made in the U.S.A." label off store shelves. Textile producers claimed that 300,000 jobs had been lost in the domestic industry from 1980 to 1985. Textile companies warned that their entire industry could disappear by the 1990s.

Opponents of the proposed legislation responded that imports would not eliminate the domestic textile industry. Critics of quotas also said that any jobs saved would be almost balanced by job losses in the retail and transportation industries.

Another key controversy concerned the possible effects of new import quotas on consumer prices. Existing restrictions on imports already added substantially to clothing costs. The textile and apparel industry was one of the better-protected sectors of the economy. Critics stressed that tight new quotas would add even more to the burden on consumers. In addition to forcing higher prices by reducing supplies, new quotas also could add to consumer prices through product upgrading. Hit by limits on the number of items they could send to the United States, foreign producers could try to preserve their profit margins by making more expensive items — exactly what happened when the Japanese imposed voluntary limits on auto exports.

Price increases would fall most heavily on the poor, quota foes argued. The deepest cutbacks in supplies would be among the inexpensive but essential items, such as children's wear, that were mostly produced overseas.

Textile producers and unions responded by noting that stores frequently put higher "markups" — the difference between the wholesale and retail price — on imported clothes. The danger posed by tight quotas, they said, was to retail profits, not consumer prices. "There is no economic rationale for relinquishing the livelihoods of hundreds of thousands of garment and textile workers," said International Ladies' Garment Workers Union president Sol C. Chaikin, "for the sake of greater retailers' and importers' profits."

The coalition opposing quotas also was concerned about the effect of quotas on the nation's overall economy. It wanted Congress to focus on the accumulating impacts that quotas have throughout the economy, including higher consumer prices and the potential for retaliation that could harm other U.S. industries. Quotas, by hurting many people in many parts of the country a little, could add up to a lot of economic damage, foes of quotas argued, ultimately undoing the benefits of import restraints.

The new refrains were heard most clearly on the West Coast, where they were being voiced by two former members of Congress, Paul N. ("Pete") McCloskey, Jr., R-Calif. (1967-83), and Joel Pritchard, R-Wash. (1973-85).

McCloskey in California and Pritchard through a Seattle-based law firm in Washington, D.C., worked with a loose association of Western retailers, importers, freight carriers, and others. They said quotas would help a narrow range of Southern and other interests at the expense of many groups around the nation, particularly in the West.

HR 1562 was aimed largely at textile-producing nations of the Pacific Rim that were a major source of Westerners' imports, as well as a potentially lucrative market for Western-state goods, such as timber.

Western quota foes feared that trade restraints, by stemming the flow of imports, could hurt Western businesses by reducing the volume of goods that those firms ship and sell in this country, lowering trade income that developing nations need to buy U.S. goods, and tempting those nations to retaliate with restrictions of their own.

Such concerns mobilized several firms, including Esprit de Corps, a clothing importer and maker, and The Gap Stores Inc., a retailer and importer, to organize an antiquota coalition of about 100 California firms. In the spring of 1985, that group helped start a similar association in Hawaii. Both associations allied with an antiquota group based in the Pacific Northwest.

The Western groups complemented the work of more-established groups such as the national Retail Industry Trade Action Coalition. Retailers formed the core of opposition to quotas at the national level. They also worked with farm and consumer groups, importers, transporters, and multinational corporations. The antiquota alliance, for instance, enlisted the backing of several aerospace firms, one of them Seattle-based Boeing Co., worried about retaliation.

The wide-ranging coalition stressed the links between economic groups. Farmers, for instance, feared they could be the indirect victims of import restraints. They claimed that quotas, by blocking shipments to the United States, would keep foreigners from earning dollars they could use to buy U.S. farm products. Farmers also feared that those nations could retaliate against U.S. agricultural goods or boycott international negotiations that U.S. farm groups sought to regulate global agricultural trade.

"It's easy for the textile industry to point to a factory closing and explain job losses because of imports," Mark Ellison of the National Association of Wheat Growers said. "But a farm is a kind of factory, too. When farm exports drop, the John Deere dealer is affected, the seed salesman is affected. It's not as easy to define, but the impact spreads through the economy."

The coalition also stressed that in an increasingly internationalized economy, the fortunes of importers and exporters were more closely related than ever. "Apparel makers are major importers of finished goods," Joseph P. O'Neill of the Retail Industry Trade Action Coalition said. "Over half the textile machinery in the country is imported."

Administration View

Administration officials repeatedly attacked the textile bill as an assault on free trade principles that would hurt American consumers and threaten relations with key Asian allies. The administration estimated that the legislation's import limits would raise the average prices of clothes and other textiles by more than 10 percent, adding $14 billion a year to consumer costs.

Reagan reiterated his strong opposition to import curbs and other restrictive trade measures in a news conference September 17, 1985. Reagan blasted proposals to erect new tariffs or quotas to protect U.S. industries as leading to a world trade war and a possible repeat of the Depression of the 1930s. "A mindless stampede toward protectionism would be a one-way trip to economic disaster," Reagan said.

Reagan warned that restrictive trade actions by the United States would inevitably lead to countermeasures by other countries — curbs that could seriously damage export-dependent industries such as aircraft production and agriculture. "Protectionist tariffs would invite retaliation that could deliver an economic death to literally tens of thousands of American family farms," he added.

Legislative History

By mid-1985 there was a growing desire in Congress for a tough overall trade policy. The proposed textile bill was a prime candidate to benefit from that sentiment, which was given an added boost August 28 by Reagan's decision not to impose industry-backed quotas on shoe imports.

Bad news from the Commerce Department in September helped intensify the mood to do something to limit imports. The department reported September 16 that the

United States had a trade deficit of $33 billion in the second quarter of 1985 — a record brought about by ever-increasing imports and continuing weakness in U.S. exports.

Even more alarming to some, the department found that the United States had become a "debtor" nation. For the first time since 1914, Americans owed more to foreigners than foreigners owed to them.

House Action

The House passed HR 1562 by a 262-159 vote October 10. The 103-vote margin of passage of the bill reflected the widespread concern among members over the future of the domestic apparel industry. "This is the last gasp of this industry," said chief sponsor Ed Jenkins, D-Ga. "Don't say you were not told."

But the vote also was a harbinger of future problems for the bill because sponsors fell 19 votes short of the two-thirds majority needed to override a veto. President Reagan repeatedly denounced the measure as dangerously protectionist and vowed to veto it if it cleared Congress.

The vote also indicated that the textile bill was losing support as time went on. A few weeks before the legislation came to the House floor, textile forces had rounded up more than 290 members as cosponsors of the bill.

Stepped-up lobbying by the Reagan administration, retail groups, and other businesses involved in international trade slowly whittled away at the bill's support. "I was wrong," said Florida republican E. Clay Shaw, Jr., who had signed on as a cosponsor but voted against the bill.

The bill also was handicapped by bad timing. It was originally scheduled to come to the floor on October 9, immediately after a speech to the House by Singapore prime minister Lee Kuan Yew, whose country would be hurt by the bill's import limits. House Speaker Thomas P. O'Neill, Jr., D-Mass., postponed action on HR 1562 one day, but the memory of Lee's fervent attack on world protectionism seemed to linger in many members' minds.

Debate on HR 1562 evoked an emotional response from House members, who trooped to the well in great numbers either to bemoan the plight of unemployed textile workers or warn of the dangers of a world trade war. At times, the House chamber almost seemed like a department store, as members waved towels, shirts, a baseball bat, and a stuffed toy bear to make points for or against the measure.

HR 1562 backers stressed both the special problems of the textile industry and the need for the House to provide a clear signal of its support for a more assertive trade stance in general.

Action on HR 1562 also showed that the textile issue was more a regional than a partisan or ideological dispute. Although Democrats had hoped for potential political gain from the emergence of trade issues, they were far from unanimous in backing the textile bill; 187 Democrats voted for the measure, while 62 opposed it. On the Republican side, the split was 75-97 against.

A clear pattern emerged, however, when the vote was broken down by states. Members from Southern states, where textile interests were particularly important, were overwhelmingly in support of the bill, regardless of party. Delegations from 15 states voted unanimously for the measure.

Similarly, members from states that were heavily dependent on international trade, particularly in the Pacific Northwest, were solidly against the bill. There were 12 state delegations that did not give the bill a single vote.

For members from textile states, lists of clothing factories that closed were a sufficient reason to vote for the bill. Cardiss Collins, D-Ill., for example, pointed to 13 firms that no longer produced textiles in Chicago because of competition from im-

Concern for U.S. textile workers helped spur legislation in the 99th Congress that would have imposed tough new import curbs.

ports. "If we continue on the present course, there will be no textile industry in Maine by 1990," warned Republican Olympia J. Snowe.

But members whose constituents transport and sell imported textiles had little interest in helping factory workers at the cost of local jobs. Thomas J. Downey, D-N.Y., for example, pointed to an estimated 3,900 jobs that would be lost in New York and New Jersey ports if imports were limited by the bill. "Don't ask us to help your workers by taking away dock workers' jobs in New York, California or Florida," said John R. Miller, R-Wash.

Critics also warned of the dangers to constituents if other nations respond in kind to new textile limits. "What right do the sponsors of this bill have to make my farmers pay the cost of retaliation?" asked Les AuCoin, D-Ore.

Senate Action

The Senate passed HR 1562 by a 60-39 vote November 13. The bill sponsors moved to shore up support for a veto override by adding protections for other industries that faced stiff foreign competition.

When the textile proposal was brought without success to the Senate floor as amendments to two bills — S J Res 77, granting limited autonomy to Micronesia, and S 1730, the budget reconciliation bill — sponsors had added a provision limiting shoe imports in order to pick up the votes of senators from shoe-producing states. The bill as approved would hold shoe imports to no more than 60 percent of the domestic market for the next eight years.

During consideration of HR 1562, sponsors also accepted an amendment calling for limits on copper imports. The move was aimed at winning support from Western states, where the hard-pressed copper industry was a major economic force.

The strategy of making alliances with other industries was sharply criticized by opponents of the textile bill, who saw the measure as a wedge opening U.S. trade policy to an array of import restraints protecting various troubled industries. "We have forgotten tin and we have forgotten nickel and we have forgotten aluminum," said Daniel J. Evans, R-Wash. "Who knows what else will come on the next Christmas tree when that comes before the Senate?"

In the process of getting their bill through the Senate, textile forces made other substantial changes in the legislation passed earlier by the House.

The House version would seriously affect the dozen nations — Brazil, China, Hong Kong, India, Indonesia, Japan, Korea, Pakistan, the Philippines, Singapore, Taiwan, and Thailand — that had the most success in capturing the U.S. market for low-price garments. The first major Senate change was to focus the bill's deepest cuts on Korea, Taiwan, and Hong Kong — the three suppliers that each provided 10 percent or more of total U.S. textile imports. China and the other major producers would be exempt from the most severe restrictions, although they would continue to face limits on future import growth.

Other changes bill made were to exempt U.S. insular possessions such as Guam and the Virgin Islands from the House measure's import limits, for example, and exempted garments made largely of silk from new restrictions. The House bill had extended import quotas for the first time to garments made of silk, linen, and other natural fibers.

Final Action

House backers of HR 1562 decided to accept the Senate-passed version of the bill, avoiding a conference. The bill was readied for Reagan after the House approved the Senate version by a 255-161 vote on December 3.

House action on the final version of HR 1562 was relatively brief and routine, with most members simply reaffirming stands on the bill they had staked out long before.

Although the bill as approved by the Senate in November was significantly less stringent in its textile import limits than the House-passed measure, there was little discussion of the changes on the floor. Nor was there any substantial increase in House support for the bill produced by the Senate's inclusion of provisions on shoe imports and copper production.

Veto and Veto Override

When HR 1562 cleared Congress, even the bill's staunchest supporters conceded that its provisions had only a slim chance of becoming law. Administration officials, led by U.S. trade representative Clayton K. Yeutter, denounced the bill repeatedly during its progress through Congress, and most observers saw a veto as almost inevitable.

Reagan vetoed the controversial measure December 17. Although he rejected HR 1562, Reagan sought to reassure members of Congress that he was concerned about the plight of import-threatened industries and their workers. "I am well aware of the difficulties of the apparel, textile, copper and shoe industries," he said, "and deeply sympathetic about the job layoffs and plant closings that have affected many workers in these industries."

Bill sponsors conceded that they did not have the two-thirds majorities in the House and Senate needed to surmount the veto. So they decided not to proceed to an immediate override vote. Instead, bill backers won House approval December 17 of a motion to push back an override attempt until August 6, 1986 — when international textile negotiations would be well under way, and the 1986 elections only three months in the future. Under the rules, there is no time limit within a Congress on when a veto override vote can occur. The point of an August 6 vote was timing.

Override Vote

The House vote on the override attempt was 276-149, eight votes shy of the two-thirds needed. The override attempt reflected a deep sense of impatience within Congress, particularly in an election year, toward Reagan's trade stance.

Backing for the override came from a mixture of Democratic liberals looking to score points against Reagan's trade policies and more conservative Democrats and Republicans from the South and Northeast, where textile and other import-affected industries were concentrated.

"This is protectionist, no question about it," Speaker O'Neill told reporters. "On an issue like this, you're voting your locale, you're voting your home."

Bill Goodling, R-Pa., described the textile bill as a "wake-up call to the White House" on trade. And Carroll A. Campbell, Jr., R-S.C., urged his colleagues to come to the aid of a domestic industry suffering under a flood of imports. "For God's sake," said Campbell, "try to vote for America one time."

Even many of those who voted to sustain the president's position acknowledged that Reagan and his top trade officials have dragged their feet in the past, only to pursue more aggressive trade actions in the face of strong congressional pressure and a record overall trade deficit. "It has taken a long time, frankly, to get the administration to face up to this problem," said House GOP leader Robert H. Michel, Ill.

Despite such comments, Yeutter called the House vote a "very gratifying victory" for the administration, which had lobbied vigorously to kill the bill. He said enactment of the textile bill would have been "devastating" to U.S. exports by inviting "massive retaliation" from foreign countries.

A series of textile trade agreements, all reached within weeks of the scheduled vote, helped the White House stave off the threatened override. U.S. trade negotiators concluded pacts with Hong Kong, South Korea, and Taiwan, the three primary targets in the textile bill. In addition, the administration negotiated a new MFA August 1, which it claimed would offer greater protection to U.S. textile and apparel producers.

House members who led the fight to override the veto said the White House trade actions in favor of U.S. wheat farmers and semiconductor manufacturers helped to shore up support for Reagan's position in Farm Belt areas and high-technology states, notably California.

Over the objections of Secretary of State George P. Shultz, Reagan decided August 1 to sell subsidized wheat to the Soviet Union under an export program for surplus U.S. commodities. The administration also reached an agreement July 31 with Japan to boost U.S. semiconductor sales in that country.

The House vote, meanwhile, demonstrated once again Reagan's uncanny ability to edge close to the brink of defeat on Capitol Hill, only to step away with a victory. In this case, he won the fight with an intensive lobbying campaign that included dozens of presidential phone calls to wavering Republican House members, accompanied by calls and visits from other high-ranking administration officials. "The president has a lot of power, a lot of bargaining chips," said Ed Jenkins. "He had to play them all to win this vote."

Appealing as strongly as Reagan did to GOP lawmakers made the difference in the override vote. While 205 Democrats — 82 percent of those who voted — went against Reagan, only 71 Republicans did so, 40 percent of those who voted. Voting to sustain the veto were 43 Democrats and 106 Republicans.

Reagan managed to win a large majority of Republicans despite energetic lobbying by key GOP lawmakers to override the president's veto. That effort was led by Minority Whip Trent Lott, R-Miss., whose district included several textile plants.

On the morning of the override vote, Lott was counting on 79 Republican votes, precisely the number he needed when combined with the votes from the Democratic side of the aisle. But 11th-hour lobbying by Reagan stripped away four GOP votes, leaving Lott and others nowhere to turn to make them up. By the time of the vote, Lott told four other Republicans who had committed to the override that they were free to vote with Reagan in order to avoid political embarrassment with the White House.

Industry Lobbying

Other members reported being the targets of very vigorous lobbying on both sides of the textile issue.

"Was I lobbied?" replied Jim Kolbe, R-Ariz., to a reporter's query on the subject. "This made the [aid to Nicaraguan] contras vote look simple by comparison. . . . I'm absolutely astounded at the level of the lobbying."

Textile union lobbyists crowded the corridors leading to the House chamber, corraling members as they walked in and out. Veteran lobbyist Evelyn Dubrow, who represented the International Ladies' Garment Workers' Union, perched herself in one of the brown leather chairs normally occupied by House employees who guard the chamber's entrances.

Kolbe voted for the textile bill in 1985, partly because of provisions to aid the domestic copper industry in Arizona and other states. This time, Kolbe voted to sustain Reagan's veto. He said one reason was Reagan's decision earlier in 1986 to set up an international group of copper producers to discuss problems in that industry. Kolbe conceded that the action would not solve the domestic industry's problems, but said it was a step in the right direction.

Selected Bibliography

Books

Adams, Gordon. *The Iron Triangle: The Politics of Defense Contracting*. New York: Council on Economic Priorities, 1981.

Alderson, George, and Everett Sentman. *How You Can Influence Congress: The Complete Handbook for the Citizen Lobbyist*. New York: E. P. Dutton, 1979.

Ashworth, William. *Under the Influence: Congress, Lobbies, and the American Pork-Barrel System*. New York: Hawthorn/Dutton, 1981.

Backrack, Stanley. *The Committee of One Million: The China Lobby and U.S. Policy, 1953-1971*. New York: Columbia University Press, 1976.

Barnes, Christopher. *The Politics of Policy Making and Pressure Groups*. Brookfield, Vt.: Gower Publishing Co., 1986.

Bauer, Raymond A. et al. *American Business and Public Policy: The Politics of Foreign Trade*. Chicago: Aldine Publishing Co., 1972.

Bedlington, Anne H., and Lynda W. Powell. "Money and Elections." In *Research in Micropolitics,* ed. Samuel Long, 161-187. Greenwich, Conn.: JAI Press, 1986.

Braam, Geert. *Influence of Business Firms on the Government: An Investigation of the Distribution of Influence in Society*. Hawthorne, N.Y.: Mouton Publishers, 1981.

Broder, David S. *Changing of the Guard: Power and Leadership in America*. New York: Simon & Schuster, 1980.

Bromley, David G., and Anson Shupe. *New Christian Politics*. Macon, Ga.: Mercer University Press, 1984.

Caplan, Marc. *Ralph Nader Presents a Citizens' Guide to Lobbying*. New York: Dembner Books, 1983.

Chelf, Carl P. *Public Policy Making in America: Difficult Choices, Limited Solutions*. Glenview, Ill.: Scott, Foresman & Co., 1981.

Cigler, Allan J., and Burdett A. Loomis. *Interest Group Politics*. 2d ed. Washington, D.C.: CQ Press, 1986.

Close, Arthur C. et al., eds. *Washington Representatives, 1986: Who Does What for Whom in the Nation's Capital*. Washington, D.C.: Columbia Books, 1986.

The Corporation in Politics: PACs, Lobbying Laws, and Public Officials. New York: Practicing Law Institute, 1983.

Crater, Flora. *The Woman Activist Guide to Lobbying*. Rev. ed. Falls Church, Va.: Woman Activist, 1977.

Crawford, Alan. *Thunder on the Right: The "New Right" and the Politics of Resentment*. New York: Pantheon Books, 1980.

Crawford, Kenneth G. *The Pressure Boys: The Inside Story of Lobbying in America*. New York: Arno Press, 1974.

Deakin, James. *The Lobbyists*. Washington, D.C.: Public Affairs Press, 1966.

DeKieffer, Donald. *How to Lobby Congress: A Guide for the Citizen Lobbyist*. New York: Dodd, 1982.

Doran, Charles F., and Joel J. Sokolsky. *Canada and Congress: Lobbying in Washington*. Halifax, Nova Scotia: Centre for Foreign Policy Studies, Dalhousie University, 1985.

Drew, Elizabeth. *Politics and Money: The New Road to Corruption*. New York: Macmillan, 1983.

Eastman, Hope. *Lobbying: A Constitutionally Protected Right.* Washington, D.C.: American Enterprise Institute for Public Policy Research, 1977.

Epstein, Edwin M. *The Corporation in American Politics.* Englewood Cliffs, N.J.: Prentice-Hall, 1969.

Findley, Paul. *They Dare to Speak Out: People and Institutions Confront Israel's Lobby.* Westport, Conn.: Hill, Lawrence & Co., 1985.

Flake, Carol. *Redemptora: Culture, Politics, and the New Evangelicalism.* Garden City, N.Y.: Anchor Press, 1984.

Goulden, Joseph C. *The Super-Lawyers: The Small and Powerful World of Great Washington Law Firms.* New York: Weybright and Talley, 1972.

Green, Mark J. *The Other Government: The Unseen Power of Washington Lawyers.* New York: W. W. Norton & Co., 1978.

Greenwald, Carol S. *Group Power: Lobbying and Public Policy.* New York: Praeger Publishers, 1977.

Greestone, J. David. *Labor in American Politics.* Chicago: University of Chicago Press, 1977.

Greevy, David U. et al., eds. *PAC Directory.* Cambridge, Mass.: Ballinger Publishing Co., 1984.

Grupenhoff, John T., and James J. Murphy. *Nonprofits' Handbook on Lobbying: The History and Impact of the New 1976 Lobbying Regulation on the Activities of Nonprofit Organizations.* Washington, D.C.: Taft Corp., 1977.

Hall, Donald R. *Cooperative Lobbying: The Power of Pressure.* Tucson: University of Arizona Press, 1969.

Halley, Laurence. *Ancient Affections: Ethnic Groups and Foreign Policy.* New York: Praeger Publishers, 1985.

Halper, Thomas. *Power, Politics, and American Democracy.* Glenview, Ill.: Scott, Foresman & Co., 1981.

Hayes, Michael T. *Lobbyists and Legislators: A Theory of Political Markets.* 2d ed. New Brunswick, N.J.: Rutgers University Press, 1984.

How Money Talks in Congress: A Common Cause Study of the Impact of Money on Congressional Decision-Making. Washington, D.C.: Common Cause, 1979.

Howe, Russell W., and Sarah H. Trott. *The Power Peddlers: How Lobbyists Mold America's Foreign Policy.* Garden City, N.Y.: Doubleday & Co., 1977.

Hrebenar, Ronald J., and Ruth K. Scott. *Interest Group Politics in America.* Englewood Cliffs, N.J.: Prentice-Hall, 1982.

Ippolito, Dennis S., and Thomas G. Walker. *Political Parties, Interest Groups, and Public Policy: Group Influence in American Politics.* Englewood Cliffs, N.J.: Prentice-Hall, 1980.

Isaacs, Stephen D. *Jews and American Politics.* Garden City, N.Y.: Doubleday & Co., 1974.

Key, V. O. *Politics, Parties, and Pressure Groups.* New York: Thomas Y. Crowell Co., 1964.

Koem, Ross Y. *The China Lobby in American Politics.* New York: Harper & Row, 1974.

Levitan, Sar A., and Martha Cooper. *Business Lobbies: The Public Good and the Bottom Line.* Baltimore: Johns Hopkins University Press, 1983.

Mahood, H. R. *Pressure Groups in American Politics.* New York: Harper & Row, 1967.

Mahood, H. R., and E. S. Maleck. *Group Politics.* New York: Charles Scribner's Sons, 1972.

Maitland, Ian. "House Divided: Business Lobbying and the 1981 Budget." In *Research in Corporate Social Performance and Policy,* ed. Lee Preston, 1-25. Greenwich, Conn.: JAI Press, 1983.

Malbin, Michael J. *Parties, Interest Groups, and Campaign Finance Laws.* Washington, D.C.: American Enterprise Institute for Public Policy Research, 1980.

Marcuss, Stanley J., ed. *Effective Washington Representation.* New York: Harcourt Brace Jovanovich, 1983.

Matasar, Ann B. *Corporate PACs and Federal Campaign Financing Laws: Use or Abuse of Power?* Westport, Conn.: Quorum Books, 1986.

Mazmanian, Daniel A., and Jeanne Nienaber. *Can Organizations Change? Environmental Protection, Citizen Participation, and the Corps of Engineers.* Washington, D.C.: The Brookings Institution, 1979.

McCormick, Robert E., and Robert D. Tollison. *Politicians, Legislation, and the Economy: An Inquiry into the Interest-Group Theory of Government.* Hingham, Mass.: Kluwer Boston, 1981.

McFarland, Andrew S. *Common Cause: Lobbying in the Public Interest.* Chatham, N.J.: Chatham House Pubs., 1984.

———. *Public Interest Lobbies: Decision Making on Energy.* Washington, D.C.: American Enterprise Institute for Public Policy Research, 1976.

Milbrath, Lester W. *The Washington Lobbyists.* Reprint. Westport, Conn.: Greenwood Press, 1978.

Miller, Stephen. *Special Interest Groups in American Politics.* New Brunswick, N.J.: Rutgers University, Transaction Books, 1983.

Minix, Dean A. *Small Groups and Foreign Policy Decision Making.* Lanham, Md.: University Press of America, 1982.

Moe, Terry M. *The Organization of Interests: Incentives and the Internal Dynamics of Political Interest Groups.* Chicago: University of Chicago Press, 1980.

Murphy, Thomas P. *Pressures upon Congress: Legislation by Lobby.* Woodbury, N.Y.: Barron's Educational Series, 1973.

Norwick, Kenneth P., ed. *Lobbying for Freedom in the Eighties: A Grass Roots Guide.* New York: The Putnam Publishing Group, 1983.

Ogene, F. Chidozie. *Interest Groups and the Shaping of Foreign Policy: Four Case Studies of United States African Policy.* New York: St. Martin's, 1984.

Oppenheimer, Bruce I. *Oil and the Congressional Process.* Lexington, Mass.: Lexington Books, 1974.

Ornstein, Norman J., and Shirley Elder. *Interest Groups, Lobbying, and Policymaking.* Washington, D.C.: CQ Press, 1978.

Renfro, William L. *The Legislative Role of Corporations.* New York: President's Association, 1983.

Sabato, Larry J. *PAC Power: Inside the World of Political Action Committees.* New York: W. W. Norton, 1984.

Schlozman, Kay L., and John T. Tierney. *Organized Interest and American Democracy.* New York: Harper & Row, 1985.

Schriftgiesser, Karl. *The Lobbyists: The Art and Business of Influencing Lawmakers.* Boston: Little, Brown & Co., 1951.

Sheppard, Burton D. *Rethinking Congressional Reform: The Reform Roots of the Special Interest Congress.* Cambridge, Mass.: Schenkman Books, 1985.

Shipper, Frank, and Marianne M. Jennings. *Business Strategy for the Political Arena.* Westport, Conn.: Quorum Books, 1984.

Trice, Robert H. *Interest Groups and the Foreign Policy Process: U.S. Policy in the Middle East.* Beverly Hills, Calif.: Sage Publications, 1977.

Truman, David B. *The Governmental Process.* New York: Alfred A. Knopf, 1964.

Washington Information Directory, 1986-87. Washington, D.C.: Congressional Quarterly, 1986.

Wilson, James Q. *Political Organizations.* New York: Basic Books, 1973.

Ziegler, L. Harmon, and Wayne G. Peak. *Interest Groups in American Politics.* 2d ed. Englewood Cliffs, N.J.: Prentice-Hall, 1972.

Ziegler, L. Harmon et al., eds. *Symposium on Interest Groups and Public Policy.* Urbana, Ill.: Policy Studies Organization, 1983.

Articles

Alexander, Herbert E. "The Role of Interest Groups in the 1984 Presidential Selection Process." *Campaigns and Elections,* Winter 1986, 21-24.

"America and South Africa: Anti-Apartheid Without Tears." *Economist,* March 30, 1985, 17-33.

Anderson, Gary. "Political Action Committees: Attaining Technical Sophistication." *Campaigns and Elections,* Summer 1983, 28-34.

Banthin, Joanna, and Leigh Stelzer. "Political Action Committees: Fact, Fancy, and Morality." *Journal of Business Ethics,* Fall 1986, 13-19.

Bole, William. "The GOP Becoming God's Own Party?" *Church and State,* January 1985, 12-13.

Boyle, Larry. "PACs and Pluralism: The Dynamics of Interest-group Politics." *Campaigns and Elections,* Spring 1985, 6-16.

Bradford, M. "Self-insurers' Group Starts Drive to Educate Legislators." *Business Insurance,* November 12, 1984, 2+.

Brewer, Lisa de Maio. "PACs on the Warpath: How Independent Efforts Reelected Jesse Helms." *Campaigns and Elections,* Summer 1985, 5-11.

Brostoff, S. "Insurer Lobbying Efforts Hit." *The National Underwriter (Property and Casualty Insurance Edition),* June 27, 1986, 1+.

Buchsbaum, Andrew P. "Campaign Finance Rereform: The Regulation of Independent Political Committees." *California Law Review,* March 1983, 673-702.

Carter, Harlon. "Here We Stand." *American Rifleman,* December 1984, 7.

"Charitable Lobbying Restraints and Tax-exempt Organizations: Old Problems, New Directions?" *Utah Law Review,* 1984, 337-364.

Chiles, Lawton. "PAC's: Congress on the Auction Block." *Journal of Legislation,* Summer 1984, 192-217.

Cingranelli, David L. "State Government Lobbies in the National Political Process." *State Government* 56 (4):122-7 (1983).

Cohen, Richard E. "New Lobbying Rules May Influence Grass-Roots Political Action." *National Journal,* May 27, 1978, 832-836.

Cooper, Ann. "Third World Insurgent Groups Learning to Play the Washington Lobbying Game." *National Journal,* February 8, 1986, 329-333.

Danas, A. M. "Grassroots Lobbying and Goodwill Advertising: Are the Regulations Implementing Section 162(3)(2)(b) Unconstitutionally Vague?" *Taxes,* October 1984, 722-740.

Dunn, Matthew Joseph et al. "The Campaign Finance Reform Act: A Measured Step to Limit the PAC's Roles in Congressional Elections." *Journal of Legislation,* Summer 1984, 497-520.

Edsall, Thomas B. "Campaign Financing: An Answer to the PAC Debate." *Management: UCLA Graduate School of Management Magazine,* Spring 1984, 10-14+.

Fialka, John J., and Brooks Jackson. "Pro-Israel Lobby." *Wall Street Journal,* February 25, 1985, 1+.

Findley, Paul. "Congress and the Pro-Israel Lobby." *Journal of Palestine Studies,* Autumn 1985, 104-113.

Forbes, James D. "Organizational and Political Dimensions of Consumer Pressure Groups." *Journal of Consumer Policy,* June 1985, 105-131.

Frendreis, John P., and Richard W. Waterman. "PAC Contributions and Legislative Behavior: Senate Voting on Trucking Deregulation." *Social Science Quarterly,* June 1985, 401-412.

Gais, T. L. "Interest Groups, Iron Triangles, and Representative Institutions in American National Government." *British Journal of Political Science,* April 1984, 161-185.

"Getting Tough About Unisex." *Fortune,* July 25, 1983, 21-22.

Gopoian, J. David. "Change and Continuity in Defense PAC Behavior." *American Politics Quarterly,* July 1985, 297-322.

——. "What Makes PACs Tick? An Analysis of the Allocation Patterns of Economic Interest Groups." *American Journal of Political Science,* May 1984, 259-281.

Grover, Ronald. "Nice Work If You Can Stand It: Lobbying for Pretoria." *Business Week,* September 30, 1985, 47.

Hadwiger, D. "Food Lobbyists: Farm and Food Policy." *Rural Sociology,* Winter 1981, 738-743.

Huwa, Randy. "Political Action Committees: Creating a Scandal." *Business Forum,* Winter 1984, 11-14.

"The Influence Industry." *National Journal,* September 14, 1986, 2030-2084.

Isaacson, Walter. "Magnum-force Lobby." *Time,* April 20, 1981, 22.

Jackson, Brooks. "Growing Anti-PAC Sentiment Leads to Proposals to Overhaul Federal Campaign-finance System." *Wall Street Journal,* January 20, 1986, 36.

Johnson, Kathryn. "How Foreign Powers Play for Status in Washington." *U.S. News & World Report,* June 17, 1985, 35-40.

Jonas, Norman, and Ronald Grover. "Tax Reform's Foes Could End Up Saving It." *Business Week,* February 4, 1985, 30-31.

Jones, Ruth S., and Warren E. Miller. "Financing Campaigns: Macro Level Innovation and Micro Level Response." *The Western Political Quarterly,* June 1985, 187-210.

Kismer, R. E. "The Persuasive Powers of Corporate Lobbyists." *Black Enterprise,* April 1984, 54-58.

Kwartler, Kenneth M. "Political Broadcasting by Independent Committees: A Proposal for Eliminating the Federal Communications Commission's PACcess Doctrine." *Boston University Law Review,* May 1984, 625-682.

"The League of Conservation Voters." *Environmental Forum,* August 1984, 19-21.

"Limit Campaign Donations by PAC's?" *U.S. News & World Report,* May 28, 1984, 51.

Lipset, Seymour Martin. "The 'Jewish Lobby' and the National Interest." *New Leader,* November 16, 1981, 8-11.

"The Lobbying Blitz That May Kill a Tax Bill." *Business Week,* November 14, 1983, 46.

"Lobbying by Charitable Organizations: Regan v. Taxation with Representation." *The Tax Lawyer,* Winter 1984, 399-408.

"Lobbying Restriction on Section 501(c)(3) Organizations Held Unconstitutional: First Amendment Implication of Taxation with Representation of Washington v. Regan." *Brigham Young University Law Review,* 1983, 442-464.

Madison, Christopher. "Arab-American Lobby Fights Rearguard Battle to Influence U.S. Mideast Policy." *National Journal,* August 31, 1985, 1934-1939.

——. "Rapidly Changing Times Keep Central America Lobbyists on Their Toes." *Na-*

tional Journal, August 11, 1984, 1517-1520.

Markowitz, Steven. "Ethical Rules for Corporate PAC-men." *Business and Society Review,* Summer 1984, 21-25.

Masters, Marick F., and Gerald D. Keim. "Determinants of PAC Participation Among Large Corporations." *Journal of Politics,* November 1985, 1158-1173.

North, James. "The Politics of Selfishness: The Effect, the Growth of Special Interests." *Washington Monthly,* October 1978, 32-36.

"PAC Spending: Getting Bigger All the Time." *Common Cause Magazine,* July/August 1983, 26-27.

"Politics, Religion, and the 1984 Campaign: A Symposium." *Chrisitianity and Crisis,* October 29, 1984, 391-406.

Poole, Isaiah J., and Elliott D. Lee. "Lobbying for Survival." *Black Enterprise,* March 1982, 52-58.

"The Powerful Lobby That Works for Japan in Washington." *Business Week,* October 17, 1983, 148+.

Rasor, Dina. "Pentagon Brass and Their Corporate Pals Team Up to Woo Congress." *Business and Society Review,* Spring 1983, 18-22.

"Religion in American Politics." *Free Inquiry,* Summer 1983, 5-50.

Ruffin, D. C., and F. D. Brown. "Clout on Capitol Hill." *Black Enterprise,* October 1984, 97-100.

Ruppert, Paul. "How to Attract PAC Support: A Guide for the Nonincumbent." *Campaigns and Elections,* May/June 1986, 6-10.

Schlozman, Kay L., and John T. Tierney. "More of the Same: Washington Pressure Group Activity in a Decade of Change." *Journal of Politics,* May 1983, 351-377.

Sethi, S. Prakash, and Nobuaki Namiki. "The Public Backlash Against PACs." *California Management Review,* Spring 1983, 133-144.

Shapiro, Walter et al. "Reagan Versus the Tax Code." *Newsweek,* June 3, 1985, 20-23.

Sheler, Jeffery L. "Is Congress for Sale?" *U.S. News & World Report,* May 28, 1984, 47-50.

——. "Lobbyists Go for It: A Breed of Powerful and Sophisticated Persuaders is Jousting with Congress over Issues Vital to America." *U.S. News & World Report,* June 17, 1985, 30-34.

——. "Lobbyists: Washington's 'Hidden Persuaders.'" *U.S. News & World Report,* September 19, 1983, 63-66.

Sligar, J. S. "Constitutionality of the Tax on Lobbying by Private Foundation Under Section 4945(d)(1) of the Internal Revenue Code." *Taxes,* May 1983, 306-318.

Smith, Richard A. "Should Government Contracts Subsidize Industry Lobbying?" *Air Force Law Review,* 1982/1983, 408-423.

Sorauf, Frank J. "Who's in Charge? Accountability in Political Action Committees." *Political Science Quarterly,* Winter 1984/85, 591-614.

Spears, M. "Why NRA Needs to be Political." *Journal of Rehabilitation,* October/December 1982, 6-7.

Srodes, J. L. "Tax Reform Eighties Style." *Financial Planning,* January 1984, 53-56.

Stokes, Bruce. "New Awareness of U.S.-Third World Ties Wins Converts to Free Trade." *National Journal,* September 22, 1984, 1758-1761.

——. "A Divided Farm Lobby." *National Journal,* March 23, 1985, 632-638.

Troyer, T. A., and A. G. Lauber. "Supreme Court's TWR Decision Provides Guidance in 501(c)(3) Lobbying." *Journal of Taxation,* August 1983, 66-69.

Ungar, Sanford J. "South Africa's Lobbyists." *New York Times Magazine,* October 13, 1985, 30+.

"The Use of Public Funds for Legislative Lobbying and Electoral Campaigning." *Vanderbilt Law Review,* March 1984, 433-472.

Ward, Bud, and Jan Floyd. "Washington's Lobbying Groups: How They Rate." *Environmental Forum,* April 1985, 9-17.

Wellisz, S., and J. D. Wilson. "Lobbying and Tariff Formation: A Deadweight Loss Consideration." *Journal of International Economics,* May 1986, 367-375.

"Whose Voice Shall Be Heard? Lobbying Limitations on Section 501(c)(3) Charitable Organizations Held Constitutional in Regan v. Taxation with Representation." *St. Louis University Law Journal,* August 1984, 1017-1033.

"Why the Democratic Process Cannot Function Without Lobbying." *Journal of American Insurance* 60 (3): 1-4 (1984).

Winkle, J. W., III. "Judges as Lobbyists: Habeas Corpus Reform in the 1940s." *Judicature,* February/March 1985, 433-472.

Government Documents

U.S. Congress. House. Committee on Armed Services. Subcommittee on Investigations. *Allegations of Improper Lobbying by De-*

partment of Defense Personnel of the C-5B and B-1B Aircraft and Sale to Saudi Arabia of the Airborne Warning and Control System: Hearings, Sept. 14-Nov. 30, 1982. Washington, D.C.: Government Printing Office, 1983.

U.S. Congress. House. Committee on the Judiciary. Subcommittee on Administrative Law and Government Relations. *Public Disclosure of Lobbying Activity: Hearings, Feb. 28-March 29, 1979.* 96th Cong., 1st sess. Washington, D.C.: Government Printing Office, 1979.

U.S. Congress. Senate. Committee on Governmental Affairs. *Lobbying Reform Act of 1977: Hearings, Aug. 2, 1977; Feb. 6, 7, 1978.* 96th Cong., 2d sess. Washington, D.C.: Government Printing Office, 1978.

Index